COGNITIVE ANALYTIC TH
AND BORDERLINE PERSONALITY DISORDER

COGNITIVE ANALYTIC THERAPY AND BORDERLINE PERSONALITY DISORDER

The Model and the Method

ANTHONY RYLE

UMDS at Guy's Hospital, Munro Clinic, London, UK

With specialist contributions from

Tim Leighton

Clouds House, Wiltshire, UK

Philip Pollock

HMP Maghaberry, N. Ireland, UK

JOHN WILEY & SONS

Chichester • New York • Weinheim • Brisbane • Singapore • Toronto

Copyright © 1997 by John Wiley & Sons Ltd,
Baffins Lane, Chichester,
West Sussex PO19 1UD, England

National 01243 779777
International (+44) 1243 779777
e-mail (for orders and customer service enquiries):
cs-books@wiley.co.uk
Visit our home page on http://www.wiley.co.uk
or http://www.wiley.com

Reprinted April 1998, February 2000, June 2001

Other Wiley Editorial Offices

John Wiley & Sons, Inc., 605 Third Avenue,
New York, NY 10158-0012, USA

WILEY-VCH Verlag GmbH, Pappelallee 3
D-69469 Weinheim, Germany

Jacaranda Wiley Ltd, 33 Park Road, Milton,
Queensland 4064, Australia

John Wiley & Sons (Asia) Pte Ltd, 2 Clementi Loop #02-01,
Jin Xing Distripark, Singapore 129809

John Wiley & Sons (Canada) Ltd, 22 Worcester Road,
Rexdale, Ontario M9W 1L1, Canada

Library of Congress Cataloging-in-Publication Data

Ryle, Anthony
    Cognitive analytical therapy and borderline personality disorder: the model and the
method / by Anthony Ryle.
        p. cm.
    Includes bibliographical references and index.
    ISGN 0–471–97617–2.—ISBN 0–471–97618–0
    1. Borderline personality disorder. 2. Cognitive-analytic therapy. I. Title.
    RC569.5.B67R95   1997
    616.85´8520651—dc21
                                                                        97–8657
                                                                        CIP

British Library Cataloguing in Publication Data

A catalogue record for this book is available from the British Library

ISBN 0–471–97617–2 (cased)
ISBN 0-471-97618-0 (paper)

Typeset in 10/12pt Times by Saxon Graphics Ltd, Derby
Printed and bound in Great Britain by Biddles Ltd, Guildford and King's Lynn
This book is printed on acid-free paper responsibly manufactured from sustainable
forestation, for which at least two trees are planted for each one used for paper production.

Contents

About the Authors

Anthony Ryle is a Senior Research Fellow and Honorary Consultant Psychotherapist at the United Medical and Dental Schools of Guy's and St Thomas's Hospitals (CAT Office, Munro Clinic, Guy's Hospital, London SE 1).

Tim Leighton is Assistant Director of Clouds House, a treatment centre for alcohol and drug dependency. He has worked as a therapist, trainer and supervisor in the addictions field for 12 years. He is a UKCP registered psychotherapist and his main clinical and research interest is the development of psychotherapeutic models appropriate for people recovering from addiction, particularly those with additional psychological problems. (Clouds House, East Knoyle, Salisbury, Wilts SP3 6BE).

Philip Pollock is a Chartered Forensic Clinical Psychologist at HMP Maghaberry, Old Road, Upper Ballinderry, Lisburn, N. Ireland.

Foreword

Nearly ten years ago I was fortunate enough, whilst editing the Wiley Series in Psychotherapy and Counselling, to be sent a Tony Ryle manuscript. I had previously admired his integration of personal construct psychology with object relations theory and so was delighted with the mature form of cognitive analytic therapy laid out in the new manuscript. In the series preface for that book, *Cognitive Analytic Therapy: Active Participation in Change*, I predicted that it would introduce many people to the possibility of an effective and theoretically coherent integration of psychodynamic, cognitive and behavioural therapies. It has.

Cognitive analytic therapy has flourished over the last decade, developing theoretically, and within its theoretical framework, discovering techniques and new applications of those techniques. It has proved equally attractive to psychodynamic therapists, wishing to practise brief, structured therapy, as to cognitive behavioural therapists seeking to develop their skills in using the therapeutic relationship as the vehicle of change. Cognitive analytic therapy is now practised in many settings within British mental health services, in psychiatric clinics, psychotherapy departments, primary care, day hospitals, forensic settings and community mental health teams. It has had a commensurate influence in private practice. A national association now regulates training and practice, and CAT courses are struggling to cope with an increasing demand for training. Research, service evaluation and audit have also been undertaken, with more formal research trials planned. The impact of CAT in the UK was certainly one of the reasons why, in 1995, the United Kingdom chapter of the Society for Psychotherapy Research honoured Tony Ryle with its Career Achievement Award, rarely conferred.

Here we see another landmark, a full description of the cognitive analytic approach to understanding and helping people with borderline personality disorder. This group of patients is often considered untreatable in psychiatric services, or is only offered treatment for the depression or anxiety problems with which they often present. When the characteristic borderline features emerge (extremely variable and volatile mood, intense relationships switching from idealization to devaluation, impulsive, self injuring or mutilating behaviour, outbursts of unmanageable rage and desperate attempts to avoid abandonment) the health care system can rarely cope. These patients present unique challenges to mental health practitioners, first demanding then rejecting help, exquisitely sensitive to failures of empathy and care, yet seeming to provoke them, inspiring powerful emotional reactions in their would-be helpers ranging from powerful compassion and a wish to rescue, to thinly disguised anger or dread. Therapists struggle to create and maintain a working alliance with someone who seems to be made worse by well-meaning efforts at empathy, someone who challenges the imposed limits of therapy and the therapist's capacity to think clearly, testing the commitment of the therapist, and, all too often, testing it to destruction.

Ryle brings a unique and valuable perspective to understanding and helping people in this predicament. He describes early trauma and inconsistent and unresponsive parenting which lead to developmental problems in the capacity for self-observation. Internal representations of interpersonal relationships, which also define the self, are fragmented, not through defensive splitting but through a developmental failure of integration. These relationship patterns are immensely powerful and self-maintaining, drawing others into reciprocal roles. Learning from experience is impaired by vulnerability to intense emotional stress triggering a switch from one self-state to another. These experiential discontinuities are addressed directly by the cognitive analytic therapist who provides explicit descriptions of the self states and state switches and gives tools for the observing self. Through these, the foundation for a coherent and continuous self is established. The basis for new learning and continuing development is created.

We have seen a trickle of books and articles on borderline personality disorder increase to a torrent over the last two decades, but this book is like no other. Tony Ryle is inimitable. His understanding of the borderline patient is highly original, and his methods are practically of great benefit. Here is a virtuoso psychotherapist and a distinguished theoretician, writing at the height of his powers.

GLENYS PARRY

Preface

This book describes the theory and practice of Cognitive Analytic Therapy (CAT) as applied to patients with Borderline Personality Disorder (BPD). Although there are many problems with this diagnosis, which will be discussed in Chapter 1, there is no doubt that patients meeting the diagnostic criteria are more damaged, more damaging and more difficult to treat than most patients accepted for psychological therapies. At the present time many of these patients receive little in the way of effective treatment.

Against Pessimism

Borderline patients are impulsive, unstable and destructive, hurting themselves and those around them, including those who seek to help them, and this has resulted in a widespread reluctance to treat them and a failure to provide appropriate services for them. This negative response has been compounded by two influences. The first is the fact that many general psychiatrists do not consider personality disorders to be illnesses and hence do not accept that they are their concern, except in so far as they make their patients uncooperative. The second is the widespread assumption among those providing psychological treatments that therapy for personality disorders must be both intensive (2–3 times weekly) and continued over years. The impracticality of providing such treatment in the public medical service, or of paying for it privately for most patients, has meant that only a small proportion of cases receive specialist help. In many psychotherapy departments cases of BPD are deemed unsuitable for the predominantly trainee therapists available, with the result that they languish unallocated on waiting lists.

I believe that this pessimism is unjustified, in that, for many borderline patients, relatively brief interventions can be effective in terms of cost and of human benefit. The intervention considered in this book, Cognitive Analytic Therapy (CAT), has been used to treat outpatients, including those with Borderline Personality Disorder, for 15 years; the results of ongoing research evaluation suggest that this treatment can achieve clinically significant changes in the course of 16–24 sessions, with fewer than one in three in this sample of patients requiring further treatment.

However, all outcome data, especially from uncontrolled studies, need careful interpretation. The results of the ongoing research, the aim of which is to describe the scope and limits of CAT and to investigate the process of therapy in this mode, will be published elsewhere. The associated process studies already carried out make it possible to define measures of 'CAT delivery' and open the way to controlled comparisons with alternative treatment approaches. Meanwhile, the results so far are considered sufficiently encouraging to justify this book presenting the therapeutic approach and describing the developmental and structural model on which it is based. Although the book is concerned to present a method of psychotherapy, many aspects of the practice and the understandings offered by the model could be of value not only to psychotherapists but to those other clinicians who, in practice, provide most of the care received by these patients.

Working with Borderline Patients

I should perhaps confess at this point that, in general, I *like* borderline patients; I have learned a great deal from them, and I have found that, once I have come to know their stories, I have usually felt moved and filled with respect for what they have endured and achieved. To be able to like them it is necessary to understand them and this demands that one has a way of making sense of their often painfully destructive experiences and acts. As this process is accomplished, as in most cases I believe it can be, one finds oneself in the room with a person less filled with anger and more aware of underlying pain and loss but also of possibility.

The methods developed in CAT for the early reformulation of patients' problems usually contain their destructiveness and allow the rapid establishment of close working relationships, with a high degree of active participation by the patient. While many aspects of practice are, of course, shared with other approaches, I believe that CAT offers a particularly high degree of integration of psychotherapy models at the theoretical and practical levels, that some important features are unique to it, and that, in contrast to many models of psychotherapy, from the beginning of treatment it offers patients a full, non-reductive acknowledgement of their experience and an accurate consideration of the extent and limits of their responsibility.

The Patients and the Setting

Most of the patients described in the book were selected from the accumulating series of patients treated in the research project in the CAT clinic at Guy's Hospital. In this study all sessions are audiotaped and psychometric testing is carried out before and after therapy and at annual follow-ups. CAT involves writing by both patient and therapist and this material too is available. Therapists are required to play through the sessional audiotapes before supervision and process notes are written on this basis. The recorded information about these patients is therefore relatively extensive and the various measures which are analysed in the formal process and outcome research can also be drawn upon in describing the illustrative case examples.

The great majority of the patients had been referred to the CAT clinic at Guy's Hospital by general practitioners, community mental health centres or (in about 60% of cases) by psychiatrists. The hospital serves a relatively deprived inner city area, and the population contains a number of ethnic minorities, but referral patterns, unfortunately, result in the fact that more educated patients are over-represented in the clinic. The cases described in this book were chosen from this patient population to illustrate the range of clinical problems encountered and the various treatment methods employed.

These patients were treated in an under-resourced department at a time when the mental health services were undergoing the stresses and disruptions of successive major reorganizations. The longstanding marginalization of psychotherapy within British psychiatry has made psychological treatment services particularly vulnerable. The competing demands of other (also under-resourced) psychiatric services, in the context of a savagely under-resourced National Health Service, have resulted in many short-term economies being made, with little reference to longer term costs, whether human or economic. These factors mean that the work reported here was done under less than ideal, if fairly typical, conditions. The patients suffered long delays between assessment and treatment, and treatment was carried out in the great majority of cases by CAT trainees, either towards the end of their two-year basic training or during their advanced training. If these factors served to generate a certain frontier spirit, they also caused a great deal of anxiety and stress.

The Scope and Contents of the Book

In this book the focus is on what CAT can do; it should be remembered that it is *not* put forward as the only, or a complete, answer to the needs of all borderline patients. It *is* claimed that it could contribute importantly to any comprehensive service designed to treat BPD. The focus is on individual psychotherapy; other possible roles which CAT might play, especially in supervision and management in inpatient and day hospital settings, are noted but not considered in any detail.

The book opens with a review of the nature of the diagnosis of BPD, concluding that, while it is now more satisfactorily discriminated from other conditions than in the past, the diagnosis does not identify a unitary group of patients and provides limited guidance to clinicians. The actual methods used to identify the patients in the study are then described. In the second chapter an outline of the general characteristics of CAT is given, followed in Chapter 3 by the first detailed published account of the CAT theoretical and practical approach to BPD. This involves the presentation of the *multiple self states model* and proposes a clarification of the relative roles of repression, dissociation and impaired self-reflection in the aetiology.

A partisan review of some of the main current approaches to BPD is provided in Chapter 4, and detailed accounts of the treatments of two patients, illustrating the CAT approach in action, are presented in Chapter 5. A crucial element in the successful treatment of borderlines is the establishment of a working alliance and the avoidance of collusive involvements; Chapter 6 proposes ways of understanding transference and countertransference, drawing on my experience as a supervisor and on therapists' self-supervision using the audiotapes of their sessions. In the following three chapters particular clinical issues arising at different stages of therapy and their management are considered. Two chapters by specialist colleagues then describe the treatment of BPD associated with substance abuse (Tim Leighton) and the use of CAT with borderline patients in forensic settings (Philip Pollock). A final chapter reviews the place of CAT in relation to other approaches and to the wider social context.

Acknowledgements

The patients in the larger study all gave written consent to audiotaping and the publication of suitably disguised material. (They were invited to audiotape sessions themselves if they wished, and it was made clear that treatment would not be withheld if they did not give consent.) The two patients whose therapies are presented in Chapter 5, and some others quoted more extensively, have read, and been invited to comment on, what was written. Detailed modifications designed to disguise the patient's identity were included in all the accounts. Given how little reason most borderline patients have had to trust others, their consent is particularly deserving of thanks. Thanks are also due to the (largely trainee) therapists who consented to their work being presented; they bore the weight of both real and imagined pressures to perform and were required to listen to the tapes of all sessions before supervision and to complete even more work between sessions than is normal in CAT practice. I think they learned from their hard work but they certainly deserve gratitude.

Case material, including some from sources other than the research series, was derived from the work of the following: Hilary Beard, John Bristow, Sangamithra Choudree, Liz Fawkes, Madelyn Freeman, Deirdre Haslam, Margaret Johnstone, Barbara Kohnstamm, Janet Mead, Stuart McCahill, Cym Ryle. Acknowledgement is also due to those others who contributed to the work as fellow members of supervision seminars, to Hilary Beard, Annalee Curran, John Field and Val Coumont, who shared with me the supervisor role, and to Katya Golynkina for her analysis of the repertory grids. Many colleagues have read drafts of parts of the book, provided material and offered comments, criticisms and clarifications; I should like to thank in particular Fierman Bennink Bolt, Mark Dunn, Michael Gopfert, Ian Kerr, Mikael Leiman, James Low, Norma Maple and Mary Tyson for related conversations and comments. I should also like to thank Mark Dunn and the resilient office staff for managing to maintain a working system in the CAT clinic at what is left of Guy's Hospital.

ANTHONY RYLE

CHAPTER 1

Diagnosis, Course and Prevalence of Borderline Personality Disorder

The diagnosis of Borderline Personality Disorder (BPD) is an unsatisfactory one, but it is also, at present, irreplaceable; the temptation to put quotation marks round 'borderline' has therefore been resisted. The issues surrounding the diagnostic process must be discussed and to ground this discussion in a concrete instance I will start this chapter by presenting the history of a patient who would be recognized by most clinicians as a typical case. The particular patient presented has been chosen because, in contrast to all the other case examples in the book, but in common with most borderline patients, she received care from many professionals but was never seen by a psychotherapist. It seemed important to acknowledge in this way that the great majority of borderline individuals never receive psychotherapy, while at the same time proposing that understandings derived from psychotherapy and the particular theoretical model proposed here can contribute to the work of the psychiatrists, psychologists and general practitioners, nurses, occupational therapists, probation officers and social workers who provide most of the available care.

Case example: Emma

Emma's parents divorced when she was aged seven. She disclosed, some 12 years later, that at that time she was being sexually abused by her cousin; this had continued over a two-year period. At the age of 16 her GP recorded 'family and teenage problems' and from this time on, for the next five years, she was involved in multiple drug use (cannabis, solvents, amphetamines, LSD and alcohol) and was sexually promiscuous. Over that period she was seen and admitted to hospital overnight on eight occasions following overdoses, receiving assessments from a psychiatrist or Community Psychiatric Nurse (CPN) and being offered follow-up appointments, which she never kept. From the age of

1

19 she lived on her own in hostels or bedsits. At the age of 21, some few months after entering an apparently stable relationship, she contacted her new GP with a request for investigation of her infertility. When he expressed doubts about whether this was indicated at this time, she angrily accused him of depriving her of care because he disapproved of her unmarried status.

She returned shortly after, depressed and angrily preoccupied with memories of her abandoning father and of her abuser and explaining that she wanted a baby 'so I can have something which is mine'. The GP suggested that it might be advisable, before embarking on parenthood, to seek counselling or to attend a sexual abuse survivors group, but her memories of her contacts with psychiatric services were not favourable and she declined. The GP also resisted her requests for investigations of abdominal pain, suggesting that this could be related to her anxiety about fertility. He then embarked on a programme of low-intensity monthly counselling, encouraging her to build on what good relationships and satisfying activities she had available, and combining this with a course of antidepressant medication. Five months later she overdosed on this and was admitted to a psychiatric ward; at this time she described hearing voices. While in the ward she told a nurse of an occasion a few years earlier when she had put a pillow over the face of a baby she had been left in charge of, because she could not stand his crying. During this admission the diagnosis of Borderline Personality Disorder was made, and she was discharged on antipsychotic medication.

During the next ten months she was in a very disturbed and angry state and there were several episodes of self-cutting. However, her partner remained loyal to her and she eventually got pregnant, only to miscarry. This provoked much grief and a flood of anger and led to frequent consultations with her GP, with her psychiatrist and with a Community Psychiatric Nurse from the hospital. This emotional turmoil subsided when she again became pregnant; at this point she got married (inviting her GP to the wedding), ceased all drug abuse and self-harm and proceeded to have a healthy baby. Emma's last contact with professional workers was her being asked to attend a Social Services Case Conference, shortly after the baby's birth, called on account of her past instability and the episode of half-smothering the crying child some years before. She and her husband were present throughout the hearing, giving an account of how marriage and the pregnancy had changed her, and both her psychiatrist and her GP were able to support this. Two years later she remains stable and well.

Reflecting on his role in this story, the GP pointed to how he had been a stable point of reference in a chaotic life, had provided safe medical care while resisting unjustified demands for investigations, home visits and so on, had received and survived much verbal abuse and, in the end, had been able to like her and to witness and applaud the progress which she made. She stayed in contact with the GP and her psychiatrist and was evidently stable until she consulted in great anger concerning a marital crisis whe the baby was aged 2. Her 'borderline career' may not be entirely over.

Emma's story will be familiar to most professional workers and illustrates something of the pain experienced by the patient, its manifestation in anger and self-destructive acts, and its impact on those involved in her care. The safety experienced in her relationship and in her baby enabled her, perhaps unusually, to contain her destructiveness.

Diagnosis of Borderline Personality Disorder

We will now proceed to a consideration of the diagnosis of BPD. Despite the evident difficulties of describing and classifying something as complex as personality there is a long history of attempts. Dimensional classifications, such as introversion—extroversion, have their historical precedents in Galen's theory of the four humours, and there is also a long tradition of more subtle descriptive approaches. An early example of the latter is provided by Simonides (in Lucas, 1956). Writing around 600 BC he grouped women into nine descriptive categories on the basis of combining ratings of their household efficiency, appetites for food and sex, speech output, social activity, temper, obedience, maliciousness, laziness and beauty. His method of deriving *categories* from the rating of selected *traits* has a modern feel to it. So, alas, does his evident sexism. None the less, students of BPD will find Simonides' description of the category 'women created from the sea' (presumably so named on account of their changeability) recognizable:

> Two persons in one body—one day laughing, so gay that any stranger seeing her at home will sing her praises: 'Never woman so sweet in all the world, so lovable.' Let a day pass and she is insufferable to come near to or look at: in a frenzy like a bitch with puppies, snapping at everyone, to friend and foe a universal shrew.

In this passage Simonides identifies three of the characteristics of BPD which appear in the list of traits in the *Diagnostic and Statistical Manual*, DSM IV (APA, 1994; the diagnostic procedure followed in this book), where they are listed as: unstable, intense interpersonal relationships, affective instability and inappropriate intense anger. Two and a half thousand years later, relying on much the same approach, the designers of the DSM have added six further items, namely: frantic efforts to avoid abandonment, identity disturbance, impulsivity, suicidal and self-mutilating behaviour, chronic feelings of emptiness, and transient stress-related paranoid ideas and dissociative symptoms. The diagnosis rests upon the presence of at least five of these nine traits.

It is easy to criticize the fruit of many years of nosological effort and, one suspects, of countless committee hours spent in search of consensus, but there are many problems with this approach. Patients diagnosed in this way differ considerably in the severity of disturbance and in the range of symptomatology. Many qualify for other diagnoses on Axis II (which seeks to classify longstanding personality patterns), particularly those listed in Cluster B (Histrionic,

Antisocial and Narcissistic Personality Disorders) and the great majority have, in addition, conditions diagnosed as illnesses on Axis I. Limited as it is by its adherence to a purely descriptive approach, the DSM could still be improved by according more salience to certain of the listed features and by quantifying the degree to which each is manifest. Nurnberg *et al.* (1991), for example, list the criteria in a hierarchy, headed by disturbed interpersonal relationships, impulsivity, feelings of emptiness and self-destructive behaviours. An addition-al problem is the overlapping between the traits; unstable interpersonal rela-tionships, affective instability and identity disturbance are hardly independent variables, and the conspicuous fact that seven of the traits are characteristical-ly intermittent surely deserves more explicit recognition by naming variability as a (higher order) trait.

This reliance on trait descriptions reflects the absence of a generally agreed theoretical model of BDP; it probably only survives because it follows the wide-ly accepted tradition of psychiatric classification. Writers in the psychoanalytic tradition, notably Kernberg (1975, 1984) have questioned the value of the DSM diagnostic approach and propose in its place a broader concept of borderline personality *organization*. This is based on Kernberg's development of classical and object relations ideas and focuses on identity diffusion and the predomi-nance of the primitive defences of splitting and projection. This model will be considered in Chapter 3. Many other writers have questioned the advisability of applying categorical methods, appropriate to the classification of butterflies and perhaps of diseases of known aetiology, to phenomena as complex as those of human personality. Berelowitz and Tarnopolsky (1993), having concluded from an extensive review that the diagnosis had been firmly established and does serve to distinguish BPD from conditions with which it had been confused in the past (schizotypal personality, schizophrenia and depression), commented that it might be better regarded as 'a measure of severe personality dysfunction rather than as a distinct diagnostic entity'. Rutter (1987), from a different per-spective, concluded that a more appropriate grouping might simply include people with major problems in making and sustaining social relationships.

Despite all these doubts and deficiencies, at the present time there is no diagnostic system which offers an alternative and more satisfactory method. In the rest of this chapter its achievements and its application in the cases described in this book will be described and the course and prevalence of cases diagnosed by it will be summarized.

Differentiating Borderline Personality Disorder from other Diagnostic Groups

One clear and historically important achievement of the DSM has been to establish the differentiation between BPD, schizophrenia and schizotypal per-sonality disorder. But the relation of BPD to the dissociative disorders, to other related (Cluster B) personality disorders and to Axis I conditions is less satisfactorily established and will be discussed here.

The Relation of Borderline Personality to Dissociative Disorders

One diagnostic issue which has attracted relatively little attention is the role of dissociation in BPD and its differentiation from dissociative disorders, notably Multiple Personality Disorder (MPD). This condition has been relabelled as Dissociative Identity Disorder (DID) but in this book the more familiar title MPD will be used. Gunderson and Sabo (1993) have reviewed the links between BPD and Post-Traumatic Stress Disorder (PTSD) and noted commonalities; in the light of the known early trauma suffered by most BPD patients this would not be surprising and the idea that aspects of BPD could be the consequence of childhood PTSD has gained some support. It is evident that many, probably the great majority, of sufferers from MPD also meet the criteria for BPD, and a high incidence of childhood abuse is found in both conditions. As the role of dissociation is central to the model of BPD proposed in Chapter 3 its neglect in most current thinking requires some attention.

The reasons are probably more to do with orthodoxies than with science. One source could be Freud's rejection of the seduction theory and his parting company with Janet, resulting in the emphasis within psychoanalysis on universal intrapsychic conflicts around sexual issues and the neglect (one might suggest *repression*) of the role of trauma. Only in the last two decades, with the rediscovery of the high incidence of physical and sexual abuse of children, has some attention been paid to this issue within psychoanalysis. A second source could be the dismissal of the idea of MPD within psychiatry; one suspects that, in some centres, to propose the diagnosis would be met with derision and might jeopardize one's career. One main source of the disrepute into which the diagnosis of MPD fell, a disrepute which is surprising given the eminence of those who first described the phenomenon, was identified by Janet himself as the attitude of some of the physicians who became interested in the condition. He wrote of one case history as follows: 'The history is strangely related; you feel in it a kind of mystic admiration for the subject, an exaggerated seeking after surprising and supranormal phenomena, which of course inspires you with some fear as to the way in which the observation has been conducted' (Janet, 1965). This strain of apparent gullibility and enthusiasm is evident in some contemporary writers on the subject (see, for example, Ross, 1994) and provokes an equally extreme rejection from critics like Mersky (1992).

What is missing from the accounts of both advocates and critics is an acknowledgement of the powerful way in which these patients (and the same is true of many borderline subjects) involve clinicians in their belief systems. Diagnosis, in such cases, must depend upon an acute awareness of one's own part in the relationship. In this context objectivity depends on experiencing and reflecting on one's own subjectivity as evoked by the patient, and calls for an awareness of one's capacity to influence the patient in turn. Putnam (1989) seems insufficiently aware of this when he describes his diagnostic process as follows: Patients who answer yes when asked 'is it as if another person is in you?' are then asked 'if that part can come out and talk to me'. Putnam observes that the more specific the description given of the invited 'alter' the more likely is it to 'come out'. This process, and the naming of increasingly elaborate platoons of 'alters' which some practitioners describe, must be a powerful reinforcement of dissociation. But to recognize this is not to deny that dissociation occurs without the help of enthusiastic clinicians.

The Differentiation of Borderline Personality from other Personality Disorders

Borderline Personality Disorder is grouped in Cluster B of the DSM Axis II classification, along with Antisocial, Histrionic and Narcissistic personality disorders. Antisocial Personality Disorder shares many features with BPD in terms of early history and associated diagnoses, the two conditions differing in that most antisocial personalities are male while most borderline personalities are female. These differences between the two diagnoses may reflect both biological and cultural factors. The basis of the other two Cluster B diagnoses seems unsatisfactory in that the Histrionic criteria reflect major cultural assumptions about the expression of emotion and the features listed for Narcissistic Personality Disorder omit any reference to the characteristic underlying, and at times expressed, self-contempt and neediness. The relative weight given to affective, cognitive, behavioural and interpersonal features in arriving at the different Cluster B diagnoses is not the same (Widiger et al., 1988), which also makes their inter-relationships difficult to interpret.

In practice, the discrimination of BPD from the other Cluster B disorders is not satisfactory and multiple diagnoses are common. Dolan et al. (1995), commenting on this, suggest that, rather than labelling such multiple diagnoses as 'co-morbidity', implying the simultaneous presence of several 'diseases', they should be regarded as examples of a greater 'breadth' of Axis II pathology. This observation lends support to the idea that Cluster B conditions might be better thought of as manifestations of personality dysfunction in which the range and severity of disturbance varies. As Tyrer (1996) observes, 'the atheoretical classification that is typical of ... DSM IV ... has been a good bricklayer in psychiatric classifications but without direction it is in danger of only making walls'.

Borderline Personality and Axis I Conditions

Psychiatric illnesses (diagnosed on Axis I) are a virtually universal accompaniment of BPD (Fyer et al., 1988); the differentiation of such disorders from long-term personality disturbances causing enduring distresses and impairments was a major aim of the DSM. Psychotherapists are likely to see this distinction between lifelong traits and transient states as of less interest than do psychiatrists, because most of their patients have longstanding problematic ways of managing their lives, even if their symptoms and consultations may be intermittent, reflecting the decompensation of longstanding coping or defensive strategies. However they, and general psychiatrists treating Axis I conditions, are well advised to be aware of the influence of destructive long-term personality traits, as identified on Axis II, on the treatment relationship and on outcome (Reich and Green, 1991).

Most borderline patients are deeply unhappy and *depression* is a feature in a large proportion of cases of BPD; the relationship of this to depressive illness has been much disputed. Given the known relationship between life events and depression and given the many life events provoked by the instability and destructiveness of borderline patients, some relationship between the two diagnoses might be expected. There is, however, no evidence for a common genetic cause for major depression and BPD and the quality of depression found in BPD and its response to medication differ from what is found in depressive illnesses. Thus Gunderson and Phillips (1991) suggest that unipolar depression is characterized by guilt, remorse, active suicidal behaviour, a preoccupation with failure and a normally stable relationship pattern, whereas the BPD patient's depression is characterized by emptiness, angry neediness, a preoccupation with loss and frequent suicidal gestures. They also contrast the depressive's proneness to long periods of low mood, suggesting a primary defect in affect control, with the borderline patient's briefer, more clearly reactive mood changes, which they suggest are better explained as due to problems with impulse control.

In conclusion, it has to be said that depression is a problem for most borderline patients but that the relation between depression and the borderline state remains incompletely clarified. Most clinicians will seek to alleviate depression in borderline patients with pharmacological means, but the response is uncertain (Soloff, 1993). To complicate the picture still more, untreated depression may sometimes make manifest, or may exaggerate, borderline features which are not normally evident and which cease to be evident once the depression is relieved, an observation which probably explains the remarkable claims made for the ability of some new drugs to change personality.

A number of other conditions are commonly found in BPD patients; these include *substance abuse, eating disorders, somatization disorders and dissociative symptoms.* (The latter have been added to the diagnostic criteria in DSM IV.) These conditions, which may all be found independently of BPD, all share with it higher than expected rates of childhood abuse.

It has already been suggested that a categorical approach to the diagnosis of BPD has many deficiencies and problems; the categorization of the various associated Axis I conditions, although less problematic, is only clarifying of the

whole picture to a certain extent. Rather than conceiving of the associated Axis
I conditions as different illnesses which happen to co-exist with the relationship,
identity and affective difficulties of borderline patients, it seems more logical to
see them as different manifestations of a common underlying disruption of personal functioning. How this association may be explained will be discussed in
Chapter 3.

Borderline Personality: Course, Prevalence and Causes

The Course

The fact that the diagnosis of BPD has only slowly become standardized and the
variability of diagnosed patients mean that no accurate and generally applica-
ble data exist about the course of BPD. The largest series is that of Stone
(1993); while the particular nature of his sample (New York, predominantly
middle class) must be borne in mind, his study and those he reviews suggest
that, while the diagnosis remains a serious one, the long-term outcome is less
universally unfavourable than was formerly believed for the majority of cases.
Ten to thirty years after diagnosis one in five patients in his sample were living
normal symptom-free lives and only one in three still showed major symptoms.
Patients described as intelligent, attractive or having artistic talent, those with
obsessive-compulsive traits and alcoholics who had become abstinent had a better prognosis. The diagnosis remains a serious one however: some 8% had committed suicide, an outcome associated with alcoholism, major affective disorders, antisocial traits and a history of parental brutality or sexual abuse. Paris
(1993) found a suicide rate of 9.5% in a follow-up study of a more socially
diverse group of patients who had been admitted to a general hospital.

Prevalence of Borderline Personality Disorder in the General Population

Estimates of the prevalence of BPD in the general population are inevitably
very approximate; it is evident, however, that women are much more frequently diagnosed than men and that the rate falls with increasing age, as would be
predicted from the known outcome data. Using the broadest interpretations of
the diagnosis, such as that provided by Kernberg's concept of borderline personality organization, the prevalence in the general population of young adults
could be as high as 10%, while applying those of DSM IV as used by clinicians
the rate is probably nearer 1–2%.

Borderline Patients in Psychiatric and Psychotherapy Services

The proportion of patients seen in psychiatric services who are diagnosed as
suffering from BPD is likely to vary greatly according to the attitudes of refer-

rers and of the psychiatrists running the services. Many psychiatrists prefer to treat Axis I disorders and pay little attention to the recognition and treatment of accompanying personality problems; many, indeed, do not accept that they are their responsibility. It is not uncommon for individuals seen after self-harm, even of a life-threatening nature, to be simply recorded as having 'no evidence of psychiatric illness'. Where severely personality-disordered individuals have committed murders, it is frequently stated in the courts (and widely quoted in the press) that there is no treatment for personality disorders.

It is a disturbing fact that similar negative attitudes are found in some psychotherapy services in which the referral of borderline patients is discouraged, often on the grounds that they are unsuitable training cases. While this is to an extent true, because they are difficult cases, it is my view that specialist psychotherapy should increasingly concern itself with treating (or supervising the treatment of) these patients, for there are now many effective treatments for less disturbed patients. If this is accepted it is essential for psychotherapy trainees in psychiatry and clinical psychology to have experience of them.

The treatment and management of BPD in general psychiatry is an issue of particular importance, given that such patients are often expensively but unsatisfactorily managed. Borderline patients are often unsatisfactorily maintained as psychiatric outpatients, where successive generations of trainee psychiatrists prescribe them successive generations of antidepressant or antipsychotic drugs. They are also commonly found, but not always identified, in non-psychiatric settings such as Accident and Emergency departments after self-harm, in substance abuse services and presenting with chronic somatic complaints to medical services. The extension of liaison psychiatry and the greater inclusion in it of a psychotherapeutic orientation could identify many of these. It is probable that at the present time the overall prevalence (and cost to the health service) of untreated BPD in various treatment settings is considerably higher than is recognized.

It is widely believed that the prevalence of BPD has increased during recent decades. Millon (1993) presents some indirect evidence that this might be so, and argues that recent rapid social changes, the fragility of the family and the greater anomie of social life, have produced a generation of poorly integrated, consumer-oriented materialists or rebels without a cause. At a more general level one could argue that the combination of the unprecedented violence of this century with its heightened competitive individualism has placed far more demands on the internal structure of the self. Whereas, in the past, damaged people might have been contained by the institutions of family and workplace, the modern individual has fewer such supports and faces more demands, being expected to continually demonstrate his or her worth by achievement (as in 'what have you done for me lately?'), while being offered decreasing security. But explanations in terms of particular historical and social factors may well be only partial, or indeed false; in considering them it is, perhaps, pertinent to note that the late Middle Ages were characterized by 'Perpetual oscillations between despair and distracted joy, between cruelty and pious tenderness' (Huizinga, 1924).

The Causes of Borderline Personality Disorder

Whatever the influence of general social factors may be, certain biological and environmental influences are generally agreed to play a part in causing BPD. While neither genetic studies nor the search for biological markers have demonstrated clear indicators, it is reasonable to suppose that genetic and organic factors will influence a developing child's reactions to environmental stresses and may also, through behavioural disturbance, play a part in provoking adverse relationship patterns with caretakers. Minor neurological damage may play such a role (van Reekum *et al.*, 1993) and an association of BPD with adverse birth experience has been reported (Soloff and Millward, 1983). Such innate or acquired organic influences are seen to lead to defects in impulse control and affect regulation and their possible presence should be borne in mind when interpreting patients' early histories.

The evidence for the association of BPD with severe early adversity is incontrovertible. Physical violence and sexual abuse have been experienced by the majority of patients (Perry and Herman, 1993) and in the remainder other forms of loss, deprivation or trauma are virtually always present. The publicity given to 'false memory syndrome' (usually in relation to forensic issues) should not distract clinicians from being alert to the occurrence of such events, which are difficult for patients to recount and for which there may be partial or complete amnesia. It is, of course, never appropriate to suggest to patients what unremembered experiences they may have had, but neither should such memories, when they emerge after periods of amnesia, be disbelieved or interpreted away, as was for so long the practice. Where memories of abuse are recovered after amnesia, whether in therapy or as a result of media reports or reminders from other family members, validating evidence is present in a large proportion of cases (Feldman-Summers and Pope, 1994). Brewin (1996), in a review of the controversy surrounding recovered memories and the 'false memory syndrome', concluded that recovered memories undoubtedly occurred and could be, but were not always, essentially accurate; his advice that one should be scrupulous in drawing inferences from such memories should be noted. Mollon (1997) offers a useful guide to evaluating recovered memories and urges a tolerance of uncertainty by clinicians. In my own experience of the assessment and psychotherapy of a very large number of borderline patients I have been more often struck by their underemphasizing the enormity of the pain they endured as children than by any sense that their accounts are exaggerated, let alone invented.

Diagnostic Procedures Used in the Present Study

The patients described in this book were identified from those referred to the CAT clinic at Guy's Hospital. Where referral data or initial assessment suggested the possibility that patients were borderline, they were interviewed by a psychiatric senior registrar with the Personality Assessment Schedule (PAS) (Tyrer *et al.*, 1987). This semi-structured interview covers a range of traits, each of which is scored for impact and intensity; the diagnosis of BPD derived from this instrument rests on the ratings of worthlessness, lability, impulsiveness and aggression.

The PAS has not been validated against other standardized interview schedules and tends to yield frequent multiple Axis II diagnoses. In view of this, patients admitted to the series of patients on which this book is based were given a final diagnosis retrospectively, on the basis of all the data collected from previous clinical reports, the assessment interviews and the therapy. Using this information, two raters independently score the presence and intensity of DSM IV features. On this basis patients in the research series will be described by a trait profile and the effect of applying more or less stringent thresholds for 'caseness' can be estimated. This process resembles, but is clearly less rigorous than, the LEAD (longitudinal, expert, all data) approach described by Spitzer (1983).

Summary

In this introductory chapter an attempt has been made to define the patient group being studied. It was considered that DSM IV, despite many drawbacks, offered the best available basis for identifying a group of patients who are undoubtedly among the more severe of those amenable to psychological treatments. The rest of the book will describe the treatment of these patients with CAT and will propose a developmental and structural model of borderline personality.

CHAPTER 2

The Evolution of Cognitive Analytic Therapy

The work with borderline patients and the theoretical model of borderline functioning described in this book evolved as part of the general evolution of Cognitive Analytic Therapy, for reviews of which see Ryle (1982, 1990, 1995b) and Leiman (1994b). CAT originated in an integration of cognitive and psychoanalytic ideas in which a main influence was my use of repertory grid techniques (Kelly, 1955) to measure and describe change in the course of psychodynamic psychotherapy. In the course of this research patients were involved, at the start of therapy, in working with the therapist at the task of identifying and describing clearly what had brought them to therapy (their *target problems* or TPs) and in elaborating descriptions of the ways in which these were caused and maintained (*target problem procedures* or TPPs). The initial purpose of the latter was to devise a description of the aims of therapy which would permit assessment not only of problem reduction but also of 'dynamic change', but in practice, it soon became apparent that this activity had a powerful therapeutic impact, and this early *joint descriptive reformulation* became, and has remained, a defining feature of the CAT approach. Later developments have included the elaboration of different methods of reformulation and the inclusion of a transformed version of object relations theory, influenced latterly by the work of Vygotsky, Voloshinov and Bakhtin (see Ryle, 1991, 1995b; Leiman, 1992, 1994a, 1995). From these various influences there emerged a mode of therapy which is collaborative in style and which emphasizes description rather than interpretation. Description acknowledges the patient's experience and provides a basis for increasing the capacity for self-reflection.

The Early Theory

An examination of the records of a series of completed therapies revealed that, in every case, the work of therapy had been concentrated on a small number of themes. It soon became apparent that these themes could be identified in the material of the first few sessions, often in the first one, from the patient's account and from the events and feelings emerging in the evolving therapy relationship. A study of these themes, seeking to identify what had prevented the revision of problematic procedures, showed that there were three main patterns whereby revision was blocked (Ryle, 1979). These were named *dilemmas, traps and snags*, defined as follows:

- In *dilemmas* the options for acting or for relating to self or others are seen to be dichotomized between polarized choices. In some cases the individual will always enact one of these, in other cases he or she may alternate between them; the essential problem is the restriction of possibility to these two.
- In *traps* negative beliefs and assumptions generate acts or roles which provoke consequences which seem to reinforce the belief or assumption.
- In *snags* appropriate goals are given up or undone, either in the (true or false) belief that others will oppose or forbid them (external snags) or as if they were dangerous or forbidden (conscious or unconscious internal snags).

These three patterns were then linked in a general model of aim-directed action, the Procedural Sequence Model (PSM) (Ryle, 1982). The unit of description is the *procedure*, which combines in sequence (1) mental processes (perception, appraisal, intention, prediction, choice of means), (2) action, including role playing, and (3) the evaluation of the consequences, leading (4) to the confirmation or revision of the aim or the means. This model was compatible with current cognitive and behavioural models but it was also possible to restate many psychoanalytic ideas in these terms. For example, dilemmas could be seen to be related to concepts of conflict and splitting, and internal snags could be seen to be the result of conscious or unconscious guilt. The aims of therapy came to be defined as the revision of the individual's dilemmas, traps and snags.

I now regard the Procedural Sequence Model as a useful analytical tool rather than as a general model of human learning; interpersonal and intrapersonal procedures are acquired in interaction, influenced by the caretaker's procedural patterns, rather than being formed and modified through rational learning, and failure to revise problem procedures has additional sources to those suggested by the model. But the focus on self-perpetuating sequences of linked mental, behavioural and environmental processes remains therapeutically valuable.

Practice

Cognitive Analytic Therapy is delivered in a predetermined time limit; this is usually 16 weekly sessions. The first four sessions are devoted to the task of *reformulation*, a process depending on the ordinary exploratory methods of dynamic therapists but also on more 'cognitive' tasks. The approach generates an informal atmosphere in which the therapist puts forward ideas for discussion which are not too far removed from the material presented and in which the patient is asked to carry out associated tasks. The main aim is *accurate description*; if 'interpretations' are offered about internal processes to which the patient has no access they will be offered as hypotheses.

At the first meeting patients are given the 'Psychotherapy File' to take away and read (see Appendix 1). This contains instructions in self-monitoring (derived from cognitive therapy), and patients will be asked to do this in respect of unwanted behaviour and variable moods or symptoms, with the aim of identifying their antecedents, accompanying thoughts and feelings and consequences. In addition, the File explains the notions of dilemmas, traps and snags and lists brief descriptions of common patterns; patients are asked to mark those that they think might apply to them and these items and the examples reported of them will be discussed at the next session. The final section describes the experience of state shifts and offers a list of possible states of mind; it is intended to act as a screening device for borderline pathology. Used in these ways the File can serve as a source of information, as a basis for exploratory conversation and as a way of introducing the patient to new forms of self-reflection. A few patients do not find it helpful; the reasons for this should be explored but it should not be imposed.

Drawing on these various sources the therapist will prepare a draft *reformulation letter* to take to the fourth session. Most of the contents of this will have been discussed in the sessions, but hearing the linked account, with its attempted clarification of inappropriate guilts and denied responsibilities and, above all, receiving an empathic acknowledgement of their life experience, usually has a powerful impact on patients. The reformulation letter ends with a list of *Target problems* (TPs) and *Target problem procedures* (TPPs), the latter expressed in the form of dilemmas, traps and snags in order to focus on the self-maintaining nature of the sequences and indicate the nature of change required. This list represents the agenda for the therapy.

Target problems will include those presented by the patient, such as anxiety or relationship problems, and additional ones which may only be identified as problems by the therapist, such as low self-esteem. The reality of what is not in the power of the patient to change, whether in the past or in present circumstances, should be acknowledged. Target problem procedures will be described in ways showing their circularity (as a non-blaming explanation of past failures to change), drawing on those identified in the File and from the history or observed in the therapy relationship; as far as possible these brief descriptions should use the patient's own words and metaphors. After discussion and any necessary alterations a copy of the letter and TP and TPP list is held by each.

The role of *description* is emphasized in CAT, in contradistinction to the role of interpretation in psychoanalysis, but it should not be supposed that a simple dead-head reproduction of the patient's story is intended; some degree of *transformation* is also implied. An imaginary conversation of the Sung dynasty painter Ching Hao (quoted in Siren, 1963) illustrates the intended difference: 'I remarked "Painting is to make beautiful things, and the important thing is to obtain their true likeness; is it not?" He answered "It is not. Painting is to paint, to estimate the shapes of things and really obtain them, to estimate the beauty of things and reach it, to estimate the reality (significance) of things and grasp it ... . He who does not understand this mystery will not obtain the truth even though his pictures may contain likeness." '

The work of these early sessions, while involving reading and writing and thinking, is also usually emotionally involving and serves to lay the foundations of a working alliance. After reformulation the emphasis on the 'homework' negotiated with the patient shifts from the monitoring of spontaneous events to the task of learning to recognize the now-identified problem procedures through self-observation, diary-keeping and other tasks. Abbreviated descriptions of these will be transferred to rating sheets to be completed at the end of sessions as a means of maintaining the focus for both patient and therapist and as an exercise in accurate self-reflection. As this work proceeds, the increased sense of safety it engenders commonly results in an extended access to memory and feeling, the relation of which to the reformulation will be considered.

The positive working alliance generated by the reformulation process is usually disrupted at some point by the emergence in the therapeutic relationship of some of the patient's negative procedures, often in a disguised and indirect form; the therapist's recognition of, and non-collusion with, these is an important moment in the change process, as Safran *et al.* (1990) have pointed out. It is usually at this point in the therapy that the third of the three Rs of CAT (Reformulation, Recognition and Revision) becomes an issue, both in relation to enactments in the therapy relationship and through the monitoring of repetitions of problem procedures in daily life. Possible 'exits' from these may be added to the descriptions of TPs and TPPs at this stage, but this should *not* be done before recognition is reliably established; both patients and therapists tend to rush to solutions before the problems are reliably recognized and understood.

Termination will have been kept on the agenda throughout the therapy; in preparation for the last session the therapist will write a *goodbye letter* and will invite the patient to do the same. This represents a way of offering and eliciting a realistic appraisal of what has been achieved, of noting and permitting both disappointment and pleasure and of suggesting how further work may continue to draw on the therapy tools and relationship. Follow-up at around three months offers a chance to see how termination has been weathered and at this time any further needs can be assessed.

The model summarized in the PSM can provide a basis for understanding a wide range of neurotic problems. Although it is essentially a cognitive model, many psychoanalytic ideas can be represented in its terms; it differs most markedly in that, rather than focusing on conflict, *sequences and non-revision* are the central concern. The conscious–unconscious division is seen as less absolute and is little emphasized, for most procedures are seen to operate automatically. Mental processes are largely unconscious (but their effects are open to reflection) and both conscious and unconscious processes derive from the early interactions of the child with caretakers. The psychoanalytic 'dynamic unconscious' is only known or hypothesized on the basis of the patient's acts, from omissions from, or intrusions into, consciousness or in the manifestation of assumed conflicts in the form of 'compromise formations'.

Human activity, in CAT theory, is organized by procedures developed in relation to a mediated version of reality acquired in joint activity with others; *all* procedures correspond, therefore, to what psychodynamic therapists would describe as 'compromise formations'. The procedures of a given individual may give evidence of the distortions or restrictions which would, in psychoanalysis, be described as the results of repression; the procedural description of these would take the form of tracing out the observable (restricted or deviant) actions or roles and describing their effects on the reciprocations offered by others. Offering possible explanations in terms of intrapsychic conflict would be of secondary importance. For example, submissive behaviour which might be attributed to castration anxiety in psychoanalysis, would, in CAT, be described as a procedure leading to negative outcomes often associated with depression or symptoms; the source (for example in the patient's perception of the reciprocal role patterns of others as threatening) would also be discussed.

The joint production of the reformulation, the subsequent use of it by the patient to develop accurate, relevant self-reflection, and the use of it by the therapist to guard against or recover from any collusion with the negative procedures, are seen as the main factors encouraging change (revision). The reformulation process combines the two modes of learning identified by Bruner, namely the 'narrative' (represented by the retelling and linking of the patient's life story) and the 'paradigmatic', in the provision of focused descriptions of ongoing processes (Bruner, 1986; Ryle, 1994b). The method combines in this way accurate, detailed empathic understanding with the 'corrective emotional experience' of an honest, thoughtful relationship which involves respect, joint work and non-collusion, enabling patients to learn new ways of reflecting upon, controlling and valuing themselves.

The Introduction and Modification of Object Relations Ideas

Although the PSM was capable of incorporating psychoanalytic ideas, some contributions from object relations theories were missing, notably the attempt to explain how early experience shaped both personality and patterns of relating to others. A first step in correcting this involved rewriting some developmental and structural ideas derived from object relations theories, using a more cognitive language (Ryle, 1985). This involved extending in particular the notion of the procedure, emphasizing how procedures concerned with maintaining relationships involve the prediction or elicitation of the response of the other. The *reciprocal role procedures* characteristic of an individual were seen to be learned and expressed in relation to others, and their origin was seen to lie in the early relationships with the mother and other caretakers. But, in a specifically human development, these same patterns become internalized and form the basis of personality and the source of *self-management procedures* also.

Personal Constructs and Social Constructivism

The initial Procedural Sequence Model owed much to Kelly's (1955) ideas and was essentially a cognitivist, personal constructivist model in which anticipation followed by validation or invalidation served to form and revise procedures. Describing problem procedures in these terms allows patients to recognize and consciously control the antecedents to damaging or ineffective acts and as such it remains a very useful technique. In offering such an account the therapist could be seen to be encouraging the patient to be a Kellyan 'personal scientist'. But he or she can also be seen to be providing a new, hopefully more useful, account (narrative) of familiar experiences and sequences and a different pattern of relating. In this respect, reformulation is a particular example of the way in which personal constructs may be acquired and modified in the course of social interaction.

The debate between personal and social constructivists (see Mancuso, 1996; discussed by Burkitt, 1996, and Wortham, 1996) seems to hang largely on the relative weight accorded to socially transmitted constructs (for a long time ignored by individual psychologists) and those personally acquired. A more fruitful concern may be to consider how the social and the personal influence each other.

Developmental Theory in CAT

The CAT model of early development is derived from the description of reciprocal role procedures as key concepts. A person's *repertoire of reciprocal role procedures*, acquired in the earliest interactions with the mother and later with other caretakers, is the product of the child's temperament in interaction with the others' procedures. From the patterns first elaborated with the mother the child progresses to an understanding of the roles of self and other and in time learns to play either role and to reverse these, for example playing the maternal role to the mother, or to dolls. In a final and distinctively human step the child comes to play the maternal or parental role towards the self and in this way an internal conversation between different 'voices', some self- and some other-derived, is initiated. With this comes the possibility of internal conflict. Personality, on a basis of innate qualities, is shaped by the internalization of reciprocal role patterns endowed with meanings. A person is characterized by his or her particular internal dialogue, a dialogue which also continues to seek expression and extension in interaction with others. Each child is unique in his or her biological endowment and in the cultural context and experience which shape personality.

This outline model, called the Procedural Sequence Object Relations Model (PSORM), offered a more accessible and reliable account than those based on psychoanalytic notions, which inextricably mix observations (often sensitive and insightful) with hypotheses depending for their validation on no more than the consent to interpretations granted by analysands (see Ryle, 1996). While incorporating some object relations ideas in CAT theory the attempt was made to be consistent with the growing body of empirical data which casts doubt on many psychoanalytic assumptions, notably those concerning the timetable of development and the relation between analytic phenomena, psychosis and normal development (e.g. Stern, 1985; Westen, 1990). In hypothesizing developmental and structural processes the mixed psychoanalytic metaphors of the 'inner world' are often confusing. Combining models of representation with notions of incorporation and identification and postulating the embodiment of instincts in quasi-autonomous 'objects' and 'part objects' relating to an 'ego' or 'part egos' provide an elaborate source of doctrinal disputes rather than a clear basis for thought. Splitting, supposed to represent a defence of the good object by separating it from the bad, can be better and less magically described in terms of contrasting, polarized reciprocal role patterns and of separate self states (see below), and projective identification can be understood as a particular example of the general mode of eliciting reciprocal responses from others (Sandler, 1976; Ryle, 1994a).

Vygotsky and Sign Mediation

A further clarification of early development, based on the work of Vygotsky, in which the social and cultural formation of mind and the crucial significance of sign mediation were emphasized, was introduced into CAT in the early 1990s (Leiman, 1992, 1994a, 1995; Ryle, 1991, 1995b). This pointed to the importance of pre-verbal sign mediation in the establishment of meanings and the development of de-contextualized thought. The child comes to inhabit a world of both physical and social realities, understood through concepts derived from the general culture. Recent work by Toomela (1996a,b) supports this view and offers a succinct analysis of the process of *internalization* as described in outline by Vygotsky. This author points out that any act or object can constitute a sign or symbol if (a) it can be directly perceived, (b) its meaning is shared with others, (c) it refers to objects, events or phenomena, and (d) the use of it as a sign differs from the use made of what it refers to. Internalization, in the proposed definition offered by this author, can only take place through the use of such symbols, the formation of which involves (1) the interaction of the child's innate capacities with the social environment and (2) the development of links between 'natural' mechanisms for non-mediated thought and the parallel acquisition of semiotic mediation.

Our first learning takes place through interaction with others; internalized in the form of mediating signs this interaction provides the basis of that internal dialogue which constitutes thought. That the essential basis for mediated thought is learned in a social context means that those aspects of thought concerned with concepts of self and other are learned from those others who provide both our first experiences and, to a considerable extent, provide the means we have of making sense of them. The unconscious mental processes on which psychoanalysis concentrates may be understood in this model as including those mediated by pre-verbal signs, those representing voices in the internal dialogue which have been silenced and those for which no mediating signs were provided or discovered.

Attachment Theory

The CAT developmental account has many similarities with models emerging from attachment theory but differs in its Vygotskian aspects. The clear discussion by Crittenden (1990) of internal models of attachment relationships may be taken as a recent example of attachment theory, with which the CAT approach may be compared. The CAT account differs from it in seeing the early attachment relationships with caretakers as the precursors, not only of attachment relationships, but of the full range of emotionally significant interactions and would emphasize how they are also formative of crucially important self processes. The representations of *self-to-other* and of *attachment figure-to-attached person* relationships, and the contrast of complementary and reciprocal patterns, would all be considered under the single concept of reciprocal roles. Reciprocal roles are described as involving action, knowledge and affect and the separate consideration of these aspects in the attachment model is seen as of uncertain value, given that the experiences which shape procedures and their expression inevitably involve all three.

Crittenden links models of relating to Tulving's description of three memory systems (Tulving, 1985). While the introduction of the word 'procedure' in CAT did not derive from Tulving's model, in many ways the use of the term is compatible. As Crittenden writes, *procedural knowledge* is acquired from experience 'although the actual experiences themselves are not remembered ... [and] ... will continue to influence behaviour even after more sophisticated and conscious memory systems develop'. Such knowledge tends to be in the form of high-level routines or patterns, operating automatically once mobilized and being, as Crittenden says, 'robust' in the face of contradictory information. In all these ways the CAT role procedure fits the description.

The CAT understanding of the role of *semantic memory* differs, however, from that proposed by Crittenden. She suggests two sources for such memory, one being information received from other people, and dependent on language, the other being 'based on direct experience'. This and the biological emphasis in attachment theory convey a neglect of the role of sign mediation in pre-verbal development. The infant's 'direct experience', whether described through concepts such as attunement and the development of RIGS (Representations of Interactions that have been Generalized) (Stern, 1985) or through attachment theory ideas, is already an experience of a world in which objects and events are imbued with meanings. These meanings are first conveyed by non-verbal signs constituting a mutually created 'vocabulary' of things, tones, gestures movements and rituals. Such semantic knowledge, structuring the child's understanding of the world and of self and others is, in this view, jointly formed by child and caretaker from the earliest stages of post-natal life and the role of language is a later, and perhaps a less formative, one. It may be that it is only with the acquisition of *episodic memory*, placing the self in relation to events through time, and with the developing capacity for self-reflection that language and other abstract conceptual tools provide, that thought can be applied to the revision of the procedural and semantic knowledge acquired in the early years.

In individual development the powerful pre-verbal forms of communication on which early semantic knowledge rests could be seen to represent the repetition in ontogeny of the modes characteristic of our primate ancestors. During the pre-linguistic stages of human evolution (phylogeny), as described in the fascinating survey of archaeological, anthropological, linguistic, neurological and psychological evidence by Donald (1991), pre-verbal, mimetic communication was the basic source of socially shared meanings. In the developing individual such communication provides a prologue to language but remains separate from it and continues to be active alongside it.

In the CAT model the early reciprocal roles, constituting actions and expectations shaped by meanings, may be further elaborated and integrated throughout childhood and adolescence, but the initial procedural patterns have a certain 'robustness' even if inadequate. Their resistance to change is reinforced by the self-confirming processes described as dilemmas, traps and snags and by the capacity we have to extract, or to think we have extracted, confirmatory responses from others. A person's basic role patterns are thus limited and are maintained largely unrevised; much individual behaviour can be understood as being constrained by the particular restricted options apparently available. For example, rather than proposing that self-harming behaviours are necessarily the result of innate drives, the enactment of which produces perverse gratification, this understanding would account for most such behaviour in terms of the persistence of old, and the failure to develop alternative, procedures, or as representing how the sense of self and identity depends upon the extracting of confirmations for the range of beliefs and values embodied in the role repertoire. Attachment theory, psychoanalysis and cognitive theories all lack an adequate emphasis on the parallels and interconnections between inner and interpersonal dialogue.

Sequential Diagrams

Descriptions of dilemmas, traps and snags are adequate for describing individual procedures but do not indicate the sources of, or the relationships between, different procedures. These can be described verbally but can be displayed more clearly in the form of flow diagrams.

Sequential Diagrammatic Reformulation (SDR) evolved from an initial ad hoc approach into a more explicitly object relations format (a development described in Ryle, 1995b). Three types of procedure can be distinguished: (1) procedures for relating to others, (2) self-management procedures, and (3) avoidant and symptomatic procedures representing transformations of feared or forbidden role procedures. In the SDR all three are depicted as being generated from a common core. In early usage some confusion arose from the equation of this core with the individual's 'inner world' or with the 'core pain' derived from childhood and equivalent to Mann's (1973) 'chronically endured pain'. In current practice the *core reciprocal role repertoire* is seen as an heuristic device, constructed or hypothesized from the patient's early history, current relationships, self-monitoring, Psychotherapy File responses and transference. In the diagram, this repertoire will be listed inside a box and procedures representing *enactments* of the core roles will be drawn as loops emanating from the box; these will indicate what is done and the consequences.

This core repertoire may be manifested directly, in the enactments of its role procedures in relation to others, in self-care and self-management. The concept of role is taken to include affect and memory as well as action. Certain roles may be replaced by avoidant and symptomatic procedures, being linked historically with feared or forbidden consequences; this corresponds to Freud's notion of primary gain. In constructing diagrams, procedural loops describing problem procedures, whether interpersonal, self-managing or defensive, will be shown to eventually provoke consequences or responses from others which lead back to the core, indicating a confirmation of the core repertoire. These descriptions are a guide to the likely effects of particular events or therapeutic interventions.

The procedures listed in the core repertoire are not, of course, a complete description of the person; the aim is to select those concerned with critically significant aspects of self-care or emotionally important relationships, and to use high-level, general forms which can be applied to different detailed situations.

Case Example

An example of how diagrams may be constructed is provided by the following case, from which three aspects or episodes will be reported:

1. Johnathon came to therapy at the age of 43 for long-term depression originating in a deprived and emotionally abused childhood. He had recently changed his career, a long-planned move which had been eased by his provoking discord at work with his authoritarian employers which led to his being sacked, following which he pursued a successful claim for wrongful dismissal. He was being seen by his therapist privately, using the compensation money to pay.
2. At session 3 he told a story of how he had just dismissed his coalman. He lived in a rural area with coal as his only source of heating and had been appalled by how much he had spent. He therefore presented the coalman with the account and said he felt that, in view of its size, he should be given some free supply. The coalman refused and he withdrew his custom (despite having previously chosen him as the cheapest and most reliable in the district).
3. At session 4 he debated whether to continue with the therapy or whether it would make more sense to spend the money on some new office equipment.

These three stories suggest that Johnathon's sense of having been abused had been dealt with by a pattern of revengeful counterabuse and by an expectation of entitlement linked with covert contempt. When this was suggested to him he reported that he had experienced a wave of envy when on the doorstep before his session and had nearly turned round and left. The core reciprocal role repertoire deduced from this and the childhood story was described as *depriving and abusing in relation to either powerlessly needy or self-righteously revengeful and envious*. Not all of these descriptions were initially acceptable to the patient; in such cases the practice is to bracket them in the core descriptions. In this case further enactments of the core negative procedures were plentiful, although it was not easy for the therapist to gain his acceptance for the descriptions without being experienced as depriving or abusive.

The diagram (see Figure 2.1) indicated clearly the main problems of the therapy which were (1) to avoid being provoked into counterattack (depriving and abusing) by the patient's continual envy and sense of entitlement and (2) to

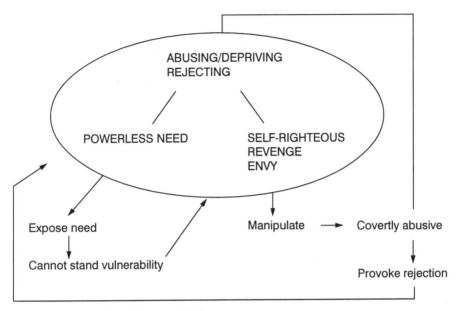

Figure 2.1   Johnathon: Sequential Diagram

help him tolerate the exposure of his need which, for him, was so strongly associated with powerlessness.

The Clinical Value of Diagrams

The detailed working out of SDRs is of value to both patient and therapist. The aim is to identify the clinically significant core reciprocal role procedures and to trace how each of the poles may be expressed by the self, elicited from others or transformed defensively. In most cases the work of elaborating the diagram is clarifying, but it may be the case that, for the purposes of its subsequent use during particular phases of the therapy, a simpler working diagram can be derived. These diagrams are kept in view during sessions and are a basis for self-monitoring by patients. One application can be the keeping of a daily diary recording significant moments, which the patient then interprets by reference to the diagram. For this purpose it is often helpful to colour code core roles and the procedures generated from them. In some therapies diagrams are elaborated or transformed by patients in original and often playful ways, as in the case described by Dunn (1994). Dynamic therapists who shudder at the thought of using writing and diagrams should be reassured by the way in which this abstract conceptual tool is employed not only to describe but also to express and to explore.

For the therapist, the diagram is first and foremost a guide which can trace and make sense of the shifting parts played by the patient and of the accompanying transference–countertransference variations. The developmental understanding points to the need to identify each role in relation to its reciprocal. As explained above, a *role*, in this theoretical context, is understood to imply a pattern of action, expectation, affect and memory. Either pole of a core reciprocal role procedure may:

1. Be enacted towards others who will be induced to play the reciprocal.
2. Be enacted towards the reciprocal aspect of the self.
3. Be transformed into an alternative avoidant, symptomatic or defensive procedure.

Core roles associated historically with unmanageable affects, or prohibited by their internalized reciprocating roles, may either be elicited from others ('projective identification') or may be replaced by avoidant or symptomatic expressions, which involve modified behaviours and lessened affective arousal. Repression and other 'ego defences' and 'compromise formations' can be described in these terms.

At its simplest, a Sequential Diagram describes a core reciprocal role procedure which generates two possible enactments. An individual could enact either role and in doing so would be seeking to elicit the corresponding reciprocal from another person or aspect of the self. For example, a core reciprocal role procedure of *conditional acceptance to striving* could generate (1) demands on others, or (2) demands on the self, or (3) could lead to efforts to meet the demands of others, or (4) the demands of the self.

This model might be complicated by the addition of an alternative response to one role (as in the case of Johnathon above). For example in relation to *conditional acceptance* there might be *either striving or resistance*. As a further complication, such resistance might be manifest directly or, if this was felt to be forbidden, might take the form of passive resistance linked with a symptom such as headache. If this were enacted and performance was impaired as a result, the level of conditionality and felt demand might well increase, thereby confirming the core pattern. Unsuccessful procedures aimed at getting emotional needs met tend to follow means such as passive resistance, idealization, indirect control, submissive guilt arousal and so on, all of which ultimately leave the needs unmet.

Notations of this sort have considerable explanatory value, and enable one to make sense of sudden changes. Thus, where alternate responses to a given role exist, there may be a *response shift*. For example, in relation to *bullying control* a shift from *abject submission* to *angry rebellion* could occur (often serving to provoke more bullying and a maintenance of the pattern). In the case of Johnathon, a similar shift occurred from *powerless need* to *self-righteous revenge*.

Another source of sudden changes might be *role reversal*, as, for example, a shift from *abused* to *abusive*. A third switch, often more disturbing, reflects a *self state shift*, representing an abrupt and apparently inappropriate shift from one reciprocal role pattern to another, for example from *idealizing–idealized* to *abandoning–abandoned*; this last form is particularly characteristic of BPD and will be discussed in the next chapter.

Reading the Psychotherapy File (Appendix 1) in relation to oneself or to a known patient can give a direct sense of the way of thinking incorporated in the basic CAT model. Although bearing signs of its unsystematic development, the File is acceptable to most patients. It is important to emphasize that it is *not* a test yielding scores, it is a way of initiating forms of self-reflection and of providing a starting point for the therapeutic conversation.

CHAPTER 3

The Multiple Self States Model of Borderline Personality

The multiple self states model was evolved in response to practical difficulties encountered in understanding and reformulating more seriously disturbed patients. As the helpfulness of mapping different reciprocal role patterns in separate self states became apparent, the theoretical understanding of how the structure so described evolved needed to be addressed. This involved in particular a consideration of the role of dissociation and a clarification of its relation to repression.

Relations between Role Procedures

Under normal circumstances individuals shift between their array of procedures in response to changes in their current activity, relationships and context. The range of reciprocal role patterns is seen to consist of mutually compatible procedures, and transitions between them are smooth and appropriate. Changes which are not apparently explicable, especially when they are abrupt, are confusing and discomforting to the individual and to others currently involved with him or her. Such abrupt changes may reflect the *role reversals* and *response shifts* described in the last chapter, representing changes within the same reciprocal role pattern, but the most disturbing ones represent apparently unprovoked and inappropriate shifts to a different reciprocal role pattern. Such changes, requiring both self and other to adopt quite different roles, are particularly characteristic of borderline patients.

The confusion caused by these changes to therapists was much reduced when it became clear that, rather than representing random and arbitrary variations or the deliberate sowing of confusion, they could be understood as *the alternate dominance of a limited range of contrasting role patterns*, each of which had stable and recognizable characteristics. In constructing diagrams, these patterns were segregated and described as the core repertoires of what came to be known as dissociated *self states*.

Moods, States, Self States and State Switches

Everyone experiences and manifests different *states*; these are each character-ized by a given *mood* but also by other features. States and moods are not eas-ily differentiated; in practice, descriptions of states should add, to an account of the mood, descriptions of cognitive and behavioural attributes. But in reality moods normally have effects in these other realms too; state-dependent mem-ory is a well-documented example of the relation between mood and cognitive functioning, and more generally it is a common observation that changes in mood affect one's view of oneself and others. Horowitz (1979) characterized *states of mind*, identified in the course of the analysis of therapy transcripts, by their dominant object relations and defensive structure as well as by mood. Influenced by this, *states* (which are better regarded as states of being than states of mind) are defined in CAT in terms of mood, access to and control of emotion, and the reciprocal role pattern of which they are one pole. A state, in this approach, will be understood in relation to its reciprocal, whether this is internal or external, implicit or explicit. When experiencing a given state one does not usually hold all these aspects in awareness; subjectively, the mood or behaviour is more central. In therapy, however, and in mapping borderline pat-terns satisfactorily, the full picture needs to be worked out.

In terms of CAT theory, therefore, a patient's *state* will be identified with a role. Roles are defined as combining memory, affect and action organized in relation to the search for, or the experience of, reciprocation. A *self state* will therefore be described in terms of its reciprocal role pattern, either pole of which may be subjectively identified with and experienced as a state. In the dis-sociated *self states* of BPD the role repertoire of each state is usually relatively narrow and the essential features of each self state can often be described in terms of a single reciprocal role pattern.

Once the different self states have been identified, transitions between them can be monitored and a *Self States Sequential Diagram* (SSSD) can be con-structed. This differs from the basic SDR by showing how procedures are gen-erated from the different self states and how some procedures may lead to state shifts. The SSSD plots the patient's self states, the transitions between them and the procedures generated by each, and allows the events or procedures trigger-ing *state switches* to be monitored.

Identifying and Characterizing Self States: Practical Procedures

A few patients will volunteer descriptions of their experiencing a markedly unstable sense of self and some may be able to offer clear discriminations between their different states. Many others find the notion of states entirely acceptable and can generate or recognize state descriptions. Screening devices, such as the questions in the last section of the Psychotherapy File, may be useful in identifying the presence of dissociated self states. High scores on Dissociation Questionnaires such as the DIS-Q (Vanderlinden *et al.*, 1993) are found in many borderline patients, but the relation of such scores to BPD has not been systematically studied as yet. Clinically, patients who present very differently at different sessions, for example leaving in an appreciative and relieved mood at the end of one session and appearing at the next resentful and suspicious, are often manifesting clearly differentiated self states. Even more directly, patients may generate confusion in therapists by state switches occurring during the session, sometimes with no evident provocation, sometimes in response to something said by the therapist or to the topic being discussed.

State switches are commonly accompanied by alterations in tone of voice and posture and may be accompanied by dissociative symptoms; in this respect they are similar to the phenomena described in Multiple Personality Disorder and reviewed by Putnam (1994). Analysis through the use of videotapes and physiological measures showed that most switches in patients with MPD occurred quickly (within five minutes) and that they were often accompanied by rapid eye blinking or upward rolling of the eyes, and by changes in pulse and respiration rates as well as by alterations in posture and facial expression.

When separate self states are suspected, patients can be asked to give some thought to recognizing and characterizing them; most patients have no difficulty in thinking about themselves in this way. It may be helpful to give the patient instructions such as the following, devised by Hilary Beard (reproduced from Ryle, 1995b).

> 1. Try to list the distinct, different states, and give each a name (for example, 'Sulky Linda' or 'Bossy').
> Take a separate page for each such name and, for each, describe (a) How I feel for others in this state (b) How I feel inside myself (c) How I think others feel about me (d) How I judge or value myself when in this state (e) What bodily feelings accompany this state? (f) What do I tend to do in this state? (g) What do I try to avoid when in this state? (h) How do I comfort myself in this state? (i) How do I get out of this state?

Therapists can begin to construct provisional, partial self state diagrams from the first session and doing so is the best way to avoid inadvertent collusion and the provocation of negative switches. The construction of a complete diagram, involving the recognition and description of the reciprocals to all the reported states, requires combining detailed self-observation by patients with careful observation and enquiry by the therapist and may take more than the usual (for CAT) four sessions. This process cannot be rushed; the reformulation letter, which initiates a piecing together of the historically divided self, should, however, be written at the usual time.

While self state diagrams can be constructed satisfactorily from the material collected in the way described, a final step, available to those prepared to use computers, is to use the identified states as the *elements* in a repertory grid, and to have the patients rate these states against a range of provided *constructs*, to which they may add their own. This *States Grid* (called the *Self* States Grid in Ryle and Marlowe, 1995, misleadingly, as the elements are the patients' dissociated *states*) can be analysed with a principal component analysis and the states can be located in relation to the constructs on a two-component 'map'. (See Appendix 2 for a brief review of repertory grid methods.) This map places each state according to its loadings on the first two principal components and demonstrates how well differentiated the different states are. Sometimes, states close together can be treated as unitary, but it may be the case that they represent recurrent sequences. The characteristics of a state are deduced from its location in the map, as indicated by the loadings of the constructs on the first two components. This information, and the work involved in completing the grid, can contribute to the final construction of a Self States Sequential Diagram (SSSD).

Bennett and Parry (in press) have demonstrated that the themes identified in therapy transcripts using the two standard methods of analysis described by Luborsky and Crits-Christoph (1990) and Schacht and Henry (1994) respectively are reliably matched with what is recorded in SSSDs and conclude that recurrent relationship patterns can be validly identified in this way.

Reformulation in terms of separate self states and the use of the States Grid is illustrated by the following case.

Case Example: John

John, a 40-year-old civil servant, was referred following an incident in which his arm had been broken in the course of a fight with his homosexual partner. That relationship had ended and he said he felt his life was falling apart. He described himself as divided between Dr Jekyll, a responsible civil servant, and Mr Hyde, prone to heavy drinking which often led to provocative behaviour and physical fights. In the past he had been promiscuous and had enjoyed risk-taking; he still preferred to keep friendships separate from emotionally uninvolved sexual encounters. John had been sexually and physically abused throughout childhood by his father in a family where surface politeness was the rule; his mother had refused to listen when he tried, in late adolescence, to speak to her about being gay and about the abuse.

John identified three states in addition to **Jekyll** and **Hyde**, namely **Abandoning**, **Soldiering on** and **Fairyland**. Of these states, Hyde was abusive, revengeful and exciting, to which the implicit reciprocal role was that of victim. This victim role was represented by two states, namely Jekyll, an uninvolved, compliant performer, and Soldiering on, mixing compliance with resentful, passive resistance. Abandoning seemed to represent a self state, one pole of the role pattern generating contempt for others and for self, the other representing the humiliated reciprocal. Fairyland was escapist and restful in relation to an undemanding reciprocal.

John rated these five states to complete the States Grid. The two-component graph of this is reproduced in Figure 3.1. In the upper left quadrant the **Jekyll**, **Abandoning** and **Soldiering on** states are described as *sad, dependent, guilty, attacked and angry.* **Fairyland**, in the contrasted lower right quadrant, is an *admired, envied, happy but unreal* state. **Hyde** is contrasted on the vertical component with the first two of these and on the horizontal component with the last, being characterized as *untrusting, unreal, uncared for, overwhelmed with feelings and wanting to hurt others*; a combination which suggests how the abusive behaviour is generated by, or at least accompanied by, distress. No states appear in the positively described upper right quadrant.

The Self States Sequential Diagram, a simplified version of which is shown in Figure 3.2, was completed before the grid had been analysed. There are two

Figure 3.1   John: States Grid—two-component graph

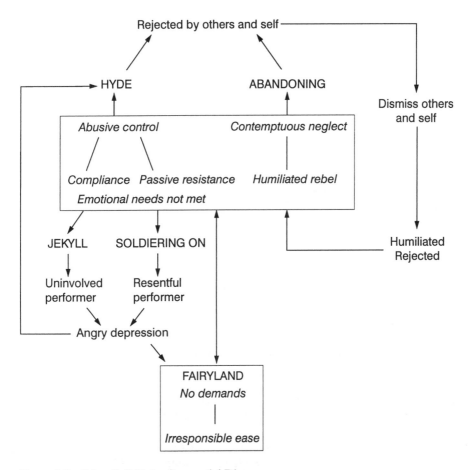

Figure 3.2   John: Self States Sequential Diagram

self states. The main one describes a reciprocal role relationship between the parentally derived *abusive control* (Father) and *contemptuous neglect* (both parents) to child-derived roles of *compliant, passively resistant and humiliated revenge*. The two parent-derived roles are those enacted in the states called Hyde and Abandoning and the child-derived roles appear as Jekyll and Soldiering on. The second self state is Fairyland, defined as irresponsible ease in relation to no demands. At the top of the diagram the therapist added a 'pop-up' observation tower to signify that, in participating in the reformulation process, John was already outside the map. Some such device—for example, the drawing of an 'observing eye'—can be helpful when patients are overwhelmed by the spelling out of their self-reinforcing negative processes, conveying a recognition of their capacity to stand outside the system and of their participation in the work of therapy. In John's case the tower became, for a time, a place to retreat to (a helpful intellectual defence) when emotional exposure was too great. The procedural loops in the diagram demonstrate how the enactment of the various roles and the Fairyland fantasy all left basic emotional needs unmet.

In terms of this SSSD, John's tendency to get into fights, and aspects of his sexual behaviour, could be understood as the result of role reversals from the child-derived to the parent-derived roles in the main self state.

The SSSD and the grid map are two different ways of looking at the dissociated structure of John's personality. The grid offers a direct account of John's self-perceptions, with closeness implying similarity, while the SSSD draws on the developmental history and is constructed to show role reciprocations and sequences and to emphasize the negative outcomes of John's procedures. The SSSD was used actively during the therapy and was an important guide to the therapist, helping him to avoid collusive entanglements. At his six-month post-therapy interview, John commented on how much more aware he had become of the consequences of his acts as a result of his use of the map.

The Uses and Value of Self State Sequential Diagrams

A completed sequential diagram, describing separate self states and characterizing each by its dominant reciprocal role pattern, and tracing transitions between self states, serves the same function as the basic sequential diagram in less disturbed patients, namely it enables both the therapist and the patient to learn to recognize where they are in terms of the map; in addition, it enables both to remain aware of currently dissociated aspects. In this way it helps the patient to gain control over damaging switches and is a crucial tool in the work of integration. For practical purposes, as a basis for self-observation or the coding of diaries in terms of the self states, colouring the self states and the procedural loops generated by them can be helpful; in many cases, self states, rather than individual procedures, become the main focus of self-monitoring.

An Alternative Way of Representing Sequences

The procedural loops drawn in sequential diagrams are described as being generated from core reciprocal roles. In the case of problem procedures, such loops either return to reinforce the core or provoke self state switches. Theoretically, such loops record the various enactments of a role in relation to the reciprocal. The acts and events occurring in the sequence portrayed by a loop may, in detail, involve role reversals or response shifts. The 'micro-analysis' of such changes, especially in the case of rapidly shifting states, may be better displayed through what Leiman (1997) has called *dialogic sequence analysis*. For the purpose of relating events in therapy as recorded in transcripts or summaries to the reformulation it is helpful to give numbers or letters to reciprocal role patterns (which in borderline cases will define self states) and procedures.

As a simplified example, dialogic sequence analysis in the case of John, described above, can be based on the following reciprocal role patterns:

1A *Bully*	– **1B** *Compliant or rebellious victim.*
2A *Neglect*	– **2B** *Humiliated rebel.*
3A *Demanding*	– **3B** *Gloomy compliance/defiance.*
4A *Hostile pressure*	– **4B** *Uninvolved performance.*
5A *No demands*	– **5B** *'Fairyland' irresponsible ease.*

These role patterns represent the 'menu' from which particular procedures will be chosen. In describing the course of an interaction the 'players' can be located in the appropriate reciprocal role As an example, the method can be applied to a brief excerpt from the therapist's account of the fourth session, as follows: 'John was on time but failed to bring any of his assignments.' (*? John in* **3B** *to therapist in* **3A**.) 'John described, in this session, in painful detail, occasions on which his father had hit him, for example for not eating his spinach, aged 3, and for refusing sex, aged 8.' (*Father in* **1A** *to John in* **1B**.) 'In telling this, John became increasingly emotional and tearful. I felt a strong need to be protective and not fail John as his mother had.' (*John in* **1B** *evoking a protective countertransference.*)

In deciding how to display procedural sequences and self state shifts the main thing is to do what works best for the particular purposes and patient. One is faced with contradictory pressures; accuracy and detail are desirable and satisfying, and necessary in research, but there is a risk of becoming obsessively overcomplicated; crude tools are often effective. For clinical purposes some simplification is desirable. In many cases the detailed working out of sequences is a valuable exercise, particularly where rapid and confusing state switches are occurring, but a simpler working diagram focusing on the key therapy issues may then be used for self-monitoring and diary-keeping.

Some Preliminary Clinical Implications

The separation of the self states described in the diagrams is understood to represent partial dissociation. On this basis it is clear that a major (*negative*) therapeutic strategy must be to avoid relating at any time to only one aspect of the patient, for to do so is an implicit reinforcement of the dissociation. The corresponding *positive* strategy is to form a relationship which recognizes but is not part of the patient's system, and here the cooperative work of reformulation initiates, for most patients, just such a new and unfamiliar way of being with another person. Everybody's sense of self is dependent on the acknowledgement and acceptance of others to some degree, and the less secure the sense of self the greater the need for such acknowledgement. Borderline subjects are both deeply insecure and profoundly destructive of the relationships they most need. Acknowledgement requires both accurate empathy (which reformulation serves to develop) and a clear differentiation of subject and object; the term mirroring does not adequately convey the complexity of these processes. As the diagram takes shape, every state and every state shift experienced can be located in relation to the (currently more or less dissociated) other states; this is the cognitive basis of accurate empathy. The continual use of the diagram in the sessions and the patient's use of it for self-monitoring is an education in the fact that all states are aspects of the self, and this in turn mitigates the narrowness and extremity of the individual states. For the therapist, the more or less inevitable appearance of the negative states in the therapy can be sooner recognized, thanks to the map, and possible countertransference pressures can be anticipated. Responding to a hostile or idealizing transference event by pointing out the location of the behaviour on the jointly created map is, in most cases, a non-punitive and assimilable way of containing these possible collusions and threats to the alliance.

The case examples presented in later chapters will give more illustrations of the construction and use of Self States Sequential Diagrams; at this point the sources of this structure in early development will be considered.

Theoretical Issues

The Origins of Self States in Borderline Subjects

As discussed earlier, there has been a longstanding neglect of the role of trauma and deprivation in psychoanalytic theorizing, because of an almost exclusive focus on issues of unconscious conflict and defence. The influential models of BPD generated from psychoanalytic sources (to be considered in the next chapter) have shown little interest in, or an unclear definition of, the role of dissociation, despite the now undeniable importance of trauma in the early lives of borderline patients and the accepted link between trauma and dissociation.

The model presented here is based on the proposition that borderline pathology can be best understood in terms of damage affecting three levels of development. It is an extension of the general model described in the last chapter. These three levels of damage are of course, a simplification of a complex and inter-related hierarchy; they are defined as follows:

Level 1. The restriction or distortion of the reciprocal role repertoire.
Level 2. The incomplete development or disruption of higher order procedures responsible for mobilizing, connecting and sequencing Level 1 procedures.
Level 3. The incomplete development or disruption of self-reflection.

Level 1

The repertoire of reciprocal roles developed by an individual child will reflect the interaction between the child's temperament, determined by genetic and organic factors, by life events such as illness and separations and by the patterns of interaction developed with caretakers, shaped by the caretaker's procedural repertoire and by factors such as parental psychiatric disorder, substance abuse or quarrelling. The predominant source of borderline patients' difficulties is the experience of cruelty and neglect; in most cases they have had little or no trustworthy, predictable care and they have usually suffered physical or sexual abuse from at least one parent. The result is that they tend to repeat what they know, accepting and inflicting on self and others the neglect and abuse which was their own constant experience. The reciprocal roles acquired through such experiences are typically those of *neglecting, abandoning and abusing* in relation to *emotionally deprived, ashamed and either rebellious or crushed*. These patterns are frequently directly re-enacted with others but, in addition, the internalization of harsh, undermining and uncaring or highly unpredictable parental voices results in internal conflict being marked. This may lead to repression of some impulses and to the development of alternative procedures, generating, for example, perfectionist, passive, submissive, placatory or avoidant behaviours, often accompanied by somatization and depression. The intrapsychic conflicts of borderline patients resemble those of less disturbed individuals but the borderline patients' experiences have usually been harsher and the distortion of their procedural patterns is correspondingly more extreme. The high incidence of Axis I disorders in borderline patients and their high levels of less specific forms of distress and dysfunction, indicated by their scores on a wide range of inventories, are a reflection of this. Other patterns, such as manic activity and idealization, which are interpreted as defensive in psychoanalysis, are described differently in CAT as representing the characteristics of dissociated self states, to be discussed below.

Level 2

The procedural system is essentially hierarchical. Just as Level 1 procedures are enacted through chains of subprocedures, so are they themselves governed by what may be called the *metaprocedures* of Level 2. The function of these metaprocedures is *connection*: they serve to mobilize and link the reciprocal role repertoire of Level 1 in ways determined by the context and the individual's aims and values. They therefore constitute an important aspect of the basic structure of the self. They are analogous to, and probably linked with, the metalinguistic processes which Donald (1991, p. 345) describes as 'superordinate cognitive structures that regulate the uses to which words and sentences are put'. From a Bakhtinian perspective one would expect language (as occurring essentially between people) to be organized in relation to the individual's social and interpersonal context and this would suggest a close connection between, and common origin for, linguistic metacognitions and the metaprocedures proposed here. Level 2 procedures are initially acquired in the same way as Level 1 procedures and their operation is largely outside consciousness, although formal education concerning rules and values may affect their later development (just as education seeks to develop metalinguistic skills). Their operation may be brought to consciousness if they fail to ensure the successful navigation of unfamiliar social situations.

The development of Level 2 procedures may be impaired by two factors, both of which are commonly present in the early lives of borderline patients. The first is exposure to *incoherent, neglectful and contradictory experiences*, such as may result from having parents who may themselves be borderline or substance abusing or are otherwise ill or chaotic. Internal coherence is normally derived from the linking and making meaningful of daily experience in the context of the relationships with parents and other family members. The second factor, derived from physical and sexual abuse and other emotionally unmanageable experiences, is *trauma-induced dissociation*. This can result in various levels and degrees of separation between split-off aspects of the self. Where, as is often the case, abuse is repeated, the threshold for dissociation becomes lower and minor retraumatization, such as may be evoked by memories or situations reminiscent of the abuse, may produce major dissociative episodes.

Dissociation varies in the range of processes affected, total interruptions of memory or of the sense of self being rare. In the proposed model of BPD it is seen to result in the segregation of different reciprocal role procedures into contrasting self states but the number of self states, the extent to which memory is impaired between them and the degree to which identity is fragmented vary. Less damaged patients may suffer from no more than unusually distinct, contrasting moods with some inappropriate state switches, whereas others, may be more prone genetically to dissociate or maybe exposed to more severe and prolonged abuse, can be fragmented into numerous states between some of which there is amnesia; these latter cases may be regarded as transitional between BPD and Multiple Personality Disorder. This description seems entirely compatible with the findings of the study of traumatized individuals carried out by van der Kolk *et al.* (1996). These authors concluded that 'PTSD, dissociation, somatization and affect dysregulation represent a spectrum of adaptations to trauma' and reported that interpersonal trauma, especially when occurring in childhood, was associated with the highest symptom levels.

The multiple self states model rests on making a major distinction between repression and dissociation. *Repression* is seen to operate at the level of the specific role procedures of Level 1; it results from intrapsychic conflict between individual wishes and prohibiting or threatening internal parentally-derived 'voices' and serves to avoid the anxiety provoked by challenging these, commonly through the elaboration of more submissive or avoidant interpersonal procedures, a process often accompanied by somatic symptoms. In contrast, *dissociation* represents the disruption of, or failure to develop, Level 2 connecting and sequencing metaprocedures. It is provoked by overwhelming emotional arousal, such as accompanies abuse, or by cues serving to bring such experiences to mind. A child exposed to repeated abuse may learn to dissociate deliberately. While serving to avoid emotional distress, such defensive dissociation *is not in any way the result of intrapsychic conflict.* In repression a less forbidden or less provocative reciprocation is offered to an unchanging internal parental figure. An example would be the replacement of expressed anger by passive aggression or avoidance. In moving between dissociated self states, on the other hand, the roles of both self and other are altered, for example between patterns of *bullying in relation to rebellion* and patterns of *ideal caregiving in relation to need.* The two processes of repression and dissociation may both operate in the same person, for in the course of development a harsh parent may both constitute an unmanageable external threat, provoking dissociation, and be internalized (in some states) as a threatening judge provoking repression.

The clinical implications of this dissociative model are important. The first aim of therapy must be to aid integration. In CAT, the states diagram is an explicit and concrete reminder to the patient that where one is at a given moment is one part of a whole system which together constitutes the person. The security offered by a connecting up of dissociated aspects is followed, in some cases, by the recovery of memory for the past trauma. In contrast, interpreting the effects of dissociation in terms of inferred motivated defence can be experienced as critical and blaming (and can repeat the childhood experience of being told what one might or might not know and feel) especially when this interpretive approach is accompanied by a disinterest in the actual traumatic experiences of the individual, a non-acknowledgement which can parallel the denials, lies and silences of the childhood abusers.

Level 3

A main function of consciousness is to allow attention to be focused on what is new or problematic; conscious self-reflection can therefore be applied to the problematic manifestations of Level 1 and Level 2 procedures, even though the origins of these are inaccessible. However, borderline patients are unable to reflect in this way, at least while in certain states. Two reasons for this will now be considered.

Firstly, self-reflection is itself a procedure which is derived from interactions from others. 'The eye sees not itself but by reflection, by some other thing' as Brutus observes to Cassius. Originating in pre-verbal communications between infant and caretakers, it comes to be mediated by language to an increasing extent. An individual's capacity for self-reflection and the range of concern and judgement involved in it will be dependent upon the forms of interest and comment provided by parents and other caretakers. Where attention is confined to the child's achievement or appearance or obedience, for example, the child's own ability to reflect on other aspects, notably on his or her subjective experience, thoughts and feelings, will be underdeveloped. Frequently, a language suitable for such concerns is lacking, as is commonly the case in patients with eating and somatization disorders. These two factors—*narrow attention* and *deficient vocabulary*—commonly co-exist; together they will impair the development of Level 3 self-reflective capacities.

A second factor affecting the capacity for self-reflection is the *discontinuity of experience and memory* consequent upon Level 2 dissociations. Borderline patients are frequently acutely aware of their own subjective states and of those of others *while in certain states* but this capacity is not sustained when either events or the subject's own actions provoke state switches. Such switches commonly repeat the original process whereby dissociation was established, in that they serve to remove the person from the memory (or perceived repetition) of the original unmanageable situation. The cost of achieving this is that procedural revision does not occur and the traumatic memory retains its force.

In terms of therapy, these Level 3 issues point to the need for serious concern with all aspects of the patient's experiences and of the meanings and values derived from them. This requires the provision and encouragement of ways of expressing and exploring memory and feeling and the constant linking up of the separate experiences, feelings and actions of the different self states. The therapist must say with Cassius:

> ... since you know you cannot see yourself
> So well as by reflection, I, your glass,
> Will modestly discover to yourself
> That of yourself which you yet know not of.

Borderline Phenomenology and the Multiple Self States Model

It seems futile to debate whether BPD and the other Cluster B personality disorders are better regarded as trauma or as deficit-induced states: they are both. These patients *are* emotionally deprived and *have* experienced persecution, both as children and, as a result of their current damaging procedures, as adults. A hostile early world has left in its wake an extensive and various array of psychological damage. The sense of self is fragmented and the predominance of angry or distancing states or unrealistic hopes serves to maintain deprivation.

The specific features which make up the DSM IV criteria of BPD can be understood in detail in terms of the proposed model as follows:

1. *Frantic efforts to avoid abandonment*, and
2. *Unstable intense interpersonal relationships alternating between idealization and devaluation* are manifestations of two dissociated self states. The *idealizing–idealized* pattern represents the search for perfect care, devoid of any disappointment or negative feeling. It is a polar contrast to the *abusing–abused* state from which it was initially dissociated. The idealizing self state is precarious for, in the face of inevitable shortcomings, or as a result of the emotional suffocation and control induced by the effort to avoid conflict, a state switch into the abusing–abused self state may occur, with either the other or the self being cast in the devalued, abused role.
3. *Indentity disturbance*. This is the manifestation of the switching between different self states. The DSM lacks any description of how this instability may be understood. The more precise description of this as due to the alternating dominance of a relatively small number of different roles and self states, each of which has stable characteristics, is of considerably more use clinically.
4. *Impulsivity*. While this symptom may be the result in part of organic factors it is also derived from the presence of dissociated states. Each self state has a narrow repertoire of role patterns, usually one that can be described in terms of a single dominant reciprocal role pattern. The maintenance of a sense of self in any self state depends on the ability to elicit from others confirming reciprocations, but in the case of dissociated self states with narrowly defined reciprocal role patterns this need is both more specific and, because of the underlying instability, more urgent. In addition, the affects and wishes operating in a given state are unmodulated by other, split-off aspects of the self and may retain a force derived from the abused child's needs and angers.
5. *Suicidal and self-mutilating behaviours*. An exact understanding of these behaviours in a given individual needs to locate them within the system of self states and procedures. They may represent, for example, the enactment of a self-punishing and abusing role towards the self, the attempt to escape from a blanked-off emotionally void state, a way of reclaiming the active role when faced with powerlessness or a form of communication with, or control of, others.
6. *Affective instability*. This reflects response shifts, role reversals and switches between sharply contrasted self states, some of which are marked by extreme moods.
7. *Chronic feelings of emptiness*. These feelings represent the effects of early, unresolved deprivation and the continuing insecurity of the sense of self and the failure to get emotional needs met because of the nature of the self-management and interpersonal procedures available.
8. *Inappropriate intense anger*. This commonly represents the mobilization of a self state linked with the experience of being powerless and abused; at times such states can have the force of the original experience, giving the

impression of a hallucinatory revisiting rather than a memory. The anger may be derived from the revengeful rage of the abused child or may reflect a role reversal into the role of the abuser.

9. *Transient stress-related paranoid ideas* can result from the perception of the world in terms of reciprocal role patterns based on early experiences of being abused or persecuted by others, on the experience of having powerful others attributing thoughts and motives, or as a means of explaining failure and low self-esteem. *Dissociative symptoms* are commonly the accompaniments of state shifts (a literal experience of 'de-personalization'). The stresses responsible for provoking paranoid or dissociative symptoms are not necessarily overt but are usually identifiable in relation to the self state reformulation, or become so through monitoring their appearance.

The proposed model proves capable of explaining the DSM features of BPD, and in addition demonstrates the inter-relations between many of them. The model could contribute to the development of a more flexible and relevant system of discriminating between patients meeting criteria for Cluster B diagnoses and a clearer way of understanding the relation between personality and Axis I diagnoses. Referring back to Chapter 1, the 'severe personality dysfunction' of Berelowitz and Tarnopolsky, the borderline personality organization of Kernberg, and Rutter's group of patients with major problems in making and sustaining social relationships could all be described and discriminated in clinically useful ways with reference to the multiple self states model and to the three levels of damage discussed above.

Level 1. The range and degree of distortion of the reciprocal role repertoire and the severity of associated Axis I conditions varies considerably. Axis I and Axis II conditions may be different results of the same early traumatic experience, but their relationship may be more complex. It is possible that some Axis I conditions (for example depression) may release borderline symptoms while some (such as anorexia nervosa) may mask them and others (such as anxiety) may be secondary to the experience of unpredictable instability.

Level 2. As diagnosed by present criteria, borderlines may be mildly or severely dissociated and may have anything from two to several main self states. The development of some form of quantifying, or at least of describing more precisely, the degree of dissociation between states, and the association of this with measures of dissociative symptomotology, would be of value. Using the methods developed so far it seems that, where patients can meaningfully distinguish between states by completing the States Grid, their mapping (in Self States Sequential Diagrams) is therapeutically valuable. The States Grid might be developed in order to contribute to a more fine-grained assessment of some aspects of dissociation. In more dissociated patients with little or no continuous self-observing capacity its completion while in the different self states, and involving the help observers, would be necessary.

Level 3. The capacity for self-reflection varies considerably in people in general, in ways reflecting inborn temperamental variables and their cultural and family background. Most BPD patients lack this capacity to a marked degree. The nature of the lack may differ, depending on how far it is the result of discontinuity due to state switches and how far the result of childhood deficiencies in attention and vocabulary.

Of the three levels considered, Level 2 damage is probably the most characteristic of patients diagnosed as borderline by current criteria and serves to separate personality disorders of Cluster B from Axis I diagnoses. Within this group of patients with major personality dysfunction, measuring the extent of disorder in the three levels may contribute to clinically useful discriminations.

Implications for Therapy

Cognitive Analytic Therapy seeks to mobilize the patients' capacity for self-reflection and control. The main challenges posed by borderline patients are their tendency to destroy what they most need, their use of anger to conceal or defend against vulnerability and the persistence of their dissociation. The therapeutic aim can only be achieved by combining a corrective (that is, non-collusive) relationship with the provision of conceptual tools. The practical working together at reformulation is an immediate and emotionally powerful new experience which serves to win patients' commitment to therapy without denying either the depth of their need or the power of their destructiveness. The production of sequential descriptions which make sense of, and plot connections between, contrasting self states is the first step in integration and provides ongoing help to both patient and therapist.

The formal tasks of the therapist include the skilful elicitation of the history and the ability to use this and the experience of being with the patient to create a transformative reconstruction of the life story. Writing the reformulation letter and constructing, with the patient's participation, the sequential diagram, together establish a safe setting within which a corrective emotional and intellectual experience is offered to the patient, in which unfinished business from the past can be completed and the replacement of damaging procedures can begin. The skilful management of the therapeutic relationship is central to this process. The CAT model of therapy is a *dialogic* model, understanding the therapeutic relationship in terms of reciprocal roles, a topic considered in detail in Chapter 6. The communications of a borderline patient in therapy are in many different voices and are addressed to many different implicit interlocutors. The task of the therapist is to identify these voices and to examine with the patient how far they may be speaking falsely, while taking care not to reply to them in collusive, reductive or distorting ways.

Therapy is a subtle educational process which aims to connect and heal the borderline's damaged self processes. It demands an understanding of the fact that the borderline's apparent inability to learn from experience and frequent failure to feel responsible or remorseful for harm done to others or the self is not due to innate weakness or viciousness. This understanding is not easily achieved and, for any therapist, may need the support of supervision as the patient's negative or idealizing pressures are applied. The patient must be helped to acquire a continuous sense of self before he or she can take responsibility for past and present actions. It is a moving achievement of therapy when pain about the past can be felt and responsibility for, and some sense of control over, the future can be accepted.

Brief therapy for borderline patients is discounted by many writers but no adequate comparative trials exist to justify this. It is my belief that therapy can have a profound effect in a relatively short time in many patients because, to use Vygotsky's term, the Zone of Proximal Development in respect of self-knowledge is extensive and the impact of new understandings is correspondingly large. The model proposed here could be of value to those working in different modes and contexts, such as day hospitals or group therapy, and could help those providing outpatient support, a form of treatment which, without a theoretical understanding, can so easily be irrelevant or collusive.

CHAPTER 4

A Critical Account of Current Theories of Borderline Pathology and their Clinical Implications

Psychoanalytic Understandings

The borderline concept emerged from psychoanalytic practice as an attempt to understand a group of more disturbed patients who failed to match conventional models and who failed to engage productively in analysis. Current psychoanalytic accounts continue to reflect this origin and, it could be argued, sometimes fail to distinguish those features intrinsic to the condition from those exacerbated or perhaps created by the psychoanalytic process. None the less, the attempt to describe borderline pathology from a developmental and structural perspective rather than on the basis of descriptive and surface characteristics was an important one. In this, a central role was played by Kernberg (1975) who offered an account of the phenomenology and who proposed theoretical understandings linking classical and object relations ideas.

Most psychoanalytic writers are critical of the DSM diagnostic process because of its failure to attend to developmental and structural factors, but, according to Higgitt and Fonagy (1992), there is a wide acceptance for a grouping of patients who show a 'stable instability' of ego functioning, a wide range of associated symptoms and diagnoses and markedly impaired interpersonal relations. Diagnosis according to Kernberg's concept of borderline *structure* is considerably more inclusive than are the DSM criteria defining borderline personality but makes more sense for those concerned with underlying processes. In Kernbergs' (1975, 1984) view, the source of these features is to be found in the intensity of the patients' destructive and aggressive drives and in intrinsic ego weakness. In association with these features there is a predominance of the 'primitive defences' of splitting and projective identification. The function of splitting is seen to be the protection of positive elements or images from hostile

43

and destructive forces. This account reifies the metaphors of 'the inner world', postulating the existence of separate, autonomous and motivated entities—fiercely opposed little ghosts in the machine—and as such, it must be questioned on philosophical grounds. I would see these ideas as an example of the general tendency in psychoanalytic thinking to equate the patient's (or analyst's) fantasy with a descriptive theory.

Kernberg's model is an object relations model, concerned largely with *internal* relations between these 'objects' (which are the bearers of instinctual forces) and paying little attention to the actual relations between the individual and others, either as formative influences in the past or as expressing and maintaining pathology in the present. The exception to this is the focus on transference, in which the internal relationships are seen to be made visible. This attitude is manifest in the following quotation: 'borderline individuals may succeed in externalising their incapacity to integrate good and bad objects by polarising people working with them and with constant attempts to attack the links between them' (Higgitt and Fonagy, 1992). This passage is noteworthy for the assumption (present in much psychoanalytic writing) that, because something occurs, it must have been intended, and manages to accuse the patient of both failure and destructive intent.

As described in the last chapter, splitting is understood in the CAT model to affect *patterns of reciprocal roles* rather than objects and the self or their representations, a point in line with the views of Ogden (1983) on internal object relations and elaborated in CAT terms in Ryle (1985). The origin is seen to lie in the actual relationships experienced by the child, either in the form of contradictory, incoherent parenting or through the effects of trauma, resulting in dissociation into separate self states. Dissociation is seen to be maintained by a continuing dynamic process involving the reinforcement of the separate self states in relationships with others and through retraumatization.

The therapeutic implications of these different understandings are major. Kernberg, while modifying psychoanalytic technique in the direction of fewer weekly sessions and a firmer discipline, confines intervention to interpretations. Interpretation, according to Kernberg *et al.* (1989), aims to extend clarifications and confrontations by '*assuming* underlying unconscious motives and defences' (my italics). In the later stages of treatment patients may graduate to the point at which they may be offered 'genetic reconstructions'. A model example of the latter reads: 'Whipping prostitutes and acting tough with me have similar functions: to behave in macho fashion like your father, rather than giving in to your wishes to be taken care of by me and to be sexually penetrated by me ...'. Interpretations (assertions) of this sort and the general emphasis on destructiveness and hostility may well, in my view, represent retraumatization; their use seems hard to defend, given the incontrovertible evidence for the role of cruelty and neglect (and in many cases actual penetration by fathers) in the genesis of borderline states (see, e.g., Perry and Herman, 1993). Yet Higgitt and

Fonagy (1992) state unambiguously that: 'Explorations of the patients' past, and interpretations using childhood experience as an explanation of current behaviour, are unlikely to do more than divert attention from the pathological nature of the patients' current behaviour.'

It is at this point that, for me, reasoned argument can easily give way to anger. The failure to acknowledge the reality of a person's experience is itself an assault, in the case of borderline subjects an assault which usually has many precedents, and the imposition of explanations of the experience of the patient (through 'penetrating' interpretations) or of their supposed unconscious wishes is similarly, in many cases, a repetition of early forceful attributions from others.

It is my view that, by imposing a theory of innate conflict and defence, developed originally with respect to 'Oedipal' issues, onto the earliest stages of development, by failing to distinguish between dissociation and the intrapsychic ego defences and by harping on the innate destructiveness of borderline patients, Kernberg's contributions to an understanding of structure have been translated into a damaging therapeutic approach.

These criticisms apply equally to the similar model offered by the Kleinians, who place borderline pathology within their general theory as being located between the paranoid-schizoid and depressive positions (Steiner, 1979). Paranoid phenomena, in CAT theory, represent the effects of actual abuse and the predominance of 'critically attributing and abusive to guilty and abused' reciprocal roles, or of procedures aiming to make sense of the experience of punishment or guilt, and schizoid phenomena reflect dissociation. The desirable transition to the depressive position would be understood in CAT to reflect the growth of new (Level 3) capacities to observe and control experience and behaviour, without which responsibility and concern cannot develop. The later-developed Kleinian concept of the 'pathological organisation' (Steiner, 1990), located in a somewhat obscure relation to the two 'positions', serves to describe intransigent resistances to the process of the analysis, usually through forms of passive resistance. I have argued, in detailed critical studies of published case histories, that this can be understood as an effect of analytic technique, in which the combination of opacity, omniscience and interpretive attributions of negative motives offered by the powerful analyst mobilize, in the patient, the least exposing reciprocal procedure available (Ryle, 1992, 1993, 1995c).

Fonagy, while largely aligning himself with the views of Kernberg and Klein, allows some reality to the persecutory experiences of borderline subjects. His main difference lies in the idea that a major defect in these patients consists of their inability to consider the psychological processes of either others or themselves. This absence of a 'theory of mind' is understood as a defensive avoidance of thinking about the actual hostility evident in their caretakers. In an illustrative case history (Fonagy, 1991) he describes the analysis of a man whose mother had been seriously depressed and whose father had been violent. In the transference, Fonagy felt himself to be alternating between being seen as threatening and cruel and being made to feel like a helpless child exposed to irrational rage. The patient also exhibited a wish for, and terror of, fusion. In terms of the CAT model this could be understood as the result of three main self states, namely the mother-derived *'out of reach in relation to helpless unmet need'*, the father-derived *'brute in relation to victim'* and the fantasy *'perfect carer to perfectly cared for and smothered'*. This patient's lack of Level 3 self-reflective capacities, representing the basis for a theory of mind, could be attributed to deficiency and dissociation rather than to conflict and defence. In CAT it would be understood to be a result of the absence of concern from others about his emotional experiences, on which self-reflection might be modelled, and of dissociation in the face of the arbitrary cruelty of his father.

In my experience this absence of a theory of mind is not a feature of all borderline patients. If a feature, it is usually true of only some states, with other states being characterized by subtle understanding. The rapid use made of reformulation by many patients during CAT would suggest that problems in this area are essentially cognitive rather than defensive, reflecting the absence of continuously available concepts. Robbins (1989) makes a similar point when he suggests that the analysis of 'primitive personalities' requires the prior clarification of their unusual cognitive processes.

Where 'thinking about thinking' appears absent (in a person or in a given self state) it is likely to be just one aspect of a reciprocal role derived from the avoidance of emotional closeness with unbearably hostile caretakers. Contacting memories of hostility and abuse can constitute retraumatization and can provoke dissociative state switches into less exposed and less reflective (angry or emotionally blank) self states. The interpretation of such switches as resistance is unlikely to be the most appropriate way in which to offer the patient an experience of a person with whom such memories can be both acknowledged and tolerated.

Kohut (1971, 1977b) offered a major challenge to psychoanalytic orthodoxy. In his second analysis of 'Mr Z' (Kohut, 1979) he recognized how the orthodox interpretations of the first analysis had been experienced as unhelpful but had been accepted by Mr Z as the price of care, in the same way as the attributions of his (possibly psychotic) mother had been accepted. This case may have contributed to the central importance placed by Kohut on empathic failure in the understanding of childhood development and to his relative neglect of trauma. After a long struggle to accommodate his new understandings within the classical structural theory and after painful confrontations with the establishment, Kohut emerged with a radically new approach, in which, to quote Mollon (1993) the analyst was called upon to recognize 'the patient's dependence on the actual responsiveness of the analyst ... . In order for development to proceed ... . Resolution of internal conflict is not enough.'

It will be clear that, in emphasizing the importance of the actual care offered to the child and to patients and, through the notion of the 'selfobject', in concentrating on the development of the self in relation to others, self psychology is more compatible with the CAT model than are the ideas of Kernberg and the Kleinians. There are, however, some problems with the theory, reflecting residual traditional assumptions and the neglect of developmental evidence, notably in respect of the importance placed on the idea of a primary state of non-differentiation or symbiosis, for which Stern (1985) finds no empirical evidence. More importantly, and perhaps reflecting the fact that, compared to Kernberg, self psychology has been more concerned with less severely disturbed patients, the model pays little attention to the rage and destructiveness characteristic of borderline patients. In a strange way Kohut and Kernberg mirror the common split in borderline patients between an 'idealizing–idealized' self state in which conflict is denied and a 'critical and abusive to guilty victim' self state in which needs are not acknowledged. Kohutian treatment risks setting up a collusive version of the first and Kernbergian treatment risks, or insists on, setting up a version of the second.

Whatever the deficiencies in self psychology, it has proved to be a healthily subversive influence in psychoanalysis, an influence nicely captured in these early comments of Pines (1975): 'There is a move afoot to discard much of the metapsychological structure of psychoanalysis. Does the complex framework not come between us and the psychic reality of the patient's existence, and fix us in the position of the detached observer ...'. Unlike previous heretics such as Ferenczi, Kohut has endured as an influence on theory and practice, countering some of the harmful effects of the more established approaches. Forceful interpretations and the presumed neutral stance of the analyst have been replaced by a more open, interactive approach in the work of some analysts (although the extent to which the intersubjective critique of classical views in fact protects patients from authoritarian interpretations is questioned by Dunn, 1995). In an interesting development, with some parallels to CAT, Patrick (1993), responding to the need for time-limited therapy, describes a combination of self psychological and cognitive behavioural methods.

This critical account of psychoanalytic approaches does not deny the central contribution made by psychoanalysis to the understanding of personality development and of the power of transference–countertransference interactions. Many of these understandings are incorporated in CAT theory and are central to its practice. However, in my view, the evolution of psychoanalysis as a treatment method has been another and largely negative story, and this is particularly clear when borderline patients are considered. Describing borderline patients as weak and vicious and claiming that only intensive and prolonged treatment can be effective has meant that, in many centres, they are not offered treatment at all. And, while psychoanalytic treatment is claimed to be the only real way of achieving change and while the contributions of other approaches are largely ignored, virtually no evidence for the effectiveness (let alone the greater effectiveness) of psychoanalysis has been published.

Cognitive and Behavioural Approaches

Interest in the disorders of personality is of recent origin in the cognitive therapy field. It grew out of the recognition of the limits of conventional cognitive therapy when faced with personality disordered patients who were uncooperative with the treatment process, a problem essentially explained as due to the existence of fixed underlying assumptions about the self and reality which generated pervasive behaviour patterns. In Beck's theory, three key basic assumptions are identified for BPD, namely: 'The world is dangerous and malevolent'; 'I am powerless and vulnerable' and 'I am inherently unacceptable' (Beck, Freeman *et al.*, 1990). In addition 'dichotomous thinking'—the tendency to see things in terms of opposed, exclusive categories—and a weak and unstable sense of identity were also described as characteristic. The combination of these factors was seen to result in repetitive cycles of behaviour tending to confirm the underlying features.

Young and Lindemann (1992) described an extension of this—a 'schema-focused model'—describing (1) *early maladaptive schemas*, (2) ways in which schemas were maintained through cognitive distortions such as *selective abstraction and overgeneralisation*, (3) *schema avoidance* involving conscious and unconscious ('volitional and automatic') cognitive and behavioural avoidance, and (4) *schema compensation*, explained as the development of schemas exaggeratedly opposite to original maladaptive schemas, a concept reminiscent of the psychoanalytic notion of reaction formation. This model lists 14 Early Maladaptive Schemas (EMS) of which the first three would seem to be a description of BPD, being concerned with instability and disconnection. They are described as involving the *perceived* unreliability of others, the *expectation* that others will hurt, abuse, etc. and the *expectation* that needs for care will not be met. The role of the actual unreliability, abuse and neglect of others is little emphasized and absence of features describing the individual's active contribution to difficulty through damaging behaviours is noteworthy.

In treating such patients the need to identify and describe harmful schemas is emphasized, affect is focused upon, using imagery techniques, and interpersonal issues are dealt with in the therapy relationship as well as in current relationships. 'Flash cards' describing particular schemas are used in a way similar to the use of diagrams in CAT, reminding the patient of the antecedents and consequences of problems. In the example quoted the card reads: '... I feel angry, drained and ignored because *schemas prevent me* from expressing my needs ...' (my italics). This form of words places schemas alongside internal objects as quasi-autonomous agents and is likely to detract from the development of a sense of responsibility and control.

While this relatively simple model describes some of the main features of BPD as defined by DSM it has little to say about the origins of these and offers only an elementary structural hypothesis. In the practice based on the model, some account is taken of the difficulties facing therapists, based largely on psychoanalytic understandings of transference and countertransference. The approach avoids the harmful intrusiveness of some analytic practice and offers a collaborative treatment relationship. In comparison with CAT, however, the understandings offered are confined to lower order, discrete behaviours and do not address the issue of integration. The model of the 'cycles' of behaviour proposed and the support given by the theory to therapists seeking to avoid collusive or provocative interventions is helpful but is less developed than the CAT model. And in terms of practice, despite the collaborative intentions, the approach conveys less respect for the patient as a person and does not recruit the patient to the work of developing new understandings.

The rediscovery of some psychoanalytic insights by cognitive therapists is more explicitly incorporated in the integrative model proposed by Safran (Safran et al., 1990; Safran and McMain, 1992). Here, the origins of 'dysfunctional cognitive interpersonal cycles' are based on Bowlby's concept of 'internal working models of relationships' and the conduct of therapy emphasizes the central importance of avoiding the confirmation of existing damaging patterns. The relationship between intra- and interpersonal role procedures is not noted. The interactional patterns in personality disorders are seen as characteristically rigid, narrow and intense, exerting powerful pressures on others to reciprocate, but there is no structural theory to account for the borderline patient's extreme variability.

The main behavioural contribution to the treatment of BPD is the work of Linehan (1993) with parasuicidal women. The approach is described as cognitive-behavioural or as 'dialectical behaviour therapy' and combines ideas and methods from many sources. The 'dialectical' elements involve a focus on process rather than structure, and are reflected in an emphasis on the need to recognize and accept opposites (for example, on the need to accept what is and also to value change), and on the use of dialogue, metaphor and paradox. One of Linehan's students described the approach to enabling patients to change as 'warmly ruthless' and this phrase captures, one suspects, Linehan's personal style, manifest also in her rejection of approaches which deny full humanity to the patient and in her emphasis on the need for therapists to receive supervision adequate to the stresses involved in treating borderline patients. She sees supervision as also being 'a balance to the arrogance that can easily accompany such a powerful position as the therapist's', and suggests that the therapist's genuine liking for the patient can only be established on the basis of the fullest possible comprehension of the patient's experience.

Linehan describes the theoretical basis of her approach as being within a 'biosocial framework', which involves her in assuming a large role for biological causes of emotional dysregulation while at the same time recognizing how far the borderline patient's problems are maintained in a social rather than an individual context. The causal role of early trauma in producing dysregulation is little emphasized. Linehan's treatment programme combines individual and group work spread over about two years. Initially, this focuses on behaviours which threaten the patient's continuing survival or which might disrupt therapy; thereafter a balance is maintained between acceptance of what, for the time being, cannot be changed and pressure to master what can be, the latter moving from an initial control of damaging behaviours to a wider emphasis on self acceptance, social participation and building a life.

There are a number of features of Linehan's approach which resemble CAT practice in some respects. Thus, in delineating problem behaviours, a process called 'chain analysis' involves identifying emotional, cognitive, behavioural and environmental features in the antecedents, enactments and consequences of the behaviour. This, however, is applied to individual behaviours and no attempt is made to identify or modify higher order processes. In instilling insight the emphasis is similarly placed on describing recurrent patterns of behaviour and their consequences, but not on understanding the overall characteristics of self processes. And in finding solutions to problems the alternative routes to desired goals are systematically explored in terms of discrete problem behaviours.

There are also a number of differences; in particular there is no model linking interpersonal and intrapersonal processes comparable to the CAT reciprocal role descriptions. In common with most authors, while acknowledging the variability and instability of personality, Linehan does not offer any way of making sense of this in terms of underlying processes and structures, offering instead the somewhat general notion of an assumed biologically-determined weakness in affect control.

Linehan's understanding of transference and countertransference, derived from psychoanalysis, seems more developed than is the case with cognitive schema therapy and there is no neglect of the patient's destructive potential. Compared to CAT, however, the absence of an early comprehensive acknowledgement of the patient's experience and of a link between this and current high-level procedures means that integration depends on the slow piecing together of numerous discrete episodes of learning, and there is no attempt to create an explanatory framework to account for the instability.

Many of the reservations expressed here about cognitive therapy and about Linehan's approach are shared by Perris (1994). While agreeing with Linehan's humanist orientation and her use of a range of therapeutic strategies, Perris sees her 'molecular' approach, with its focus on modifying specific behaviours, as limited compared with his own aim of promoting personality integration and of restructuring underlying dysfunctional schemata. As with Safran, such schemata are understood to be derived from the 'working models of organism and environment' described by Bowlby and, as with CAT, their persistence is attributed to the constant reconfirmation of maladaptive strategies. In these ways Perris seems the closest to CAT of the cognitive behavioural models, lacking only a model of dissociated self states in the theory and the use of reformulatory tools in the practice. These differences may explain the relatively long time required in his approach.

None of the authors discussed here consider language and the role of sign mediation in development and none includes as extensive a use of writing and diagrams by patients and therapists as does CAT. The 'top-down' understandings offered by CAT, in which the events of therapy are understood in terms of the overall model created jointly early in therapy, may be the explanation for the evident speed with which change can occur in many patients and for the ability of CAT methods to encourage integration and self-reflection.

Conclusion

Psychoanalysis, self psychology, cognitive therapy and dialectical behaviour therapy have all made contributions to the understanding of BPD: psychoanalysis through the attempt to understand it in terms of development and structure; self psychology by its emphasis on the impact of relationships with others in its formation and in its treatment; and cognitive and behavioural approaches in their focus on observable sequences linking cognition, affect and behaviour and in some of their specific techniques. These approaches have been considered in this chapter from a CAT orientation and both convergences and differences have been noted. I have argued that psychoanalysis can be actively harmful and would add to that criticism the fact that its intensity and duration make it totally impracticable for most patients. Less intensive therapies based on psychoanalytic ideas, such as that of Safran, may have a part to play, particularly because transference and countertransference issues are of crucial importance in the treatment of a condition marked by interpersonal destructiveness. The degree to which these are adequately understood and managed in cognitive therapy is uncertain; its underlying assumptions about learning being based on rational deductions from evidence and its elementary structural model are a serious limitation. Both Linehan and Perris address these issues more adequately, by borrowing psychoanalytic notions and, in the case of Perris, by including Bowlby's developmental theory.

I would (understandably) argue that the model and the methods of CAT provide a more comprehensive understanding and a more rapidly effective treatment. The CAT contribution includes (1) its critical revision of key understandings from psychoanalysis, (2) its linking this with the cognitive and behavioural focus on sequences, (3) the introduction of the model of dissociated self states and the use of the self state sequential diagram. Through these features it is able to offer a more powerful understanding of borderline phenomena and a more accessible guide to clinical intervention than the existing models reviewed in this chapter. But this is not to say that the last word has been said; while research may in due course help indicate the scope and limits of different methods of treatment, an equally important task is to clarify, through discussion, the conceptual basis of our understanding of borderline phenomena. This chapter is intended to be part of that clarifying debate.

CHAPTER 5

An Outline of Practice and Two Case Illustrations

This chapter presents a brief summary of the CAT treatment of borderline patients, followed by accounts of the therapies of two such patients, one at the mild end of the borderline spectrum, the other more seriously disturbed. Later chapters will provide a full discussion of the issues arising at different stages of therapy. A more detailed account of basic CAT procedures will be found in Chapter 2 of Ryle (1995b). It should be noted that a wide range of therapeutic methods may be included in CAT provided that their relation to the overall understanding summarized in the reformulation is clear; for example, behavioural methods or role play techniques could be employed in order to aid the revision of identified problem procedures.

The purpose of the various CAT-specific procedures described is to enable therapists to maintain an acknowledging and non-collusive relationship with their patients and to develop with them new concepts and understandings. This transforming relationship is the foundation on which integration and the learning of new procedures can commence. The stages of treatment are summarized below.

Assessment

The patient's diagnosis in terms of Axis II and Axis I (DSM IV) diagnoses needs to be established, current medication needs to be reviewed and arrangements for its supervision confirmed, and the risks of self-harm, suicide, or violence assessed. Other clinicians (for example, general practitioners or psychiatrists) involved with the patient should be informed if treatment is offered. Relevant questionnaires may be administered.

Contract

A written description of the proposed length of the therapy, arrangements for cancelled sessions, expectations as regards homework and an account of the scope and limits of what the clinic can offer is provided.

Early Sessions: Reformulation

In addition to noting information given by the referrer, the therapist will gather information from clinical history-taking and by noting the evolving therapy relationship, and patients may be involved in self-monitoring and will be invited to read and discuss the Psychotherapy File and maybe to carry out other assignments. The purpose of each of these exercises should be explained. As information is gathered, therapists need to show that they have heard and understood the patient's story and can begin to reformulate it in provisional written or diagrammatic form. With borderline patients the most useful descriptions will be those of variable *states* and those identifying the contrasting *reciprocal role patterns* which will characterize the different *self states* in most cases. Once the patient understands the idea of separate states (this is usually accepted without difficulty) he or she should be involved in their identification and characterization.

The *reformulation letter*, linking the history to the patient's present difficulties, can usually be discussed verbally, written out and offered for discussion and possible revision by the fourth session. Preliminary, partial diagrammatic reformulation may be usefully sketched out from the first session onwards, either to illustrate predominant reciprocal role patterns or to offer preliminary models of different states, on the basis of which the reciprocals can be identified and self states described. This latter procedure will, in most cases, delineate one self state based on the dominant pattern of childhood on the lines of *abusing and neglecting in relation to guilty or rebellious victim*. Other self states commonly include (1) forms of idealization, (2) emotionally blank states, (3) placation and perfectionism or (4) frenetic overactivity. The individual states as identified and characterized by the patient must be the basis of the final diagram, in which the reciprocal patterns will be described and the procedures generated from each self state will also be shown. This full mapping commonly needs six or more sessions. The work involved in this plays an important part in developing the alliance and in initiating a more continuous observing capacity.

The Working Phase of Therapy

In most cases the completion of the reformulation phase ushers in a period of active use of the diagram to trace the daily manifestations of problem procedures, a parallel process also being used during sessions. For this purpose adequately simple colour-coded diagrams should be used. During this phase patients often report increased dreaming and greater access to memory. This phase is often the manifestation of either striving to please or idealizing procedural patterns and these need to be identified. Some time around the 12th session out of 24, there is frequently a switch to more ambivalent or hostile patterns, usually indirectly expressed; the acknowledgement of these, locating them in terms of the diagram and avoiding hurt or counterhostile responses is a key moment in the therapy. Such mixed feelings will recur around termination.

Termination and Follow-up

Therapists write a 'goodbye letter' and invite patients to do the same. The therapist's aim is to estimate realistically what has been achieved and to acknowledge and allow both disappointment and appreciation. At this stage most patients have learned to understand themselves and to recognize where they are in terms of their old procedures and are feeling less fragmented but few have yet established alternatives. Change requires that they can continue to draw on the conceptual tools developed during therapy and can internalize the therapist as an accurate, honest and imperfect figure to stand alongside their historical abusive, neglecting or idealized ones. Follow-up at 1, 2, 3 and 6 months can make termination more tolerable and can contribute to a more balanced internalization of the therapist. The following case histories illustrate the application of these procedures.

Case 1: Barbara (Therapist: Madelyn Freeman)

Barbara was a 27-year-old clerical worker referred by her general practitioner on account of long-term depression, low self-esteem, phases of impulsive spending and binge eating, and moodiness. These problems were associated with a physical deformity; Barbara had been born with an encephelocoele (a developmental abnormality affecting the spine) which had been successfully operated on but which had left her of small stature and with a markedly short neck.

Barbara lived in her own flat and was in a long-term but still insecure relationship with a boyfriend who was a few years younger. She had seen a psychiatrist for a 6-month period three years previously; she had felt supported but did not feel that her underlying problems had been solved. Her pre-therapy assessment with the Personality Assessment Schedule (PAS) showed a number of borderline traits, notably impulsiveness, instability of her sense of self and feelings of worthlessness. Retrospective diagnosis based on this and on the additional data gathered during the therapy, which included her describing some paranoid features, suggested that she met the criteria for BPD, but she was one of the least severe cases in the project.

The first therapy session was devoted to an explanation of the form of the therapy and to the exploration of her early history. This continued in the second meeting, supplemented by the discussion of her completion of the Psychotherapy File. A key issue in the history was the effect of her congenital defect. This had exposed her to cruel teasing at school and to friction with her brothers at home. Other details of the history are summarized in the reformulation letter, reproduced below. From this history and from her responses on the Psychotherapy File, a preliminary identification was made of two states, labelled *Powerless Victim* and *The Bitch*; the former was representative of how she often felt with others and the latter of how she felt and behaved towards both herself and others. Her self-descriptions included the following, from the first session (this is an edited excerpt; omissions are indicated by ...):

PT   I know I react differently in situations where I can sometimes be totally irrational ...
TH   Can you give me an example?
PT   Like yesterday with my boyfriend. I was picking on him ... he sometimes flips ... I'll go for him. I'll smack him ... Then he'll go to tears. I hate the thought of this. I feel I have to continually prove myself to him. When he does show me affection, I don't trust him, you see, so he can't win, really, I suppose, but I'm never sure about it but I think he has the upper hand.

The theme of fearing rejection was discussed again in session 3:

PT   It keeps coming back to primary school; I was put in a separate class because my learning ability was lower ... I felt I was constantly reminded ... taking away the fact of what I physically am ... I'm still proving to people that I'm normal. I felt that barriers were put upon me ... like a punishment in a way. In secondary school I couldn't do child care because I couldn't carry children ... I carry shopping! I do everything! ...

The aspect of Barbara's nature evident in the last remark was identified as *Defiant Coper*; it had been apparent to the first assessor who, commenting on her evident strengths in the context of her other more disturbed features, noted that she did not convey a 'borderline feel'. While in this state she felt able to assert herself and gain advantage over others, but it often left her feeling vulnerable and insecure. Two other states were subsequently identified. One was called after an uncle (now dead) who seemed, in many ways, to have been a closer and more reliable figure than her father but who was, in the nature of things, only sometimes available. This state was labelled *Uncle Bob Island*; it stood for possible but precarious depending. A fifth state emerged later, based on fantasies of giving and receiving perfect care (especially in relation to her mother); this was woven around the thought of winning the lottery and was called *Pink Spectacles (the Ideal)*.

At the fourth session the therapist read out the reformulation letter:

Dear Barbara,
The purpose of writing this letter is to help us clarify the feelings you have spoken about concerning yourself, how you feel about others and the way in which you perceive other people feel about you ... . It is often helpful to remember family histories in order to understand how you came to feel the

way you do ... . Being born with your abnormality made you feel inadequate and especially vulnerable. In early days your Mum said you were perfect, but in the picture you drew for me of yourself you gave no definition of your hands, feet, face, breasts or hips, and in another you were so overweight as to be unrecognizable. And you told me how being placed in special classes at school did little to confirm your Mum's statement.

At home, when there were angry scenes involving your parents and brothers, you felt irrationally guilty for being the cause of family troubles and felt you were the one who should be blamed. Because your parents were always working very hard ... they do not seem to have recognized how lonely you had come to feel ... and your dad seems to have been a remote and unapproachable kind of person ... so you may have come to feel that there was no one to turn to and no one you could trust.

As you grew older you also felt that others, outside the family, could not be trusted. They appeared to be more powerful than you and more in control, even to the extent of controlling your thoughts, so you became suspicious about their motives in befriending you, as if they would humiliate you ... which angered you and possibly encouraged you to act rebelliously. This in turn could cause others to reject you, which could seem to confirm your underlying fear of being a victim ... . So your choices seem limited to EITHER angry, upset, rebellious, needing to feel in control of others OR feeling a powerless victim controlled by others.

In therapy you have been able to hear your inner voice, which seems 95% angry and critical and contemptuous of yourself; we have named this voice 'the Bitch' to show how it is a part of you which makes you feel powerless. We have also seen in relation to your boyfriend how you act rebelliously, feeling angry, hurt, let down but eventually guilty. You also feel he is unable or unwilling to respond to your deepest feelings of emptiness and isolation ... In this therapy ... we can continue to place the thoughts and feelings you have about yourself and others on the map we have drawn, in order to see how these recurring patterns cause you to suffer from changing moods or states. It is possible that you may also come to feel angry or powerless in relation to me; I could become, for example, 'the Bitch' ... it is very helpful to recognize these changing feelings about me and about therapy ... .

This letter follows the basic form of (a) a retelling of the story in a way that acknowledges past pains, (b) noting the persistent strategies which were the results of early experience or of attempts to make sense of and deal with such experience. In this case these are identified as reciprocal role patterns evident in relationships with others and with self. The accompanying diagram listed identified states. In addition (c) the letter notes the ways in which these procedures might be manifest in the therapy relationship.

Barbara described this letter as 'spot on' and over the next few meetings cooperated enthusiastically in developing her Sequential Diagram. This never reached a static, final form, as she quickly used redrawing of it as a metaphor for change. After one session in which objects were dispersed in the room to stand for her different states, Barbara built on the notion of these states as 'islands' and began to draw bridges between them and later increasingly overlapped them.

Barbara agreed to do two main homework tasks between sessions. The first was to work on the diagram, using different colours for each state, and the second was to keep diaries in which the events of the week could be recorded and located in relation to the colour-coded states.

At the start of this phase she had completed the 'States Grid' (see Appendix 2), rating the first four states identified (*Pink Spectacles* had not then been named) against a range of provided constructs. The two-component graph derived from a principal component analysis of this is given in Figure 5.1 and serves to confirm the characterization of these different states. (This graph can be read as a map in

Figure 5.1   Barbara: States Grid—two-component graph

which the descriptions written round the edge indicate the nature of the territory; the nature of each state is described by the descriptions of the area it occupies,
and will be opposite to the descriptions it is furthest away from.) *The Bitch* and
the *Powerless Victim* can be understood as complementary poles of a reciprocal
role procedure. *Defiant Coper* and *Uncle Bob Island* represent alternative ways of
relating to others who might offer care, the first an untrusting doing without, the
second a cautious acceptance of limited care.

Barbara's elaborations and use of her diagram and diary increasingly included instructions to herself and accounts of new ways of coping. The therapist's
suggestion of the need to develop an 'observing eye' ('the eye which becomes
an I') through these activities and the accompanying connecting up of the states
were enthusiastically pursued. In a late version of her diagram four coloured
states are depicted overlapping a central, multi-coloured one labelled *'I'm me'*.
The four states were commented on as follows: (1) (**Pink Spectacles, the ideal
state**) *Take those glasses off, life doesn't go as you plan. Come down to earth and
be fair to yourself.* (2) (**Uncle Bob Island**) *No one can compare to yourself for
looking after yourself.* (3) (**Bitch**) *Use only as necessary.* (4) (**Powerless Victim**)
*This starts every bad thought off. You're hurting yourself. Stop building walls and
blaming everyone else.* **Defiant Coper** did not appear in this diagram, perhaps
assimilated in the central 'I'm me'; the page was headed 'LOOK AT ME; I AM
WHAT I WANT TO BE'.

These changes took place in the context of a positive therapeutic relationship in which Barbara clearly felt safe and to which she brought admirable
determination. During this time Barbara had to deal with two important life
events and these provided many of the themes of her sessions and diary-keeping and were a test of her developing confidence. One was a sudden, potentially serious illness in her mother, and the other was deciding with her boyfriend
that he should move in with her, which he proceeded to do about halfway
through her therapy. In the past what she perceived as her boyfriend's uncertain commitment had been a source of much pain; her own contribution to their
difficulties now became clearer and at the same time she was able to be more
direct and firm about issues that concerned her. An example from her diary
written before he moved in reads:

> He was tired and I asked did he want an early night. I really wanted him to
> stay but I was quick to phone a cab.

Another example from later on, when she was recording episodes on separate
sheets for each state, reads (on the *Bitch* sheet):

> Got home from work, rushing round tidying things up, while he was lying
> around not helping me. He asked me for a pin and I shouted 'for fuck's sake
> can't you see I'm doing something. Care for yourself'.

Later in the week another entry on the same sheet reads:

> Wanting him to hurt like me, physical punishment towards him (why can't you see what you're doing to me). I react over the top, use his anger against my own and return the anger.

The illness of Barbara's mother served to bring into focus a range of feelings. Earlier in the therapy she had been struck to recognize that a very negative and distorted drawing of herself had in fact been a drawing of her mother. Now, in preparing for her boyfriend's moving in, issues were addressed which were linked to her relation with her mother and to her sense of herself. In particular they referred back to the time, four years previously, when she had moved out of the family home in protest, after a row when she had resisted the pressure she was under to do a far larger share of household tasks than was demanded of her brothers. This argument had become so heated that her mother had called the police. It seemed that, apart from this episode, there was a smouldering under-current of anger in the home, seldom expressed directly. It is possible that, since leaving home, Barbara had dealt with her mixed feelings towards her mother by denying their differences. She now began to feel more separate, although still clearly concerned about her mother's illness. An entry in her diary reads:

> I get really annoyed when I'm at home doing the housework. I see myself as my Mum and I fear my future will be like hers, no rewards for breaking your back to get things done and keeping everyone happy ... I do a lot of protest-ing against this happening ... she, I think, isn't as disappointed about the way her life has ended up as I am ... I've stopped taking responsibility for the rest of the family.

The therapeutic relationship was a positive working alliance (maybe pink-tinged) and there came a point when the therapist felt that she had not fully contacted the depth of Barbara's core feelings of emptiness and powerless anger. (The work component of CAT, while creating the understanding which makes it safe to feel, can also serve to keep painful emotions at bay.) The ther-apist therefore suggested that they might explore what was *not* written on the map. At the next session Barbara reported a week of intense dreams which had woken her from deep sleep. The most important dream was of a man entering her room and raping her; she woke screaming and calling out for help and want-ing her mother. At this stage Barbara was keeping her diary with a separate page for each state. The dream was described on the *Helpless Victim* page:

> I dreamt I was raped but all I saw was my emotional state—breaking down crying as I tried to tell my Mum (the pain in my heart full of such sadness, it hurts, crying all the time).

The therapist noticed that while this dream was being recounted Barbara was gripping her neck with both hands; she pointed this out and suggested that perhaps in some way the image of rape was a parallel to the sense of violation involved in her physical deformity. This led to Barbara discussing the meaning of this with much greater intensity of feeling than had been the case previously. A second dream was concerned with anger with a work colleague; she banged her head repeatedly on a school desk and felt pleasure at causing her pain. This dream was clearly of *The Bitch* in action.

Barbara opened the 14th session with some reflections on her progress:

> I'm feeling more relaxed and trusting of myself. I come away and think about things; I'm thinking differently. It's like analysing my own thoughts and finding my own answers ... it's two lines of thought and then trying to find the best route to take. It's trying to analyse something before it happens and trying to set up, like we discussed, a cautioning measure before the reaction or situations happen. So I don't feel upset about the way I carry out things ... And I also find, in triggering situations, a lot relates to when I was a child, and a lot of things flash in my head ... how I felt, the emotions and everything, and that starts things off and makes my line of thought be that way. I still go into that routine, but I'm arguing the case in my head and giving myself verbal reasoning compared to other people ... .

During the remaining weeks of therapy the problems provoked by her mother's illness and the adjustments called for by the presence of the boyfriend in her flat were discussed in relation to the understandings recorded in the diagram. Her diary yielded some wry self-observations, for example on one occasion the large statement 'I'M IN A MOOD' had appended to it 'Leave me alone, don't go'. The sheet monitoring *Uncle Bob Island* (described as 'feels pretty risky but maybe it'll be OK') had one simple entry: 'My Dad said on the phone he loves me and he's being more expressive to me. I didn't react coldly; I laughed lightly and replied in the same way.'

The approach of termination (a reminder of imperfect care) generated tearful anxiety but there was also growing confidence. Goodbye letters were exchanged at the last session. The therapist offered a brief recapitulation of the work done and noted the effort and intelligence which Barbara had brought to the tasks, concluding:

> I think you have said you find it very difficult to think positively about yourself. Perhaps we did set down a foundation not only for future self-monitoring but for feelings of self-acceptance. The qualities you possess have been rewarding to work with. I also accompanied you as you faced serious life events. Throughout, you cared for and expressed deep affection for others. I hope the possibility of caring deeply for yourself will continue to evolve, long after the memory of therapy fades.

Barbara's goodbye letter included the following:

> Thank you for the following: Opening my eyes to myself. My Observing
> Eye. What triggers the moods. Stop blaming myself. Stop putting people on
> that high stool. I am their equal. They have different moods too. I have
> rights. I'm gaining confidence and I am trying to teach myself to trust
> myself. To understand myself is to understand others. We all have differ-
> ent behaviour patterns but do experience the same emotions. I have been
> blinded by the inner mood which changes the outer appearance of myself
> and my opinion of myself. Recognizing the danger signs. By using the ideal,
> Uncle Bob island, Defiant coping, the Bitch. When I looked back at the
> past I was shocked how I saw myself—i.e. the two pictures I drew—they
> looked different. You said a few words and I saw 'That's my mother, not
> me'—and then at the other picture; 'Wow! Don't I look nice. That's me,
> Barbara.' ... I'm a lot happier and in the past day I have noticed I smile
> quite a bit more ... I could go on and on about what I have learned about
> myself ... You have taught me to use my observing eye, recognize my
> behaviour and moods. I will miss your help ... You didn't give me advice
> you encouraged me to find my own answers and to believe in my own
> judgement ...

Barbara attended for three follow-up sessions at monthly intervals with her
therapist, reporting continuing progress and, at the third, delighted to
announce that she was pregnant. A last meeting was arranged to be after the
birth. I saw her for her post-therapy assessment interview about 6 months
after termination. She was glowing with pleasure at her pregnancy and at her
sense of having achieved real changes in her therapy. She rated herself as
much improved as regards her presenting complaints and in terms of the procedures identified at the start of therapy, and the reported changes supported that judgement. She felt good about herself but, she insisted, in a realistic
not a 'pink spectacles' way. She was more stable and less irritable at work,
where colleagues had commented on the change, and with her boyfriend, who
was now the more moody of the two. She seldom thought about her neck. The
only evidence for suspiciousness was hypothetical; she wondered if she would
feel insecure if her (currently unemployed) boyfriend were to go to work.
There had been no episodes of impulsive spending or eating. The instabilities
of her sense of self and of her view of others were much less marked and were
understood and her sense of emptiness was no longer apparent. Her scores on
the symptom questionnaires were near zero. In discussing her pregnancy, she
announced with great firmness that, even if she were to have a Caesarean
delivery (on account of her small stature this was quite likely) she was going
to insist that she was the first one in the family to see her baby. In this and
other ways she conveyed the impression that defiant coping had been modified to proper assertion.

Comment

Despite Barbara's insistence to the contrary there was probably an element of euphoria in her state, but overall there seemed no doubt that a considerable change and integration had been achieved, and that her capacity to meet whatever life presented her with and to avoid old patterns of self-limitation seemed assured.

In many ways this was a relatively easy therapy, in so far as negative procedures did not, at any time, interrupt the therapeutic process. The therapist offered a warm, respecting, professional presence, and Barbara responded with trust and commitment. It could be that her *Uncle Bob Island* offered a basis for making use of what was available and doing without what was not, and it seems that her *Defiant Coping* was recruited to the therapeutic work and contributed to the development of her observing eye. Within the context of the early reformulation and of her elaboration of it, the drawings had had a major impact on her sense of her self and on her revision of her relationship with (or identification with) her mother.

One technical point needs to be made: the diagrams in this case were based on the descriptions of *states* rather than of *self states*. The latter would have been identified in terms of reciprocal roles, such as *The Bitch in relation to the Powerless Victim*. In this therapy this was not important, but in general the use of *self state* descriptions is preferable, in that it ensures that patients know, when in a given state, how they are perceiving the other (person or part of themselves), as well as how they are feeling, and can question that. In addition, therapists are better able to anticipate and identify occasions when they are under pressure to enact or feel any one of the possible reciprocations to the patient's behaviour.

Case 2: Tom (Therapist: Anthony Ryle)

Tom missed his first appointment, having been admitted to the ward after being brought to the hospital by the police. A passer-by had found him wearing a rock-filled rucksack, having climbed over the parapet of a Thames bridge. He had attended the hospital 18 months previously, following a paracetamol overdose, and had been seen again a month later in the Accident and Emergency department. On that occasion the Duty Psychiatrist recorded that he was preoccupied with thoughts of killing himself or others, in particular his mother and stepfather, and that he had been enquiring about how to obtain a gun. He was carrying a knife but handed it over without argument. Tom was referred for CAT at this time but did not pursue the appointment. Seven months later his general practitioner referred him to Outpatients with persisting suicidal preoccupations. He had described having prepared to electrocute himself in the bath; the thought of his two friends (Anna, an ex-partner, and Peter, an ex-work colleague) had made him change his mind. He was again referred for CAT and on this occasion confirmed that he wanted to be seen and returned the questionnaires. He was offered his first appointment five months later. (I took him on personally, partly as an act of solidarity with the trainees who were carrying out most of the research therapies, partly because of the history of possible violence and the absence of available male therapists and despite the fact that I was only going to be available for 18 weeks.)

The main history was well documented. His father had left home before he could remember and over the next 16 years his mother had many partners, of whom three were relatively long term. The third, who married his mother, was violent to both Tom and his mother and Tom finally left home aged 19, having hit him on the head with a hammer. Moving to London he had lived in a squat, taken many (non-opiate) drugs and had continued an established pattern of drinking heavily. Tom's schooling had been badly disrupted by his mother's frequent moves, but he had obtained some GCSEs and after coming to London had been employed most of the time in various jobs, most recently as an unqualified care assistant in a hostel for rehabilitated alcoholics. At the time of starting therapy he had been unemployed for nearly a year. During this period he had sought alcohol counselling and had reduced his intake considerably. He had had one court appearance for being drunk and disorderly at a football match. He lived alone in a poorly maintained flat and his social contacts were largely confined to his two friends.

Tom remained in the ward during the first weeks of his therapy and also began to attend Art Therapy, which he valued. At the first session I explained in outline what I knew from the notes and did not seek to take a systematic history. Tom described feeling humiliated in seeking therapy and also untrusting. He spoke of practical problems, in particular major rent arrears, and about the depressing nature of his semi-basement flat, painted black and dark blue by the last tenant. He went on to describe how he had always been a loner but was now, for the first time, lonely; he saw nobody apart from his friends Anna and Peter. He described his disillusion with the people with whom he had worked, how they were after power and had lost concern for their clients; a similar disillusion had spoiled an earlier involvement with an anti-racist political group.

By this stage of the session I had the sense of being with a sensitive and intelligent man and had seen no sign of the violent side. He went on to speak of his fear of being rejected should he reach out in therapy and of losing one of the few good things about him, his independence. The other good thing he could name was that he was 'loyal and compassionate'; my comment that this was not so in relation to himself led on to dismissive remarks about his lack of education and to his reporting his mother's frequent comment that he was 'a waste of space'.

At this point the form of the therapy was described in some detail and the need to guard against disrupting it through the probable emergence of his negative patterns was emphasized. He expressed anxiety about what to do if he felt upset after a session when he was no longer an inpatient; he was already aware that a duty psychiatrist was always available in the A and E department and had already been able to call his friends, and understood that the Psychotherapy Unit was not able to offer support outside his sessions. At this point I also explained that I would be available for only 18 weeks and would not be able to offer follow-up meetings.

Towards the end of the session diary-keeping around his mood shifts was agreed (and the likelihood of non-compliance mentioned) and he was invited to comment on how it had felt to be starting therapy. He replied that he felt overwhelmed to look at the confusion of his life, and angry at the injustice of it, especially at his mother's unconcern for his needs as a child. He was given the Psychotherapy File to take away.

At the second session he described having felt drained by the first meeting, though also hopeful (but 'it's bound to go'). He spoke with difficulty about his powerful feelings for a female staff member, feelings which he knew were bound to lead to disappointment, and he linked this with previous examples, saying 'I need to be adored to make up for all the hurts and for all I've missed; but I know it can't be like that'. He described how, of his past relationships with women, it was only with Anna that the disillusion had been lived through and a real friendship maintained.

He went on to tell some detailed stories about his mother; for example, how he had been beaten for vomiting on leaving the dentist, and how he had been left for hours with appendicitis until an uncle insisted on calling the doctor. He described how his fears at school had led him to truant regularly; to avoid criticism he would climb over the school wall and spend the day alone on the sand dunes.

Towards the end of the session I offered a preliminary verbal reformulation, and drafted some elements of a sequential diagram. He responded by feeling close to tears and by saying that he felt privileged and that someone else should have the time; I rejected this view of himself as a 'waste of space' (his mother's phrase) and promised a written reformulation next time.

The following is the final version of the reformulation letter, which was revised in some details after session 3:

Dear Tom,
Here's my letter summarizing how I understand the story of your life that you have told me.
Your childhood was a desert; your father disappeared without trace and your mother was too busy with her own affairs to attend to your emotional needs, often showing brutal indifference or incomprehension of your experiences, for example when you vomited after the dentist or had appendicitis. Because of frequent moves you were unable to make use of school and once you were behind you found the teacher's criticisms unbearable ... you also

got into fights and found it better to be on the cold and lonely sand dunes ... from this you acquired a capacity to be independent and began to store up pain and anger ... while your mother's previous suitors had been experienced as threats to what little security you had, they were men you could have liked, but your stepfather's brutality and your mother's acceptance of it added more pain and anger; feelings which culminated in the hammer-blow that led to your coming to London.

The baggage you brought with you was a capacity for independence (denying your own needs) and an expectation that relationships offered largely indifference or abuse. Your solutions were to cut off, to revenge or to fight randomly, and to use drugs and alcohol. However, you found some mutual support among others around you who were also displaced or outside society and ... in your involvement in politics and in your last job you made an attempt to put yourself and others right ... but you experienced disillusion as you found care and concern submerged by ... petty personal ambitions. This pattern of disillusion also characterized your love affairs where ... as others failed to fulfil the role you asked of them you would become withdrawn, a zombie (like your mother)—when the other became cross about your withdrawal you would respond with self-righteous anger and spoil the relationship. But not always; with Anna you went on to a loyal, compassionate friendship and she and Peter have stood by you ... and do not see you as a 'waste of space'.

The letter continued with a discussion of the issues identified in the Psychotherapy File. These consisted of three traps (depression maintained by placation, low self-esteem and avoidance) and dilemmas of self-care which were summarized as the reciprocal role pattern 'Indifferent critical rejection to guilty waste of space'. The letter concluded with a list of the tasks of therapy.

The self states sequential diagram was elaborated over the ensuing sessions. The final version is given in Figure 5.2.

Tom came to the fourth session saying he had nearly decided not to come. Preparing to cut himself off was a reaction to feeling guilty towards his friends and a preparation for another suicide bid. He reported daydreams: 'being rocked in a woman's arms like a child and being able to cry'. In Art Therapy he had felt good but went on to see 'ugly meanings' in what he had painted, but he could see this as being the effect of having become more aware since drinking less. The negative feelings were more dominant in session 5; he did not want therapy, he wanted to draw the logical conclusion from not coming, namely suicide. He described images which flashed through his mind in a train of himself with a machine gun, blowing off peoples' heads, 'it was great'. He recalled with bitterness his sense of betrayal and his rage, expressed by random vandalism, when a love affair had ended. He brought to this sesson a letter (not for posting) written at my suggestion, telling his mother of his feelings:

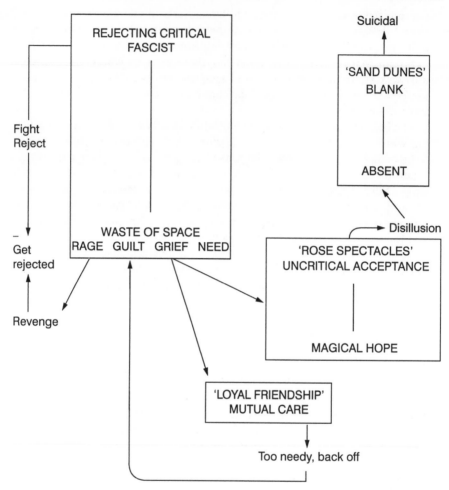

Figure 5.2   Tom: Self States Sequential Diagram

Dear Bitch,
I am glad you have loads of shit in your life as you failed to notice all the shit
in mine. You always complained about having no money ... how the hell was
I supposed to help—all the time at school I wore second-hand clothes, you
fucking didn't—I fucking hate you. It doesn't take any money to give love—
you always worried more about how you looked than how I felt—I hope you
have a slow painful death ... .

This was a painful and anxious session; the next meeting was to be the last
before the Christmas closure of the department, and he assured me he would

not come. The relation of this to the fascist voice in the diagram, and the path he was following to the sand dunes, were pointed out and I wrote a letter to him after the session reiterating these points and repeating that one thing he needed to learn was that getting less than you want and need is still getting something. He came to the session, telling how in Art Therapy he had achieved a sense of his depression being less than all of him, but none the less he presented a weary, hopeless air. I took him through what we understood as summarized in the reformulation letter and diagram and spoke about the pace and nature of change, but also sensed and described how I felt distanced by him.

I was distressed but not altogether surprised to discover, when the department reopened, that Tom had presented to the A and E department 'in order to leave a goodbye message' for the Art Therapist, the ward doctor and me, and had been compulsorily admitted. I visited him in the ward, to find him utterly bleak. Later that day his consultant took him off the section, whereupon he returned to his flat and again set up the wiring to electrocute himself in his bath. As he explained at our next meeting (session 8), having trashed his flat and had a last cigarette, he had got into the bath only to be overcome with weeping. He got out of the bath and phoned Anna who had come round, given him a hug and arranged for his readmission.

From this sequence Tom discovered the extent to which his anger had served as a cover for his sadness. Some sessions later, he linked this with an episode when he was six or seven years old when he had begged his mother not to leave the house and she had belted him; his uncle had remonstrated with her and he had vowed 'never to cry again'.

Thereafter, when upset, he would 'go out, pick up a brick and find a smaller child'. Referring back to my saying that he had been busy 'going to the sand dunes' he said:

> I thought about it ... I'd just sat there in the bath because you were all getting too close ... I thought fuck it, I don't give a shit.
>
> TH You felt like you didn't care, then, by saying that?
> PT I felt I had to do it then or I wouldn't do it at all.

After exploration about how the anger had kept grief at bay and how the grief had come through, I acknowledged how hard it must have been to change his mind and phone Anna:

> ... I just cried, got out of the bath, wet through, felt such an idiot and didn't know what to do, sat for half an hour, then went to the phone—I felt such an idiot, it was like me 'Mr Know-it all,'—whom no one can tell how he feels.

The discussion turned later to Tom's feelings about therapy:

You can't care that much or you would not take me to the end and say 'bang, bang, bang all solved—'

This was responded to in part by reminding Tom of his unrealistic Pink Spectacles hopes and of the use of incomplete offers, and in part by an acknowledgement of his realistic anxieties about termination, with a preliminary consideration of possible continuing help, such as joining a group.

The next few sessions were marked by optimism and energy and also by a realization of how he had harmed others: 'There are so many people I want to say sorry to.' He could not forgive his mother 'for passing it on to me' but added 'But I pass it on to others.' He felt now able to do things from wanting to inside, not from intention, and began to make realistic moves about his debts and the dingy state of his flat. Reviewing the changes in session 12 with reference to the diagram he felt he was not wearing rose-coloured spectacles, he was being real with his friends and not backing off and 'the fascist in my head never stays more than half an hour'. He felt he had needed both this therapy and Art Therapy, which provided another way to represent and then think about his feelings. He could still put himself down, however. He had seen the group therapist and accepted a place in the group, to start a few weeks after termination with me.

This positive phase gradually faded over the last four sessions; I found myself increasingly offering encouragement and reminders of progress (and a small loan to buy paint so he could get on with decorating his flat, which he refused), only to be faced with sluggishness and emptiness and a sense of being held at bay.

This was obviously linked with termination and this point was made in the goodbye letter which I gave at the last meeting (he 'forgot' to bring his). I wrote:

... I have felt myself pitted against the 'fascist in your head', both in my work with you to clarify and recognize the ways in which your past strategies have kept you down and in my being with you, along with the Art Therapist, the ward staff and your friends, on terms which challenge the assumptions of the fascist. In the middle phase of therapy you were able ... to use this and felt realistic, not magical, hope, and became aware of the ways in which you could begin to use your own resources ... But over the last 3–4 weeks you have lost that sense and stopped doing many of the things you had been able to do to combat negative feelings and thoughts. The old ways are familiar and automatic and the new ones need conscious attention and you have felt it to be precarious, like walking on soft sand—the fascist voice has started to murmur again that it is a shit world and that you lack the strength to take it on ... you hear my words, as you said, but not my meaning—But there are new voices in your head, human voices addressing you as a fellow human with respect and affection. You may grieve and curse that, after so much pain, we gave you so little, but I believe you will discover that we gave you enough and that these voices will increasingly become your own ...

At this last meeting he described how a small retiling job in the bathroom had, in the end, needed a complete stripping down and redoing; he was proud to have completed it and to have kept his temper. I took some comfort from this story.

Tom missed his last appointment with the Art Therapist. He attended one group therapy meeting but then neither returned nor replied to letters. He attended his six month post-therapy assessment interview; at this time he still met borderline criteria on the PAS interview and his inventory scores were virtually unchanged. At this assessment interview he reported no change from therapy and said he had torn up his diagram and reformulation and goodbye letters as being 'superficial'. He was, however, free of active suicidal preoccupations. He was living an isolated life, mostly staying in his flat.

Shortly after this assessment, about eight months after termination, Tom came to see me at my request. He remained adamantly opposed to any further treatment apart from agreeing to consider further Art Therapy; after three meetings with the Art Therapist he turned this down too. At this stage I assumed that the account of Tom's therapy would appear in this book as an example of failures and limitations. I was glad to be found mistaken in this, however.

Follow-up

One year later (20 months after termination) I telephoned Tom for his annual follow-up; his response was friendly and he said he had been about to get in touch. We met a week later, Tom bringing in his questionnaires, now all scoring in the normal range. He described how, some 6 months previously, it had 'suddenly all clicked'. He thought to himself that 'they all showed me what I was doing, but I don't have to go on doing it'. He had started work in a small restaurant and was now the part-time chef and was beginning to think about getting some more education. And he had a girlfriend, met through Peter, who was 'imperfect and autonomous and I love her'; he described this as a quite different sort of relationship, in which things could be talked through. He gave an example of this; he had felt a little suffocated in the relationship, had first blamed her, then seen it was in him and had then realized that he could survive it if she went. His mother had visited recently; he had looked across the room and thought 'well, she has some difficult habits, but so do I; anyway I am Tom, aged 31!' These dramatic changes had 'just happened', he felt free, the weight of lifelong anger had lifted, he felt responsible and in charge of himself and was in the process of stopping smoking and, as for the 'fascist in his head', it was now more of a disciplinarian than a brute.

Comment

As a result of the pilot study preceding the main project, CAT for borderline patients was modified from the normal 16 sessions with one follow-up to 24 ses-

sions with follow-up at 1, 2, 3 and 6 months, in recognition of the extreme difficulties around termination faced by these needy patients. It was a wrong decision on my part to take Tom on when I knew that I could only offer 18 sessions
and no follow-up. The offer of a group a few weeks after his therapy was no substitute for follow-up meetings, for these are often the occasion when anger and
disappointment with the therapist can be more directly expressed. Having said
that, the therapy itself felt mostly good, if difficult and anxious; the work on
reformulation had given me a good sense of his predicament and had helped
provide him with a new way of thinking about himself. It did not save him from
the episode in the bath but may have helped him learn from that, although the
availability of Anna on the phone was fortunate. The distancing from me over
the last sessions and the ensuing long period of isolation were clearly expressions of Tom preferring the 'sand dunes' to the pains of my incomplete and
abandoning human presence. Tom's anger with me had never been directly
expressed in the sessions; had it been spoken and survived during the therapy
or during the follow-up six months the subsequent long retreat to the sand
dunes might have been avoided. How far I may have made anger difficult to
express is something I am uncertain about; in common with others who dealt
with him, I felt a lot of compassion and affection for him, which may have disarmed him. On the other hand, a controlling or distant approach would have
almost certainly provoked early termination. At this last follow-up meeting I
asked whether my offer of the loan for paint had had such an effect; he replied
that the main impact had been to make him ask himself why he had arranged a
life of such poverty.

How much CAT contributed to the ultimately happy ending is difficult to
know; I think it was important, I think it combined well with Art Therapy and I
think the two together ultimately enabled Tom to find his way to a real independence, in which his needs as well as those of others can be accepted. But I
also believe that without the gift of the reliable friendships of Peter and Anna
Tom might not have survived.

*(Tom was happy with the above account. A year later he wrote: 'For the first time
in my life I am able to face problems without any bad mood swings and all the
problems that that causes. And I am very hopeful about my life. My relationship
with my girlfriend is going very well; I put this down to not being full of hate, anger
and pain.')*

CHAPTER 6

Understanding the Treatment Relationship in Work with Borderline Patients

Given that unstable and extreme interpersonal behaviours are a central characteristic of borderline patients it is not surprising that the main challenge they represent to psychotherapists and other clinicians is how to establish and maintain a working relationship. While most patients accepting treatment acknowledge the possibility of being helped and accept the helping role of the clinician (although an occasional patient may appear to be more concerned to demonstrate that all help is useless), there is seldom any strong, realistic expectation of therapy and mistrust, dismissiveness or magical hopes are usually manifest before long. A main aim of the CAT techniques described in earlier chapters is to foresee, contain and learn from these processes. The present chapter offers a more detailed application of the theory to the therapeutic relationship with borderlines.

Preliminary Considerations

The theoretical framework for this examination is the dialogic understanding of personality and relationships whereby, in communicating or playing a role, there is always assumed to be another (external person or part of the self) from whom reciprocation is experienced or sought. The therapy relationship is examined, therefore, as one particular example of a dialogic or reciprocal role relationship and transference and countertransference are each seen to imply the other. In CAT usage these interactive processes are understood to involve some fully conscious aspects and others which are reflected upon only sometimes or never; these latter can be inferred from their manifestations. Contradictory or conflicted feelings may co-exist or alternate for expression, especially in borderline patients; in many ways it would be better to speak of transferences and countertransferences.

Both patients and therapist bring their own procedural patterns to their relationship. The patient's role procedures (transferences) are the source of the pressures applied to, and responses sought from, the therapist. The therapist's responses to the patient include both *elicited countertransference feelings*, which are of diagnostic and therapeutic significance, and the *personal countertransference feelings* which express the therapist's history and personality and which may be unhelpful to the therapy, needing, therefore, to be understood and their expression controlled.

Varieties of Transference

The transfer of attitudes implied by the term transference originally implied a wholesale transposition of perceptions and attitudes from a parental figure to the therapist, or to the contrasting negative and positive transferences of polarized versions of such a figure. With the development of object relations notions of splitting and projection, the use of the term has increasingly implied the effects of unconscious internal processes on the therapy relationship, often with no direct reference to the actual parenting experienced. In CAT this object relations approach is modified in that: (1) the origin of the reciprocal role repertoire is seen to lie in the relationship with caretakers, (2) it is also seen to be constantly re-enacted and confirmed in later relationships, and (3) transference and projective identification are seen as no more than particular examples of the general way in which role reciprocation is elicited.

The role procedures enacted by patients in relation to their therapists will be influenced by the nature of the clinical situation and the somewhat unfamiliar way the therapist behaves but it is generally the case that much of the everyday repertoire of role procedures identified during reformulation will be manifest at some time in the therapy relationship. Recognizing the links between therapy and 'real world' manifestations of procedures is aided in CAT by the fact that both are understood in relation to the core repertoire, which, of course, is itself deduced from both reported and enacted patient behaviours.

Transference is not a static phenomenon; in the case of borderline patients particularly, as was suggested above, it would be better to speak of transferences. There are as many potential transferences from a given patient as there are reciprocal role patterns in the core repertoire or, to be more exact, there are twice as many, given that either pole of a reciprocal role may be enacted in relation to the therapist. In fact there are more still, for some of the roles in the core repertoire may be replaced by avoidant or defensive procedures, which will elicit different responses, without necessarily obliterating all traces of the replaced role. For example, a patient may speak in a placatory way to a therapist while simultaneously, by clenching his or her jaw muscles, conveying non-verbally the anger which placation has replaced. Over a short period of time during a session a patient, as well as simultaneously conveying two or more possibly contradictory roles, may (1) switch in a bewildering way from one self state to another (for example from *vulnerable and needy in relation to idealized* to *cut off and blank in relation to out of reach and rejecting*) or (2) may, while remaining in one self state, manifest response shifts (for example from *submissive* to *rebellious* in relation to *powerful control*) and role reversals (for example, from *abused victim* to *abusive bully*). Such shifts can be bewildering to both patient and therapist and the latter's common sense or generalized understandings will not be an adequate guide in such situations. If inadvertent collusions are to be avoided, and if as much as possible is to be learned, a way of describing, analysing and recognizing these different transference manifestations (and their parallel occurrences in the patient's reported experiences) must be developed.

The active, living interchange of therapeutic discourse is frequently too rapid for a deliberate, conscious reflective process to be possible. But, just as a fencer or tennis player can develop spontaneous (that is, unreflected upon) new skills through deliberate practice, so can a therapist acquire a more accurate perception of where each patient is operating from and a more precise set of differential responses. The basic reformulation can contribute to this level of understanding, and the more fine-grained Dialogic Sequence Analysis (Leiman, 1997), applied to segments of the therapy, offers a more detailed understanding.

Case Example: Philip

Philip was a long-term unemployed 42-year-old man, living marginally and using cannabis heavily (6–8 joints daily). His emotionally unavailable mother used to masturbate him when he was a young child. He was currently suffering from a fractured right wrist and the plaster cast made dressing and basic self-care difficult. From the start of his therapy he showed a capacity to sow confusion while apparently being cooperative, a general mode which was identified as 'smokescreening' in supervision. Edited verbatim excerpts taken from the fourth and seventh sessions show how this process, which largely blocked any felt contact with the therapist, could be characterized in reciprocal role terms. The dialogic sequence analysis was based on the following reciprocal role patterns as identified in the (still incomplete) reformulation:

Self state 1
A: Critical demand to: **B1**: guilt, striving placation
                         or **B2**: pseudo compliance, passive resistance
                         or **B3**: rebellion, revenge

Self state 2
C: Disarming contempt to **D**: dismissed, humiliated

Self state 3
E: Abusing to **F**: abused

Session 4

PT   You ask me how I feel ... I feel fucking horrible since the last session. You
      asked me to say when I smoked to block out feelings, well I did then, but
      I have not bothered to smoke since and I've felt like shit ... there's some-
      thing you said really upset me.
TH   What was that?
PT   You made a criticism about my appearance ... it's on the tape if you want
      to check. I was talking about how people look at me and you said 'You've
      got to admit you do look a daunting sight' ... I took it as criticism and I lost
      a lot of trust in you. I wanted to write to express my feelings but I can't
      with the wrist ... what you had not seen was that I could not shave or comb
      my hair, with my wrist as it is ...
(Patient either in **D** *to therapist seen as in* **C** *or in* **B3** *to therapist in* **A**.*)*

A bit later in the session:

PT   I'm glad you have seen me angry, because you can see how I behave when
      angry; I'm not violent. The thing that annoys me is that you've got a red
      button *(a security alarm, actually not functional)* but I haven't.
TH   I see *(laughs)*.
PT   Yes, it really annoys me. Never been attacked by a psychologist, but there
      must be a first time ...
(Here, the patient has turned the tables, humorously dismissing (**C**) *the therapist*
(**D**).*)*

Session 7

The session started with the patient entering the therapist's room 10 minutes
early, bearing two cups of tea.

PT   I was 15 minutes late two weeks ago so I resolved never to be late again
      (Patient **B1** *to therapist's* **A**) but I have to admit that I got here today only
      by having a smoke first, which is a let down from something I resolved
      myself ... *(this is breaking an agreement about cannabis use before sessions:*
      patient **B3** *to therapist's* **A***; the therapist does not comment)*. I felt quite
      depressed all week ... that's what caused the smoking. But I started work

on your map. (*The patient produces a much worked-over, or rather scrawled over, draft diagram: Patient* **B2** *to therapist* **A**.)

TH You've done a lot of work on it.

PT Yeah—I've been burying myself in bullshit ... I've been so detailed — how is this going to help me have a bonk? (*patient* **C**) ... three days ago I felt less depressed but I burst into tears ... so I went and had a tattoo (*laughs, and shows tattoo on his arm*). Otherwise I'd have slashed myself or hung myself ... (*patient to self* **E** *to* **F**).

The session continued with the patient wondering if the research component of his therapy meant it was not for his benefit (hinting at **B3**), and then returned to his multiple scrawled additions to the draft diagram:

PT My great ambition, as you can see from that page, is to make it neat, and do it thoroughly ... but in the end I wanted it to be jolly and drew a map in the shape of Treasure Island ...

TH You show a lot of humour.

PT One of my defences too ... it's disarming; it stops people coming near me for a start. If you don't believe me, walk down the street laughing and see how long it is before you're arrested ... (*patient* **C** *to therapist* **D**).

Here the patient gives a good example and explanation of his use of disarming contempt. The supervision group to which the therapist came with this case pointed out how, during these early sessions, the therapist seemed to be unable to recognize or acknowledge the hostility being expressed. This was probably due to the indirect, disarming mode employed by the patient interacting with a personal countertransference tendency in the therapist. In reflecting later on what he had learned from listening to the sessional tapes and from supervision, the therapist highlighted his proneness to be disarmed.

Reciprocating and Identifying Transference

The analysis of the above excerpts was made in terms of *reciprocating transference*, describing how the patient perceived the therapist to be at the opposite pole of one or other of his reciprocal roles, or attempted to draw him into such a role. This type of transference is the predominant one, especially in borderline patients in whom the narrowly defined and precarious self states generate powerful pressures on others for reciprocation. A simple refusal or failure to reciprocate can provoke state switches and the value of the diagram is that such events can be recognized and named and linked to the whole picture. Identifying the pressures to reciprocate is, in the early sessions, a source of understanding and contributes to the reformulation process. The patient Philip, described above, had an extensive range of ways of confusing the therapist, such as the overelaborate pseudo-compliance with tasks and the deflection of anger with humour, and these had to be clearly delineated as part of the reformulation process in order to provide a way through to the real anger and pain they had replaced.

A different pattern of transference, which can be described as an *identifying transference*, is one in which the patient, rather than seeking a relationship with the therapist, seeks to become like him or her, in a way denying separation, differentiation and the possibility of conflict. This may be associated with the patient being intrusively concerned with the therapist's life and whereabouts between sessions, in the patient imitating aspects of the therapist's dress or speech or, in one of my patients, in inflicting on herself a minor cut imitating one which I had accidently sustained. In these cases it is as if separate existence were impossible. Intense identifying transference can be one source of the loss of self–other differentiation; another can be rapid oscillation between the two poles of a reciprocal role pattern. The grandiose narcissistic *seeking special admiration from a special, admired other*, combines reciprocal and identifying elements. The experience of therapy should show patients how self–other boundaries are maintained by complex and accurate reciprocal role procedures, which involve differentiation of roles and may include conflict. Across such boundaries, identification provides the basis of accurate empathy.

Forms of Countertransference

Therapists respond to patients in ways determined by their own personality and procedures (personal countertransference) and by the patient's communications and actions (elicited countertransference). These two forms of countertransference will be discussed separately. In practice, of course, personal factors will influence what the patient is able to induce in the therapist.

Personal Countertransference

It is the therapist's responsibility to structure the relationship in ways which help the patient. This involves a highly self-conscious awareness of both professional issues and personal idiosyncrasies. Every therapist brings personal restrictions, sensitivities, vulnerabilities and preconceptions to the work; training and personal therapy aim to bring these into awareness and under control, but they cannot be eliminated and borderline patients, more than most, are adept at discovering them. For this reason supervision is essential for therapists working with borderlines; supervisors, like therapists with their patients, can often see what the individual cannot see for him or herself, and can notice when normal practice is departed from or collusions entered into. Self-supervision using audiotapes is also helpful, preferably linked with work with an external supervisor or (better, in my view) supervision group. Personal countertransference may be a general tendency, or may be evident only in relation to particular kinds of patient; either way a therapist and his or her supervisor or supervision group need to get to know one another and need to establish an atmosphere of trust in which all assume that, at times, they will get drawn into some collusion with their patients. The possible contribution of Dialogic Sequence Analysis to supervision or self-supervision is discussed in Chapter 9. A supervision group (or some members of it) will also, at times, be drawn into feelings and enactments echoing those of the patient or the patient–therapist pair ('parallel process'), a kind of group countertransference which can be illuminating and which may serve to identify co-existing or contradictory feelings.

Elicited Countertransference

Accurate recognition of the shifting countertransference reactions evoked by the borderline patient demands openness, self-awareness and conceptual clarity. Careful reformulation provides the framework within which direct responses can be experienced and reflected upon. Such reflections are initially a source of, and are later referred to, the descriptive reformulation of the patient's procedures and self states. In contrast to psychoanalytic practice they are not the basis for assertions about unconscious processes in the patient.

It is useful to discriminate between two different forms of countertransference, which parallel the distinction made between the two forms of transference. One involves the therapist in feeling, or being induced to play, a reciprocating response, the other consists of an identification with the role played (experiences reported) by the patient. In the latter case, which up until now has not been well described in CAT theory, there is an implicit shared perception of the part played by a third (external or internalized) person or persons playing the reciprocal role.

These two forms of countertransference can be called *reciprocating* and *identifying* respectively. *Reciprocating countertransference* does not imply an exact response to the patient's expectation, nor does *identifying countertransference* imply an exact echoing of the patient's experience. To a varying extent the therapist's countertransference reactions are modified, partly by personal factors, partly by reflection based on professional understanding of the patient's history and personality. The therapist's recognition of, and response to, the role transmitted by the patient is sometimes restricted by these professional factors and sometimes extended; a common example of the latter would be a compensatory feeling of care towards a patient expecting rejection.

This analysis of elicited countertransference responses can be summarized as follows. A patient in a state dominated by the reciprocal role pattern of **A in relation to B** who is enacting role **A** may evoke in the therapist either **B**, a *reciprocating* countertransference or **A**, an *identifying* countertransference. In either case the countertransference may be (1) *echoing* more or less accurately, (2) *extending*, or (3) *restricting*.

Elicited Identifying Countertransference

Identifying countertransference is a source of empathic understanding in therapy; it can be communicated to the patient in ways which make the experience and memory associated with the role concerned more tolerable, especially where what is conveyed is painful or unacceptable feeling. In some cases the identification induced in the therapist is with an avoidant or defensive role; extension in this case may involve recognizing both the defence and also what is defended against. The recognition, naming, placing in context and acceptance of *identifying countertransference* feelings induced by the patient in respect of destructive roles makes them less frightening. Psychoanalysts of an object relations persuasion would describe this as the 'metabolizing' of the patient's projections.

Countertransference is, necessarily, as complex and discontinuous as is transference. In some cases identifying and reciprocal countertransference may be experienced simultaneously; for example, *identifying* with the vulnerable or defended role of an abused person may mobilize the *reciprocal extending countertransference* of a reparative response to (unstated) need, as is exemplified by the case vignettes of Paul and Lesley, below.

Elicited Reciprocating Countertransference

In the case of *reciprocating countertransference* the therapist can learn to recognize the patient's indirectly conveyed role from the reciprocal feelings being induced. The main task, following recognition, is to avoid any response which can be seen to reciprocate (collude with) the patient's damaging procedures, whether, for example, these are inviting the therapist to punish, be punished or to provide perfect care. In these cases it is often appropriate to describe what the patient evokes, for this may throw light on similar reactions provoked from others in daily life and at the same time can convey that what was communicated was tolerated. On the (inevitable) occasions when collusive responses are elicited, the therapist's frank acknowledgement and correction of this and locating the event in the diagram can be a learning experience and can also provide an example of shared and tolerated human frailty. Where the therapist's feelings seem to be reciprocations to indirectly expressed or unacknowledged roles and feelings, whether destructive or needy, it is important to explore these and to avoid any emphatic claims to know what the patient feels or what is 'in the patient's unconscious'.

Uses of Countertransference

In describing and discussing any form of countertransference the therapist provides an example of being able both to feel and to reflect upon feeling. In treating borderline patients such reflection may serve to extend and refine the patient's 'emotional vocabulary' and can also include examining the context and the scale of the response and the connecting up of the roles and affects of particular self states with other, currently dissociated, aspects. This contact with other ways of acting and feeling can make memory more accessible, experiences more manageable and actions more appropriate.

In the course of a session with a borderline patient it is probable that a range of countertransference reactions will be elicited as the patient goes through *response shifts*, *role reversals* and *self state shifts*. Where patients induce confusion by rapid switches between self states or roles it is helpful to both patient and therapist to halt this (for example, by the use of a metaphoric 'pause button') and to concentrate on the analysis of a segment of the exchange, either in the session or on audiotapes subsequently, using dialogic sequence analysis. The Self State Sequential Diagram provides a constant visible reminder of how the person contains, and must in due course accommodate, all his or her dissociated self states, while detailed dialogic sequence analysis makes sense of very confusing exchanges.

In order to be alert to the meaning of evoked countertransference reactions, it can be helpful, especially for trainees, to make a transparent overlay of the patient's SSSD on which the feelings experienced by the therapist in response to each of the different roles played by the patient can be mapped. Confusion evoked in the therapist is usually shared by the patient and it is neither true nor helpful to interpret it as a form of motivated defence designed to damage the therapy or undermine the therapist.

Sources of Transference Communications

Patients may elicit reactions by obvious behaviours but, especially in the case of difficult feelings and experiences, the communications are often indirect. How such subtle influences are transmitted, and the powerful impact they may have, can feel somewhat mysterious. Therapists need to be open to experiencing these communications as well as being skilled in mapping them. The process of mapping, in common with other cognitive tasks, can be carried out in ways which are a manifestation of the therapist's countertransference, for instance serving as an obstacle to, or defence against, emotion, but done sensitively it provides both patients and therapists with a safe framework which allows greater access to feeling. This indirect transmission of transference feelings must rest on non-verbal means, such as voice tone and rhythm, posture and expression. These forms of communication are also, of course, evident between babies and mothers long before words are used. Some light is thrown on this process as it occurs in therapy by the discrepancies reported by some therapists between their experience of being with patients in the session and of listening to the audiotapes subsequently; examples of this are given in the two cases illustrating countertransference issues with which this chapter ends.

Case Example: Paul

Paul was 43 when he was referred with a history of longstanding depression accompanied by repeated self-injury (cutting his arms) and by occasional episodes of violence towards others. He was stably employed and was married with three children but found little joy in any of these contexts.

Paul had no memories before the age of seven, at which time his mother had left home. His father had been a cruel man and he recalled being locked in the house with his younger brothers for long periods. He had learned to climb through the window to dig up the toys his father had buried in the garden (reburying them before his father returned) and he had also learned how to get into the locked larder for food.

Paul told his story in an inexpressive and unreflective way; more striking than the painful content was his therapist's response to it. During the early sessions she reported losing herself in a trance-like state and saying things she did not intend to say and had not reflected on, and while playing the sessional tapes she frequently fell asleep. This powerful blanking out effect was even transmitted to some degree to the supervision group. This clearly reflected an *identifying countertransference*, echoing the patient's dissociation from feeling; by recognizing it as such, the therapist was able to communicate her sense of the degree to which Paul had had to close himself off from unbearable feelings. Once this state had been clearly identified, his switches from this blankness into frightening rage accompanied by flashing lights and blurred vision, or into self-cutting, were traced.

A second strand of countertransference emerged as the therapist increasingly felt herself to be the champion of the deprived and abused child Paul had been. This was expressed by her helping him realize how, far from being useless and stupid as he had been made to feel, he had been brave and resourceful in coping for himself and his brothers. This is an example of an *extending, reciprocating countertransference* in which the therapist responded to a deep, unstated need in the patient for recognition. As therapy progressed the therapist's trance-like feelings dissipated and a strong and playful working alliance developed. The diagram (SSSD) evolved in the form of two main sections, recording negative and positive procedural sequences respectively, and by chance these took on the form of two figures. As therapy progressed Paul successively redrew this, shrinking the negative half until it became no more than a parrot, perched on the shoulder of the positive figure, whose repeated negative phrases became less and less powerful.

Paul found termination difficult and in the weeks following it had some return of symptoms, including one episode of self-cutting. At the post-therapy assessment at six months, however, he said he felt much more in charge of his life and referred to his parrot as being under control.

The powerful induction of blankness in the therapist and its occurring also when she listened to the audiotapes suggest that in this case the tone of voice and mode of telling the story must have been the main way in which the identifying countertransference was induced. The transmission of a similar blankness to the supervision group was probably induced by the therapist remaining cut off from her feelings in relation to Paul and by her conveying this both by reporting it and by *her* style and tone of speech.

Case Example: Lesley

Lesley was a 22-year-old graduate, currently a temporary office worker, referred on account of a longstanding depression and an associated eating disorder consisting of strict limitation of food intake alternating with bingeing, the latter sometimes associated with self-cutting. Her weight was maintained in the low normal range. She had had therapy in the past with little lasting benefit.

Her therapist came to the supervision seminar after her first meeting with Lesley reporting a strange experience. During this session, as Lesley told a bleak and despairing story, the therapist found herself emotionally cold and unresponsive in a way quite uncharacteristic for her. On playing through the audiotape, however, she had been close to tears, and this strong emotional response was shared by the other seminar members.

This would seem to represent the operation of a powerful *identifying countertransference* occurring in the room, echoing the patient's extreme distancing from her feelings, followed by the transformation of this on playing the audiotape to an *extending reciprocating countertransference* responding to the pained and needy feelings which the patient could not bear. The induction of the defensive distancing in the therapist must have been conveyed by non-verbal means in the room, blocking the felt response to the patient's words. This understanding was of central importance in the construction of the diagram and in the subsequent management of a difficult therapy.

The SSSD (Figure 6.1) describes four self states labelled *Crazy*, '*Smile and get on with it*', *Normal* and *Numb*. Lesley described her Crazy state as filled with a degree of terror and confusion which she would do anything to avoid. The safe alternative was to be in the Numb state, but being numb was also being petrified, in the sense of being turned to stone, and to escape this she would either enact the bulimic and self-cutting procedural loop or would shift to the compliant, dutiful, socially acceptable but need-denying 'Smile and get on with it' state. This could edge towards the Normal state in which spontaneous enjoyment of life and of food were possible, but this was never sustained and loss of control over eating and guilt would provoke a return to the Numb state.

An already difficult therapy was complicated when Lesley discovered she was pregnant (the result of impulsive, emotionally meaningless sex) and chose to have a termination, and by the fact that her therapist was (visibly) pregnant. The maintaining of a therapeutic relationship under these circumstances, when any feeling was perilously close to craziness for Lesley, involved a skilful use of

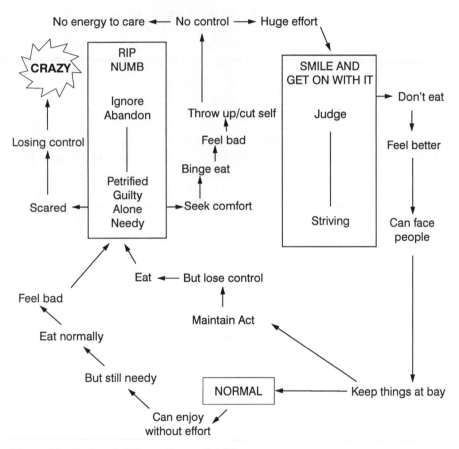

Figure 6.1   Lesley: Self States Sequential Diagram

the diagram and a very sensitive reading of countertransference feelings which now involved the *reciprocating countertransference* to unexpressed need, an *extending identifying countertransference* with what Lesley was sometimes able to feel, and an *identifying* awareness of the defensive blocking which still operated most of the time.

CHAPTER 7

Referral, Assessment, Contracts and Containment

The cases presented in Chapter 5 and the discussion of the treatment relationship in Chapter 6 will have conveyed the main features of the CAT treatment of patients with BPD; the aim of the next three chapters is to give more detailed attention to clinical issues arising at different stages.

The capacity of borderline patients to arouse anxiety and to disrupt arrangements is frequently evident during the process of referral and assessment, as the following case illustrates.

Case example: Ivy

Ivy, a 26-year-old mother of two, married to a Malaysian immigrant factory worker, was seen at the urgent request of the experienced CAT counsellor attached to the general practice with which Ivy was registered. She had formed a dependent and increasingly demanding relationship with the Health Visitor attached to the practice and was now disrupting the work of the practice by daily unscheduled visits, constant phone calls, damaging the waiting room furniture and threatening staff members. After consultation with the general practitioner the counsellor requested an urgent assessment for Ivy and forwarded copies of past records; these recorded drug use and promiscuity in adolescence and a history of heavy drinking for which she had been admitted for detoxification on a number of occasions. Assessment confirmed the diagnosis of borderline personality disorder. The current alcohol intake was uncertain but it was suspected that she was drinking vodka most days while her husband was at work and her children were at nursery school.

Ivy was taken on for therapy on the condition that she observed clear limits on her access to the Health Visitor and she was given predetermined times at which she might telephone the counsellor. She quickly formed an intense relationship with her experienced therapist and had disturbing and at times seemingly hallucinatory recollections of both physical and sexual abuse in childhood. After six sessions, during which she became increasingly regressed and decreasingly able to cooperate with the work of reformulation, she brought a knife to the clinic and then locked herself in the toilet with a rope, threatening to hang herself. At this point a compulsory psychiatric admission was arranged and the therapist made it clear that therapy could not continue or be resumed.

The psychiatrist under whose care Ivy was admitted was less than pleased with this outcome. It transpired that there had been a similar episode three years previously, involving threats of violence and the use of a knife to damage furniture in the outpatient department, following which he had ruled that the patient should not again be offered treatment or admission. However, no letter conveying this decision had been received by the general practitioner.

Reviewing this story, it is clear that, in responding to the urgency of the referral, many normal and necessary assessment practices had been omitted or curtailed. The case had not been discussed at the unit assessment meeting, the level of drinking had not been clearly established and the potential for violence, despite the fact that she had already done damage at the practice, had not been carefully considered. The lack of the crucial letter from the psychiatrist was unfortunate, but in such a case it would be normal practice to contact the appropriate psychiatric resource in case admission should become necessary. In this instance the psychiatrist was angry that a staff member had been exposed to risk and angry that a bed was occupied by what he deemed to be an unsuitable patient. The CAT team, on the other hand, while acknowledging the deficiencies in the assessment, felt that the staff at the general practice were *already* at risk. As Health Service underfunding had resulted in the virtual absence of day hospital or inpatient services prepared to take responsibility for out-of-control personality-disordered patients, we had felt obliged to accept the referral. Ivy had successfully provoked rejection from one resource and an unrealistic offer of care from another.

Ivy spent a month as an inpatient and was then discharged to the care of the general practice team. Two years later she remains contained, with no further acts of violence or self-injury, an outcome attributed by the team in part to the shared understandings of her different states derived from her reformulation.

With this cautionary tale in mind, some of the issues around diagnosis, assessment and contracting therapy with borderline patients will now be considered.

The Purposes of Diagnostic Interviewing

The pre-therapy diagnostic interview involves confirming the diagnosis, including that of associated Axis I conditions, and estimating the severity of the disturbance and the patient's capacity to use treatment. It also aims to give the patient a sense of what therapy is about. The final test of a patient's ability to benefit from therapy is the use made of the assessment interview and of the early sessions, and requirements for prior 'psychological mindedness' or high motivation are, in my view, inappropriate. Most borderline patients have had negative experiences of professional help and of relationships in general and will need to be persuaded by experience that anything of value is being offered. 'Psychological mindedness' will be underdeveloped or disrupted by the nature of the borderline state, despite which self-reflective capacities may be mobilized remarkably quickly by the reformulation process. In view of this, the *creation* of psychological mindedness and motivation is one of the main tasks of the early sessions and should be initiated at the assessment meeting by the offer of a pre-liminary reformulation which links past and present and provisionally describes some of the main procedures. If this is done in an open and collaborative way, the anxiety aroused by the situation is less likely to provoke shifts into negative states and, if such shifts occur, they can at once be considered jointly as mani-festations of the patient's problems. It is easy, but not helpful or necessary, to confirm the diagnosis by provoking hostile or paranoid responses through adopting a confronting or withholding interviewing style.

The patient's motivation depends essentially on the therapist being experi-enced as genuinely attending and as offering back something useful, under-standable and hitherto unknown. By focusing on problem procedures, including in particular those which may impede therapy, the assessment and reformula-tion process develops psychological mindedness and establishes the meaning and value of therapy. Only a small minority of patients seen in specialist psy-chotherapy settings need preliminary education about the nature of therapy, perhaps because only patients with some understanding will actually attend for assessment. The problem is different in other contexts, notably general practice, where, before formal treatment or referral is proposed, there is a need to avoid confirming false explanations of the patient's distress and a chance of extend-ing patients' psychological awareness.

Medication and Axis I Disorders

Another function of the assessment procedure is to establish the need for med-ication and to ensure that any prescribed drugs are appropriate and are super-vised properly by somebody other than the therapist. Medication may have a part to play in the control of some borderline patients' biological predisposition to affect dyscontrol and impulsivity (Soloff, 1993; Stein, 1992), but this should be initiated before therapy is offered; the simultaneous psychological and pharmacological treatment of borderline symptoms is likely to be problematic (Brockman, 1990). There are, however, no contraindications to combining ther-apy with the medical treatment of associated *depression*. Where it is effective (which is by no means always the case) antidepressant medication may decrease borderline symptoms other than depression. The interaction of BPD, depression and medication can, however, be confusing, as the following case illustrates.

Case Example: Georgina

Georgina, the mother of three adolescent children, was already being prescribed an antidepressant when she was referred for CAT. She gave a long history of depression and anxiety, some of it centred on a long past serious illness of her son, much of it on her current loneliness, the family's relative poverty, and her (unexpressed) resentment derived from a deep, lifelong sense of deprivation. Her main state was one of imposing *self-sacrificing, controlling care* on *dependent and submissive* others, and her main alternative self state was one of 'depression', more properly described as emotional blankness (*out of touch with self and others*).

Georgina was a puzzling patient, largely because of her difficulty in accepting the help-receiving (to her, powerless) role and because of her frequent blankness, but a fair amount of progress was made in the second half of therapy when, in relation to her husband and children, she was able to revise her main procedure and allow them more independence and herself a little respite. These changes were still evident at her three-month follow-up with her therapist, but at the clinic review at six months her symptom scores on all the inventories were at the initial level and she reported herself as little changed compared to before therapy.

During the therapy the possibility that her inaccessibility might be due to persisting depression had been raised in supervision, and the therapist had enquired closely about Georgina's adherence to the medication. It emerged that she used to omit the tablets when things were going well but would, on other occasions, take them in many times the prescribed dosage, in order to induce her emotionally blanked-off state; often at those times she also ate compulsively. After this had been revealed she had been asked to discuss the matter with her prescribing doctor, but unfortunately no direct contact had been made. It seemed possible, therefore, that the recurrence of her depression at follow-up might be the result of non-adherence to the medication. She was returned to the care of the mental health centre from which she had been referred with a letter describing how her drug use was linked with her procedures, and over the next year, with the support of her psychiatric nurse, she regained many of the changes achieved in therapy.

Anxiety, Substance Abuse, Eating Disorders

The drug treatment of *anxiety* in borderline patients is seldom helpful and minor tranquillizers are liable to be abused. Heavy use of these is, like alcohol, a contraindication to therapy, a prior withdrawal programme being necessary. More modest use should be monitored with the aim of reducing intake and identifying where, on the patient's diagram, the wish to use the drug occurs. Major tranquillizers may be helpful in patients experiencing frightening state shifts with accompanying dissociative or paranoid symptoms, but here too use should be monitored and linked to the diagram.

Active *substance abuse* is associated with a poor outcome and regular heroin or alcohol use makes therapy impossible. But a policy of automatically excluding from treatment any patient still showing intermittent abuse, or of relying on cannabis or prescribed drugs to maintain abstinence from major drugs, seems unduly harsh in that it requires, in effect, that the patient must get well before treatment is offered. A number of patients, on giving up or greatly reducing their dependence on drugs or alcohol, are faced with the memories and emotions which led to their substance abuse in the first place, and need help in understanding and containing these raw feelings (see e.g. Tom in Chapter 5). More generally, any patient whose use is evidently associated with personality and relationship factors may only achieve stable cure if the personality factors are dealt with. Such patients must be required to record their intake, plan to reduce drug use and must come substance-free to their sessions; treatment outcome will still often be disappointing. Detoxification, behavioural and CAT treatments will often need to be combined sequentially. In Chapter 10, Tim Leighton discusses the place of CAT in the treatment of substance-abusing borderline patients.

Many borderline patients will have associated *eating disorders*. Where these are severe, prior cognitive behavioural treatment or possibly admission to hospital may be indicated, but in most cases, especially of bulimia nervosa, the symptom can be linked to the borderline phenomena and located on the patient's diagram (see e.g. the case of Lesley in Chapter 6) and can be expected to fade as the general problems resolve; if it does not, subsequent cognitive-behavioural treatment can build on the CAT. In practice it is seldom possible to treat eating disorders without addressing the personality factors which underlie the symptoms and which so often undermine treatment; the best way to combine approaches will become clearer as CAT is incorporated in specialist treatment programmes. CAT has been shown to be as effective as, and quicker than, other treatment approaches in a controlled trial with severely anorectic outpatients, many of whom had borderline features (Treasure and Ward, 1997).

Risk Assessment: Suicide

Many borderline patients have a history of parasuicidal or failed suicidal episodes and many continue with forms of deliberate self-harm; in the series reported by Stone (1993) 8% ultimately killed themselves. The evaluation of the risk of serious suicidal behaviour is not easy and therapists must expect to carry anxiety in this respect. Soloff *et al.* (1994) found the risk to be higher in older patients with a history of previous attempts and of impulsive acts, but judgement concerning individual cases must depend primarily on the detailed understanding of the antecedents of active suicidal thinking or acts. In CAT these will be portrayed as soon as possible by locating suicidal impulses on the self state diagram. Connors (1996a) provides a valuable review of the various possible meanings of self-injury.

It is important to discuss this issue at the start of therapy, with no pretence of therapeutic neutrality; the aim is to establish the view that therapy is about finding reasons for living and that, while the patient's intense wish to die is acknowledged, it is seen to be generated from beliefs and experiences and transient states which therapy can modify. Ways of countering suicidal thinking need to be explored and rehearsed at this stage, including listing the availability of friends, if any, and of resources such as the Samaritans' telephone service. It is not usually practicable for therapists to offer telephone access to patients and in any case the offer can generate unreasonable expectations, and later disappointment; in some cases it may be appropriate to offer scheduled telephone contact between sessions. The availability of duty psychiatrists and the possibility of admission should be explained. Ultimately both patient and therapist must acknowledge that patients who are determined to die will do so, and therapists, while doing all they can to generate hope and institute change, cannot be controlled by suicidal threats. If therapists become seriously concerned about a possibly increasing suicidal risk during therapy, an independent psychiatric assessment should be sought.

Risk Assessment: Violence

Uncontrolled anger is a common feature of BPD and many patients will have been physically violent at some stage of their lives. Such patients should only be seen in hospital settings and only by willing therapists and after full discussion with colleagues. The small number of therapists who have been killed by patients should not be forgotten. Patients with persistent paranoid beliefs are probably unsuitable for therapy in outpatient settings; interesting developments in the understanding and cognitive therapy of such patients are discussed by Trower and Chadwick (1995), and to me this seems an area where management might be helpfully informed by the CAT model.

The possibility of violence is greater where there have been previous unprovoked, impulsive physical assaults on others. Such episodes may represent a state shift, involving the mobilization of usually dissociated impulses rooted in the experience of childhood abuse, and they may be provoked by therapy. For this reason, the rate at which patients are encouraged to recall and discuss early trauma should not be accelerated and should, as far as possible, be left to the patient to determine. Such memories are less likely to be unmanageable, and more likely to become available, once a good therapeutic alliance has been established. Clearly all patients with a history of violence must know that any episodes in the clinic will lead to the end of therapy, but such contractual arrangements are of uncertain use in controlling impulsive behaviour. The only real safety comes from the early establishment of a therapeutic alliance in which the therapist's attention and acknowledgement of the patient's experience have established a degree of trust. The best basis for this is the early joint reformulation of the patient's personality problems in which procedures or events liable to lead to violence are identified and alternatives are rehearsed.

Case Example: Nick

Nick (described in Ryle, 1995a) was a powerfully built man with a history of physical violence (including a dangerously violent fight with a man and beating up his ex-girlfriend) who had continuing problems with anger control. His (female) therapist began to develop a diagram in the first session, describing how anger followed disappointment after striving. The patient made good use of this, and the therapist linked it with a simple behavioural procedure: she proposed that the patient (a keen watcher of football) should carry in his pocket a referee's yellow card to serve as a warning if anger were mounting and a red card indicating that he must 'leave the field' if the anger persisted. There were no further episodes of loss of control of anger either during therapy or in the subsequent three years.

Some abused patients are in the habit of carrying weapons. No male patient with a violent history should be allowed to carry offensive weapons in the clinic. In the case of female patients weapons are more likely to be symbolic of their intention not to allow further abuse than they are indications of violent intent, but therapists are liable to find their concentration impaired and with women too it is an appropriate policy to refuse to allow weapons in the clinic. There may be exceptions, however, and I have, on one occasion, allowed a female patient to bring a knife to her sessions, after an early prohibition had been followed by her producing, at the next session, five or six scalpels from various folds of her clothing. We negotiated an agreement which required her to leave the knife in sight and out of reach. Once an early history of physical and sexual abuse had been remembered in detail and discussed she no longer brought the knife.

Potentially violent patients should not be seen in private practice or in remote areas of the clinic; colleagues and all clinic staff should be aware of the situation.

Treatment Contracts

All patients seen in the CAT clinic at Guy's Hospital receive a letter explaining the nature and length of the proposed therapy and describing what is offered and what is expected. Patients are also requested to sign consent to audiotaping of their sessions and to the use of material from their therapies, suitably disguised, in research and publications, but it is made clear that treatment will still be offered if this consent is withheld. This consent is again obtained at the first session. Patients are invited to record the sessions for themselves if they wish to do so.

A formal, mutual contract offering explicit descriptions which may be expanded verbally represents a civilized arrangement, but probably contributes little to the control of patients' impulsive, or compulsive, undermining or destruction of the therapeutic process. None the less, by having an explicit set of expectations, one can consider departures from the contract as examples of problem procedures and can understand and use them therapeutically. The only real sanction open to therapists is to discontinue therapy and this is very rarely needed.

Yeomans *et al.* (1993) report on the impact of a specific form of contracting in the psychoanalytic (Kernbergian) treatment of borderline patients. This contract is arrived at after several sessions and seeks to identify the specific issues likely to emerge in the therapy; its aim is 'to protect the work of therapy and contain the intense affects and inner dynamics of the patient as they get played out in the observable and relatively safe space of the therapy. The contract can also help the therapist monitor his/her countertransference ...'. This form of contracting also serves to clarify the limits of what the therapist is prepared to offer or tolerate and also makes clear to the patient his or her responsibility for the treatment. In this preliminary report the authors record that the patients of therapists who presented and negotiated the contract effectively were less likely to drop out. This was an important observation given that previously 9 out of 14 patients had dropped out in the first year.

The procedure which these authors describe involves the early consideration of possible transference–countertransference events and the provision of a detailed account of the issues likely to arise in therapy, such as missed sessions, arriving drunk or failing to pay. In some respects this form of contracting resembles aspects of the reformulation letter and procedural descriptions written by CAT therapists. The latter, however, will describe particular potential problems as examples of the higher level procedures which constitute the patient's problems and which therapy aims to modify. In CAT, therefore, the role of formal contracting is limited; the emphasis being on the creation, maintenance and use of the reformulation to create a therapeutic working alliance and to protect it from disruption by the patient's procedures. Thus the important 'contract' is reformulation, a jointly created understanding through which the patient's destructiveness is contained and trust is established. Only in the case of very disruptive patients may this need to be combined with a more disciplinary approach, as in the case described below.

Containment

This chapter started with a cautionary tale; to end it, here is an account of how CAT methods were used successfully to provide a framework for the containment of a disruptive patient. I am grateful to the supervisor (Jane Blunden, Senior Registrar in Psychotherapy) and the CAT trainee therapist concerned (Sally Gray, Clinical Nurse Specialist in CAT), of the Psychological Therapies Service, Royal South Hants Hospital, for providing this account and to the patient for agreeing to its appearance.

Case Example: Jim

Jim was a 34-year-old patient who was unemployed. His childhood had been lacking in affection and riven with physical and emotional abuse from his father. His mother had been emotionally cold and neglecting. Jim described himself as being 'addicted to failure and the pain that it brings'; he had made 35 abortive attempts at educational courses. His wish for therapy came from this and from his inability to sustain intimate relationships. During his teens he had been prone to frequent angry outbursts and had been in court charged with grievous bodily harm. He began to use drugs and alcohol to manage his distress and during his early twenties he was a heroin addict whilst continuing to be violent, seeking fights. At the time of referral it was clear that his problems with drugs and alcohol, although better, were still not fully resolved. He went on drinking binges when he could afford it. He had undergone previous courses of counselling, but with only limited success.

The original referral from his general practitioner was unremarkable, citing only 'depressive neurosis' and an 'impoverished childhood', but the subsequent course of his assessment through our Psychological Therapies Service proved to be a stormy one. The usual procedure would have been for Jim to have a single assessment appointment approximately 20 weeks after referral and then to be placed on a waiting list for the appropriate therapy. Soon after referral, however, there was a letter from the college he was attending expressing concern and requesting urgency. Before this could be answered Jim made the first of two unannounced visits to our consultant psychotherapists in which he angrily demanded immediate assessment. This resulted in him being referred to a psychologist within the department for Anger Management. He continued to demand psychotherapy however, with the result that he was referred back and forth between several professionals who in due course became involved in angry exchanges amongst themselves. He was eventually assessed and placed on the waiting list for CAT, largely since he was considered unsuitable for psychoanalytic work because of his uncontained and unbounded anger, yet was considered too disturbed for a simple cognitive-behavioural approach such as anger management. The protracted referral process raised anxieties within many members of our department, including the secretaries who had felt intimidated by his telephone calls and his visits. It also slowed his progress through the department—he was eventually seen for his first therapy session 16 months after the original referral letter!

Jim posed a challenge both to the therapist and to the supervisor as this was the first case of potential violence that either had treated. The therapy is therefore described in the form of two separate accounts in order to convey the thoughts and feelings of both those involved.

Supervisor's Account

I first heard about Jim at our weekly supervision group when Sally, to whom he had been allocated, reported the first session. She had felt that she was being interviewed for a job as a therapist. Jim came in overly confident and self-assured. He put her in the position of defending herself (for example, by asking what her qualifications were) and of defending CAT. Sally's thought had been 'Whoa, he's frightened'. He brought in a diagram to the session and had obviously been reading up on CAT. He dismissed Sally's comment that he seemed to be trying very hard to control the session. During the interview he flitted from one subject to another without finishing anything. Sally pointed out that the pattern he described, for example in terms of his academic record, was being acted out within the session. He denied this and continued to control the session, arguing with every boundary that Sally tried to set.

In the supervision I gave Sally lots of positive feedback, thinking that she had handled a difficult situation well. The supervision group agreed. There was discussion in the group about the possible meaning of his behaviour. Our conclusion was that the overwhelming nature of his 'attack' was similar to his pre-therapy presentation and might be understood as an aspect of his personality. However, we also felt that anyone who had experienced what he had, since referral, had a right to be angry and it would be understandable if they were anxious about the quality of therapy they were about to receive! We therefore reserved judgement.

The next week there was no supervision group and the week after that only Sally and I were in the group. She presented sessions 2 and 3, which included his history as summarized above. Sally's experience of him was that he had lots of self-blame and self-hate. At times he seemed to be like a little 8-year-old boy, at other times he was angry and intimidating. He produced writing and drawings between sessions which he brought in for the therapist; these were sometimes disjointed, occasionally very angry, once or twice sadistically horrific; some were sexually explicit. Sally wondered whether he got a sexual thrill from this and she felt quite abused by it. At times the anger and intimidation would be directed at Sally. He told her that he did not want to be vulnerable in front of her, and called her cold, hard, clinical, and abusive. On more than one occasion he got up from his chair and walked around the room, sometimes coming around behind her chair and leaning over to point to one of his drawings. On each occasion, she firmly asked him to sit down again and he complied. Jim wore large steel-capped boots and would sit with one leg crossed over the other, jiggling his boot within Sally's direct visual gaze.

On hearing all this, I thought 'Oh, my God!' I was alarmed at his threatening and intimidating manner and his past history of violence raised my anxiety enormously. I did my best to remain outwardly calm, while feeling anything but, and asked Sally which number CAT training case this was for her. 'Five', she said. I asked how she felt about taking it on; she replied that he was certainly going to be a difficult challenge, but that she could work with him. I accepted that, and made reassuring noises.

Then I asked her to talk in more detail about how it actually felt for her to be in the room with this man; my personal countertransference was primarily that of feeling worried about her physical safety. She talked at some length. I asked her outright if she was frightened of him physically. She said that she didn't *think* he would actually hit her but the *feeling* was that he had the potential to do so. I said that I thought it was very difficult to do psychotherapy under that kind of anxiety. I invited her to explore ways in which *she* might feel more comfortable in the sessions. She talked about obvious ones which she was already using, like always sitting nearest the door and making sure that she only saw him when she knew other people were in nearby offices. I was very relieved that she considered these obvious and my own anxiety began to reduce a little. I realized that I was willing to trust Sally's ability as a therapist, which I already knew was considerable.

I then started to think about ways in which I and the wider department might help. I thought that the need for safety and containment was paramount and remembered his route through our referral process. One interpretation of this was that he had somehow managed to create splits within the staff of our department and created quite violent arguments—something which I knew to be very unusual. There was therefore a possibility that splits might occur within the therapeutic relationship, within the supervision group and, once again, within the wider department. The need was clearly for containment, to prevent these splits happening. It then occurred to me that this man had very little experience as a child of feeling secure by being able to predict reliably what other people would do. The idea of agreeing a contract with him came to mind and I mentioned this to Sally, with some of my reasoning. She thought this was a good idea and took it forward with enthusiasm. We discussed the measures to go into the contract, and Sally then took it away to work on before the next session.

Before finishing supervision, I made two other decisions. One was that I decided that the reformulation should consist primarily of identifying Jim's repertoire

of reciprocal role procedures. The other was that we decided to share an understanding of possible problems with management and with the rest of the department. This was done both verbally and in official letter form. Our colleagues were
subsequently very supportive and this proved to be containing not only for the
therapist and me, but also for the secretaries who dealt with Jim face to face.

Therapist's Account

My anxieties had increased between the two supervision sessions described
above. During the first session, I felt that I had been interviewed but had also felt
that I had made good interventions, for example by suggesting he was frightened. I hoped that he would just settle down. However, the next two sessions
were the worrying ones for me. When he got out of his chair and walked about,
I felt extremely intimidated. There were also numerous verbal assaults, and, to
make matters worse, I did not like him! I began to wonder whether I could work
with him—an unusual experience for me. I felt overwhelmed; it was difficult to
empathize with the vulnerable part of him in the midst of such attacks.

I was looking forward to the second supervision session because I needed
help. It is difficult for me to remember exactly what I thought or felt during that
supervision session because I was so caught up in my own countertransference
feelings. I felt not only guilty about my feelings of dislike, but also worried
about my ability to contain the therapy and work properly. I was totally unaware
of my supervisor's anxieties at that time and it was a shock to discover two years
later what they had been! I knew at the time that I wanted clear direction about
how to handle the therapy, in particular the threat of violence, and also that I
needed to somehow establish clear boundaries with Jim. It seemed that I was
already employing everything that I knew, but it was not enough.

I felt great relief when the idea of a contract was proposed, and it was suggested that reformulation could focus on reciprocal role procedures. I did not
think of outside matters, but only the situation between Jim and me. I had had
a fantasy beforehand that I could easily get into an argument with him and he
would end up hitting me.

Over the next week I wrote the reformulation letter, linking up his early life
with his current problems and procedures, and describing the reciprocal role
patterns we had identified—now an easier task because we had worked out the
reciprocal role procedures within the supervision session. The main reciprocal
role procedures we identified were as follows.

1. Sadistic, unpredictable and demanding to terrorizing, withdrawing,
   masochistic and hypervigilant.
2. Demanding, critical, humiliating and cold to crushed, angry, withdrawn and
   betrayed.

3. Ideal care to ideally cared for.

I remembered a behavioural contract that had been used at a day hospital I used to work in and based the contract for Jim on this. The contract was added to the end of the reformulation letter and read as follows:

> The aim of therapy will be about enabling a safe and trusting, mutually respecting therapeutic relationship where you understand the 'expectations and rules'. For this reason I have listed four rules which form the basis of our contract for therapy:
>
> 1. No taking of drugs other than medication you are prescribed by your GP.
> 2. No drinking alcohol to excess, as this will interfere with your weekly therapy. Should you come to the Department intoxicated with either alcohol or drugs, you would not be seen, and would be asked to leave. If this was at a time when you were due to have a session I would not see you and you would lose the session.
> 3. No violence or threatening behaviour towards any member of staff in the Department. Evidence of this would result in the termination of your therapy.
> 4. Therapy Time
>   (a) Should you feel the need for support outside of the therapy sessions, it would be important that you contact your GP.
>   (b) No other therapies should run concurrent with the CAT.
>   (c) I would recommend a therapy-free period post-CAT, as in the past you have engaged in therapy in the search for idealized care.

I was really worried about presenting this contract to him; I thought that he would get angry. In the event I was surprised because he was relieved by it. Furthermore, he was moved by the reformulation letter and now seemed ready to work with me. I presented the contract as a necessity—providing security and predictability for both of us. He said that he was really pleased, because now he knew exactly where he stood. I then reflected on my feelings of intimidation in earlier sessions and he admitted that he had done this on purpose. The sadistic pleasure he got from this fitted in perfectly with one of his reciprocal role procedures, and naming this in relation to the reformulation produced an even greater sense of relief for him.

Concluding Comment

The rest of the therapy was much less anxious for both the therapist and the supervisor. Any elements of violence could be discussed and these gradually diminished. His writing and drawing became more reflective, involving whole people instead of fragmented images. Jim was able to apologize to someone he had previously threatened. Sally came to admire his courage and motivation enormously as he faced the painful issues during the therapy. Her dislike of him diminished rapidly after reformulation and by the end of the therapy she felt that he had been a pleasure to work with. A later major issue in the therapy was Jim's idealization of Sally, understandable as this was his first experience of emotional containment. The details of this aspect of the work are not relevant here, but this issue was dealt with appropriately.

He was given an extended follow-up over one year. He was angrily depressed for the first six months, but recognized this as grieving and gradually began to recover. He even passed a GCSE.

Since working on this case, we have been involved in two other CAT cases involving men presenting with extreme levels of potential violence. We have used a similar formula involving a formal contract with the therapist concentrating on the identification of the dominant reciprocal role patterns of the patient's self states and on state switches between them. The descriptions of more 'neurotic' procedures seem at best to be largely irrelevant and at worst to divert from the main work which is a process of continually monitoring and feeding back transference and countertransference issues by reference to the self states. The content and timing of interventions concerning countertransference need careful thought and sensitive presentation. The degree of intense concentration which the therapist requires for this can only, in our opinion, be achieved if a sufficient degree of containment has been established. It is difficult to imagine this being possible in the isolation of private practice and work with this client group should probably only be contemplated within a larger organization such as the NHS. The anxiety is diluted at each step up the organization such that it loses destructive power: the patient feels safe with the therapist because the therapist feels safe with the supervisor, who feels safe with other clinical colleagues. Another major element is that of honesty; using this formula neither the patient nor the therapist need be inhibited about expressing their fears. These thoughts are elaborated further in Blunden and Gray (in preparation).

CHAPTER 8

The Early Sessions

Reformulation is the main task of the early sessions in CAT. It is a process through which the therapist seeks to gain a real sense of what it is like to be the patient and a clear understanding of the ways in which the patient's distress and unwanted behaviours are maintained. It is also an activity involving the patient in working and thinking and initiates the heightening of self-awareness. Much of the therapist's understanding is derived from the patient's biographical account and from devices such as the Psychotherapy File and the construction of life charts or family trees. But in all cases, and most markedly in BPD, this unfamiliar activity and the requirement to be self-exposing serve to mobilize some of the patient's problem procedures. The therapist offers or constructs a stage on which the patient's utterances and acts evoke unfamiliar responses, and on which such responses are themselves subjected to unfamiliar reflection. This process is made particularly explicit in CAT, where the use of writing and diagrams serves to generate and sustain a process of reflection which continues between the sessions. In more dissociated and impulsive borderline patients, the therapist's offering of provisional written or diagrammatic understandings of the patient's states and state shifts needs to begin at the first meeting if inadvertent collusion or the provocation of negative procedures is to be avoided or at least quickly recognized and corrected.

The Impact of Assessment

The assessment or first session can have a profound impact; for example Malan *et al.* (1975) found that many patients who did not return for therapy after their (dynamic) assessment interviews showed major changes when followed-up. While psychoanalytic writers warn against premature *interpretations*, there is no evidence to suggest that early *reformulation* has a harmful effect; the provision of descriptions which begin to make sense of experience and imply the possibility of change, and the involvement of the patient in the creation of these descriptions, is usually relieving. It has not been established how much effect

97

offering borderline patients provisional reformulation at the time of assessment might have but, given the long delays between assessment and therapy which are currently inevitable, it is a question which we intend to research. The following is an example of an early reformulation aimed to contain active problems during an anticipated six-month wait for therapy.

Case Example: Karen

Karen, a 29-year-old journalist, was referred for depression following a termination of pregnancy seven months previously. The relationship with the father continued but she felt uncertainly committed, describing him as supportive, kind but unexciting and herself as bored and liable to provoke frequent rows, some accompanied by her physical violence.

Karen was the eldest of four children. She described her mother as totally unmaternal and she remembered many instances of neglect and unkindness when she was a child; at one stage social services had been involved. From the age of 10 she became fiercely independent ('if I wanted to know something I would go to the library') and took on a protective role with her siblings. She was rebellious but academically successful at school. She described her father as warm and loving but unavailable.

At college she saw a counsellor for a year; he was going through a divorce and they remained in contact after her treatment; after a short time she went to live with him and his two children, staying for the next three years. Thereafter, she had a number of relationships, often with older work colleagues; these were described as exciting, in contrast to her current relationship, but they were all time-limited and she avoided the 'claustrophobia' of living with any of her partners.

Karen gave her early history in a matter-of-fact way but was tearful when discussing her recent termination. She described an intense urge to get pregnant again; she was worried that she might arrange for this to happen, despite knowing that it would be an irrational act. In view of this, and of the anticipated six month wait for therapy, a second assessment interview was suggested.

At this, the therapist read out a draft reformulation letter in which the early deprivation and premature autonomy were highlighted and the way in which her relationship with the counsellor had again deprived her of the experience of being cared for was pointed out. A preliminary diagram was then sketched out, based on three childhood-derived self states, as follows:

1. A state derived from her relationship with her mother, described as *either crushed or excitedly rebellious in relation to involved and intrusive but neglectful*. Karen saw how she had played the former role as a child and how the reverse pattern was evident in her adult relationships with men.

2. The second self state, derived from her relationship with her father, was described as *loving but unavailable* in relation to *idealizing but unprotected*. This pattern had possible relevance to her relationship with her current boyfriend, but rather than feeling unprotected she felt *unexcited*. In considering this she was struck by the realization that her mother would never have permitted her an intense (exciting) connection with her father. For Karen, lovingness had become equated with mildness.

3. The third pattern of *protective to protected* was derived from her adoption of the strong caring role with her younger siblings and was reflected in a reluctance to seek care herself. The relationship with the counsellor could be understood psychoanalytically as an 'Oedipal victory' but equally may have represented her taking on of the protective role to him and his children. The current intensity of her wish for a baby might also reflect, in part, this procedural pattern.

It seemed likely that the understandings arrived at in this second assessment meeting might reduce the chances of Karen's acting impulsively in respect of her relationship and her urge to become pregnant, and might also generate constructive self-reflection during her long wait for therapy.

Just before starting her therapy, eight months later, Karen was sent the above account with a request for permission to publish and any comments. She had not got pregnant and had not resolved the relationship with her boyfriend and she was buoyed up by new developments in her professional career. She recalled that the diagram had been helpful at the time but was now lost and that the main impact had been receiving her transformed life history in the reformulation letter.

Difficulties in the Reformulation Process

The reformulation process is often relatively unproblematic and the recruitment of patients to the task of identifying and describing their different states can be a source of early understanding and control. But this is not always the case; the problems arising with more impulsive and disintegrated patients are well portrayed in the following case examples.

Case Example: Elaine

This account is written by Elaine's experienced therapist (Hilary Beard): 'I am sitting waiting anxiously for Elaine; it is our first session and she is 20 minutes late. The phone rings; she is lost in the wrong part of the hospital. Ten minutes later a tornado arrives; she hates London, she's been sent to me because nobody in the part of the hospital she knows wants her, she's depressed but "what the hell can *you* do about it". Then she bursts into tears: "this is one part of me, it's because I'm late". Then she rages again, paces about the room, lights a cigarette and ends up talking with her back turned, looking out of the window, for the next 20 minutes. During this she displays or describes in turn emotional blankness, persecutory anxiety, rage, control and concern that her smoking might harm me. She admits with contempt her reliance on "happiness pills" which her GP (who has "given up on her") prescribes, and speaks of how she cuts herself with scissors to "help her to cry" and of how she would like to murder her partner. Finally, she sits down and looks at me and says "that's some of the worst".'

'Elaine cancelled the second appointment due to illness but thereafter was always on time. At our second meeting she described having hit her partner with a rolling pin because he had been emotionally upset; she felt she wanted to die and then cut herself: "I was punishing my body ... well, myself, it's just hard luck my body gets it". This partner was the first man she had been with for some years; she could not bear seeing him out of control when she was so near losing control herself. I suggested that it would be helpful to know about this loss of control and the changes of state she experienced, and she settled down to the task of describing these with great directness in a way which I came later to recognize as one of her strengths. The first "mood" she described was called "*horrified*"; it was accompanied by images of animals being slaughtered: "I can't watch but I know its there ... I've seen awful things ... I want to stab myself and die the way they die." Later, we called this "*the slaughterhouse*". A second "mood" was called "*humiliated*" and followed arguments: "it seems the only thing I can do to prove I'm not going to back down is to try and commit suicide or cut myself ..." Associated with this was the *depressed* mood of hopelessness, gloom and despair. It led to self-cutting; "nothing on earth can stop me apart from someone hitting me; if only someone could flog all the badness and hatred out of me". Sometimes her partner was seen as an intimidating bully, making her feel *intimidated and paranoid* (a state with clear origins in her early life), but it was evident that she too could be this *bully* to herself and to others. She went on to summarize herself in terms of opposites: either as "*a thing that curls up in the corner*" or as "*arrogant and awful*". And finally, she was able to find one description of feeling good; one way of finding this was through her long-term interest in visiting the uncared-for and abandoned Lidos of London's parks. This state was symbolized by, and called after, a small *glass globe* which she would hold and look at: "it makes my mind feel good".'

This second session had served to introduce seven or eight states and had begun the task of establishing an understanding of how the extensive range of mostly painful experiences might be studied and controlled. From it, and from further explorations over several sessions, a Self States Sequential Diagram was elaborated which served as a guide through the therapy. This identified a number of negative states in which subjectively she identified with the victimized roles which were the reciprocations of humiliation, torture, oppressive control, abandonment and condemnation. These destructive and punishing roles were enacted in her self-cutting and in head-banging. Her escapes from this involved a no-feeling state and a fragile positive 'secret garden' for which the glass globe was a token.

Reformulation is the beginning of change only. Elaine continued to alternate thoughtful and courageous self-exploration with symptoms, self-cutting and desperate lurchings between her states. Without the containment and orientation provided by the joint reformulatory work of the first sessions it is doubtful if she could have used therapy at all.

The process of her growing internalization of the reformulation, was summarized by her therapist as follows (the therapist's account is recorded in normal type, the patient's state and achievements in italics).

*Naming each state. *Differentiating between the different states.* *Describing feeling, images, words associated with all states, including those largely dissociated. *Beginning to recognize states.* *Linking states and relating them to key figures and to symptoms. *All seen to be connected, not just chaos.* *Linking history to states. *Some sense of continuity.* *Paths between states identified. *More flexible, less disconnected.* *Differentiation of self from different states. *Sense of an 'I' beyond the states.* *Clarity about what belongs to self, what to other. *Sense of self as having control, possibility of getting what only others seemed to have.* *Often can predict, control, avoid, alter, contain and soothe. *Growing sense of power. State switches less frequent and intense.* * Hope and intense fear of loss. *Separation anxiety.*

(In the event, her intense distress at termination was responded to by the offer of a second 24-session CAT, following which she was seen by her therapist at slowly increasing intervals. During this time she consolidated her gains and became able to envisage and develop new ways of being and to manage and contain herself.)

Case Example: Claudia

Claudia was the daughter of an Italian woman who, at the age of 18, while working as an au pair in London, became pregnant by the father of the family. He eventually divorced his wife and married Claudia's mother. During the 13 years that the marriage lasted Claudia's father sexually abused her and subjected both her and her mother to a range of sexual, physical and psychological assaults.

Claudia had had previous therapies and at her first two sessions presented this story in a way that seemed rehearsed and left her therapist strangely untouched (a similar experience to that of Lesley's therapist described in

Chapter 6, representing an identifying countertransference to the patient's defensive distancing). This sense of distance was overcome when Claudia brought, at the therapist's request, a very moving written account of her early years; as is often the case she was able to be far more expressive in writing than in direct speech. The ensuing sessions were often overwhelming, not only because of their painful content but also because of the rapidity with which Claudia spoke and her constant shifting between states. This instability later became identified as a lifelong response to anxiety, occurring when her normally precarious ability to stay in one of her more adaptive states was lost.

Claudia described very clearly how, as a child on her way to school, she would deliberately distance herself from the abused child at home and become a different, largely competent, person but this facility for dissociation had left many experiences unassimilated. This led to another difficulty for the therapist; it was often very difficult to know, when she was describing experiences or when she was enacting one of her range of states, what period of her life was being referred to or re-experienced. In such cases the use of grid techniques can be clarifying. Claudia completed two dyad grids (see Appendix 2) in each of which her relationships to her parents, herself and a number of other people were rated, in one grid as she had experienced them as an adolescent and in the other as an adult. The results of this, expressed as a two-component map in which only key relationships are included (namely self-to-father, father-to-self, self-to-mother, mother-to-self, mother-to-father, father-to-mother, and self-to-self) are given in Figures 8.1 and 8.2. These results, of course, represent Claudia's views on a particular occasion and might well vary according to her state when doing the ratings. In the adolescent map it will be seen that father is described as *sexually and physically abusive and emotionally exploitive* to both Claudia and her mother, who are *forgiving, giving in to and guilty*. Self-to-self is seen as *cross, blaming and confusing*. In the adult map, in contrast, father is described as *dependent on and forgiving* to mother and Claudia, who are seen as *blaming* of him, and self-to self is seen as *abusive, exploitive and controlling*. It would seem from this that, as an adult, Claudia was critical of herself and did not see herself as having suffered abuse. This is parallel to the findings reported by Pollock (1996) from his study, in a forensic setting, of abused women who had attacked their current abusive partners; these women showed an inability to acknowledge their victim status, having themselves committed acts of abuse.

The Value of Early Reformulation

These two cases illustrate some of the ways in which the early stages of therapy can be complicated by confusion reflecting rapid shifts between states, and demonstrate how the work of reformulation can clarify this. Therapists need to be able to think and should feel entitled to set limits on the degree to which they are exposed to overwhelming floods of emotion and confusion. It can be help-

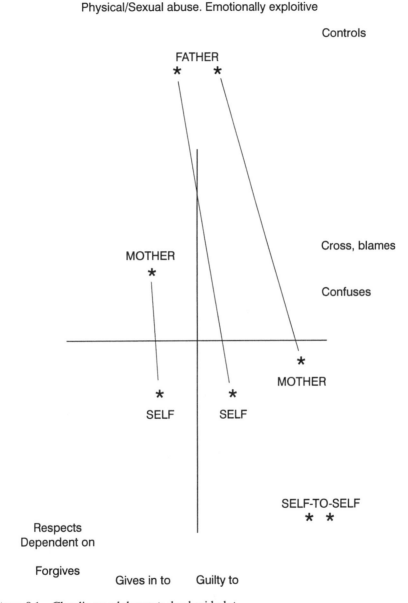

Figure 8.1   Claudia as adolescent: dyad grid plot

ful to both patient and therapist to devise ways of slowing down, such as the institution of a metaphoric 'pause button', for as well as controlling the session this can teach patients how to slow down their own thoughts for themselves. It may also be helpful to focus down on a short segment of the session and trace

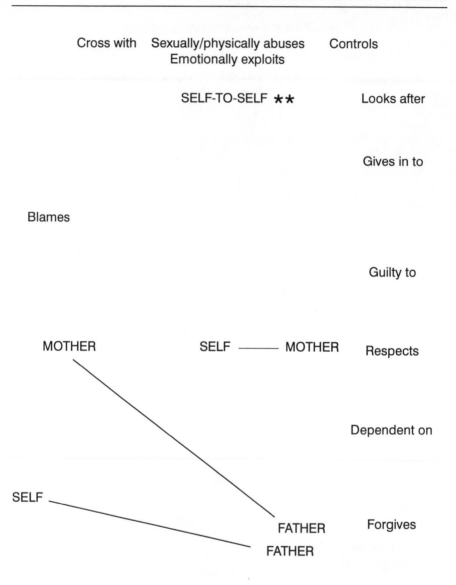

Figure 8.2   Claudia as adult: dyad grid plot

in detail the shifts in roles and self states; an example of this procedure is given below.

Just listening to, reflecting back or offering interpretations of the jumbled material brought by very dissociated patients is seldom helpful. The CAT refor-

mulatory process offers an effective means of controlling and of using therapeutically the chaos such patients bring. In most cases, as in the two described
above, the chaos represents uncontrolled shifting between states and is not a
motivated attack on the therapeutic process, as some psychoanalysts seem to
suggest. In some ways this makes borderline patients easier to reformulate than
more constricted, defended patients; provided one can moderate the pace and
recruit the patient to the task, the reformulation process can be accomplished
relatively quickly and will then serve to further contain the patient and guide
the therapist.

Case Formulation: Comparing CAT and Conventional Psychodynamic Approaches

At this point it may be helpful to consider the relation of these early interventions
of CAT to the mode of work characteristic of dynamic therapists. One immediate issue concerns the speed of the work; some dynamic therapists question the
possibility of basing any accurate understanding on the first few hours' contact
with the patient. These doubts are rooted in part in the traditional model of psychoanalysis, in which principled inactivity is seen to allow the slow 'gathering' of
the transference. This is clearly not an appropriate method for conducting once-
weekly or time-limited therapy. (How far the regression induced by such a procedure may *create* primitive patterns of relating rather than *reveal* them is, to me,
an open question.) Of course many pioneer short-term therapists working within
psychodynamic theory relied upon forms of early 'reformulation' (e.g. Malan,
1976; Mann, 1973), but they tended to regard borderline patients as unsuitable
for brief work. The immediate fostering of integration through the active and collaborative work of CAT (which, to use a surgical metaphor, is relatively non-inva-
sive) makes these patients accessible to brief work and is, I believe, safer than the
potentially disintegrative impact of long-term, intensive psychoanalytic work,
even supposing that that were available.

There are many aspects of CAT which parallel the 'here and now' focus of
psychoanalysis by constantly linking the patient's past and present difficulties to
the evolving therapy relationship and by referring all the material to the reformulation. New understandings are achieved by, and incorporated in, procedural descriptions; in contrast to psychodynamic practice this is done without the
need to offer interpretations of unconscious forces. Another difference is the
fact that, in CAT, the approach is 'top-down', offering very general descriptions
early in the therapy, whereas in psychoanalytic psychotherapy attention is more
on low-level examples of conflict and defence.

Early reformulation is possible because patients (particularly borderline
patients) do not usually require time or regression to make their problem procedures manifest; the clinical need is to identify and describe them quickly and
to avoid collusion with them. The CAT practice of reformulation through the

direct acknowledgement of feelings and meanings and the production of clear descriptions of processes and the linking together of dissociated aspects is, in my view, the explanation of the ability of CAT to produce rapid change.

There are some further aspects of the early sessions in relation to which CAT and psychodynamic psychotherapy may be compared. There are many similarities: thus reformulation in CAT involves the descriptive retelling of the patient's life history and present procedures in ways involving transformations whereby the meanings and the consequences of the patient's ways of experiencing and acting are altered. These descriptions resemble what Freud (1933) described as 'constructions'. They serve to provide 'a structured and organised conceptual and affective framework within which the patient can effectively place himself and his subjective experience of himself and others' (Sandler *et al.*, 1973). The CAT process differs in that this transformation does not refer to unconscious motives and gratifications, and is developed and checked out for accuracy and value with the patient. This difference does not reflect a rejection of the notion of unconscious mental processes (we clearly do not have access to most of our mental processes), neither are the phenomena attributed to the 'dynamic unconscious' neglected; ideas of internal conflict (as one form of internal dialogue) and the avoidance of anxiety by means of the replacement of some acts and the suppression of some memories and desires by 'compromise formations' (alternative procedures) are fully incorporated in the CAT model. But they are described in terms of observable phenomena (actions, omissions, indirect and often non-verbal communications and the avoidance or replacement of procedures) rather than through conjectures about unconscious processes. The use of the notion of 'the unconscious', a hardy reification in psychoanalysis, is avoided because it implies a far more absolute distinction between what is and is not accessible to reflection than is appropriate and assumes a quite different formation for conscious and unconscious thought. In the CAT model actually reflected upon thought, potentially reflected upon thought, and thought processes out of reach of reflection are all seen to be the products of the individual's endowment and life experience, as mediated by the signs and language developed in the context of early relationships. What *is* avoided in CAT is interpretation; by investing 'the unconscious' with mysteries to which he or she holds the key, the psychoanalyst claims a unique and powerful role, whereas the CAT therapist would seek to influence patients by less opaque, authoritarian and potentially disabling forms of discourse.

In these respects, I have a certain sympathy for the fictional General von Stumm in *The Man without Qualities* when he observes: 'In the old days it was also often true that you didn't know something ... but you didn't think anything of it, and if it didn't happen during an examination it didn't harm anyone. But suddenly this was turned into the so-called unconscious, and now everyone's unconscious is the size of all the things he doesn't know, and it's much more important to know why you don't know something than what it is you don't know!' (Musil, 1995, p.1341). The aim of reducing 'what it is you don't know' is shared by psychodynamic and CAT therapy, but the explicit, written and mutually discussed descriptions developed in CAT are more able to recruit the patient to the task of describing and elaborating what he or she almost knows, once 'given permission' to know, or can know once the necessary concepts are available, than are the psychodynamic therapist's interpretations of 'why you don't know' or claims to know it for you.

In CAT, the early high-level descriptions of a patient's procedures are supplemented, in the case of borderline patients, with the mapping of separate, dissociated self states. This attempt to describe the effects of deficient (Level 2) metaprocedures has no equivalent in psychoanalytic practice, where the phenomena are understood in terms of conflict and defence or of intrapsychic splitting of ego and object. Once reformulation in these terms has been accomplished, the work of therapy proceeds in ways that are quite distinct from psychodynamic therapy. CAT therapists use the descriptions to teach patients to recognize and control their shifting self states and to create a central observing capacity and also to guide themselves through their complex countertransference reactions, providing concepts and experiences which recruit the patient to the task of integration.

Case Formulation: Comparing CAT and Cognitive Approaches

CAT and cognitive formulations resemble each other in their emphasis on the description of sequences linking outside events, mental contents and behaviour. The cognitive ABC approach, linking A (Activating event), B (Beliefs and meanings) and C (Consequences in terms of distress or destructive behaviours), is summarized by Chadwick *et al.* (1996) as involving the following eight steps: (1) focus on a problem, (2) assess C, (3) assess A, (4) confirm that the problem is described in C, (5) assess B, (6) link Bs to Cs and connect current ABC sequence to childhood, (7) explore goals and list options, (8) challenge the beliefs (B).

One main difference from CAT is the molecular approach of addressing the range of problems volunteered by the patient one by one, rather than seeking from the start to link these, and their origins (the cognitive stage 6) through overarching, more general descriptions of patterns. Another difference lies in the explanations offered for the persistence of negative procedures; although it is acknowledged that Cs can operate as As, that is to say that the consequences of one's acts may serve to activate new sequences, the circular, self-reinforcing nature of many damaging sequences is less clearly described than in CAT reformulation. A third difference lies in the absence, in cognitive approaches, of an understanding of early development, relationships and personality in terms of reciprocal roles. Cognitive therapists seek to persuade and to confront and not reinforce their patients' negative beliefs or to demonstrate their unhelpful or false inferences (and CAT therapists should do the same) but they do not have a way of using the therapy relationship, whether cooperative or destructive, as a learning experience, and they do not systematically link how they are seen and treated with the historical and current reciprocal role patterns determining the patients' self-management and relationship patterns. These limitations are, however, increasingly recognized. Chadwick *et al.* (1996), in applying cognitive therapy to the treatment of psychotic symptoms, conclude that in this and other aspects of cognitive work the symptom model is due for replacement by a person model. In my view CAT offers the basis for such a person model, while itself needing to incorporate more effectively many of the detailed cognitive techniques developed in recent years.

Drop-outs during the Reformulation Stage

Therapy begins to generate changes even before the first assessment interview, through its effect on morale; the reformulation process, during which the patient acquires new understandings and the beginning of new ways of thinking (usually accompanied by powerful feelings), continues and extends these changes. During these first few sessions it will become apparent that a small proportion of patients need to be referred for other forms of treatment, because of features not picked up during the assessment procedures. Some others may drop out because they find the approach too demanding or uncongenial or because inexperienced therapists fail to contain negativity adequately; compared to most reported series of the treatment of borderline patients, however, the drop-out rate with CAT is low.

For most patients the finalization of the agreed letter and diagram marks the end of this first phase and the establishment of a working alliance. At this stage there is a change in the nature of the work; from now on the task is to apply the new understandings and to explore their implications. This phase, ending in termination, is the topic of the next chapter.

CHAPTER 9

From Reformulation to Termination

As the working phase of therapy gets under way, two interlinked processes are involved. The first consists of the patient consciously using the understandings summarized in the reformulation to understand the past, daily life, and the evolving relationship with the therapist. The greater security derived from the new perceptions summarized in the reformulation and from the more trusting relationship with the therapist allows the second process to occur, whereby the patient experiences a fuller access to memory and feeling. This second change seems to be a consequence of the provision of new, high-level understandings, rather than the recollections being the source from which the new understandings are derived, and for this reason speculations as to what might be repressed or dissociated play little part in the CAT therapist's work. As these new memories and feelings emerge they will, of course, be considered in relation to the broad patterns indicated by the letter and diagram; sometimes (but surprisingly infrequently) this leads to the revision of the procedural descriptions.

The general principles on which therapy is based have been described and illustrated in earlier chapters; the aim here is to consider these in more detail. Successful therapy depends on the establishment of a strong therapeutic alliance; to establish such an alliance with a borderline patient good intentions and basic therapeutic empathy are not enough, it is necessary from the beginning to acknowledge, describe and not collude with negative procedures. Such a process requires the therapist to combine cognitive work with emotional availability, with each enhancing the other. The main task for the patient is to learn to recognize how events and acts are located within the system of self states and procedures, and for this purpose it is usually appropriate to encourage patients to use the diagram for daily self-monitoring. Only when conscious attention to the felt experience of following a described procedure has become possible can conscious change be initiated. Sometimes self-monitoring may be focused on particular procedures, but more often the patient can be asked to keep a daily diary of whatever significant events happen or important acts are undertaken and then to locate these in terms of the self state or procedure involved. This task is helped by using adequately simple diagrams in which summary descriptions are used and in which self states and procedures are colour-coded. Letting patients choose the colours is a good idea; usually the choices are conventional, as is exemplified by the association of idealized states with pink in both cases in Chapter 5. This kind of diary-keeping establishes the diagram as a mnemonic device, so that, in a relatively short time patients, in their reports of internal conversations, begin to use the shorthand descriptions, such as 'I realized I was in the brown state' or 'at that point I started to follow the purple loop'. Such diary-keeping is of particular use in identifying the antecedents of negative shifts, while serving also to locate each particular experience within the whole system of self states.

The spontaneous recovery of memory, of dreaming and of unfamiliar feeling may be supplemented by other kinds of task, particularly where memory of the traumatic events which played a part in establishing dissociation remains incompletely accessed. While therapists may challenge avoidances or reluctances on the part of patients in respect of such issues, the pace of access should be explicitly discussed and, as far as possible, should remain under the patient's control. Too much pressure may provoke shifts to defensive procedures or to cut-off or angry self states, while too little may represent a collusion with avoidant procedures. Therapists often feel that they are walking a knife-edge between being experienced as violently intrusive on the one hand and out of reach and abandoning on the other; it is helpful to discuss this dilemma with the patient and to work out ways of maintaining a manageable pace. In exploring dissociated feelings the use of writing may be helpful; for example in the form of letters to past abusers or to lost or dead people who have been incompletely mourned. Painting and drawing may also provide a way of externalizing and getting more understanding of, distance from, and control of, difficult feelings. While the existence of forgotten memories may be hypothesized, their nature should not be suggested. Where it is hypothesized that current procedures represent defensive or symptomatic alternatives to core roles associated with avoided affects and memories, the phrase 'unmanageable feelings' can be applied to the core role in the diagram; this both accepts that the formative experiences were unmanageable and invites exploration of them.

Linked with these activities, the patient's feelings (or avoidance of feeling) in relation to the therapist can become an accepted part of the conversation. Rather than insisting that transference manifestations are the only topic and rather than attributing them to unconscious forces requiring interpretation, they can be understood as one of the various actions and experiences which can be linked to the past and present through the use of the diagram. In most cases the transference feelings of borderline patients are powerful and polarized and need to be experienced and acknowledged if therapy is to have a profound impact. Therapists must be aware of the patient's role procedures if they are to avoid being drawn into the unintended repetition of negative patterns. Only on that basis can the therapist give the patient the lived and felt experience of an emotionally charged relationship (which can stand at different times as a metaphor for all emotionally significant relationships) in which old patterns are not confirmed and in which trust and truth are valued. Through this, the therapist comes to fill a role in the patient's repertoire which has been largely vacant.

Those patients who do have some current significant relationships will need to apply their new understandings to them, in order to counter established patterns which might otherwise serve to confirm negative procedures. In some cases joint work with partners may be appropriate, but most borderline patients are so deprived that they need their own therapy first. Those emotionally involved with borderline patients may be collusive and themselves disturbed but may, on the other hand, offer affection and resilience and a relatively firm sense of self. Work done in relation to others can be as powerful and valid as that accomplished in relation to the therapist but such others will inevitably be vulnerable. It can be helpful (and it is not uncommon) for patients to show their reformulations to those close to them.

The emergence of negative, destructive feelings and of mistrust in relation to the therapist will have been anticipated in the reformulation letter, so that their appearance can be greeted in a relatively matter-of-fact way. In the same way, powerful or potentially shameful dependent feelings, including those with regressive or erotic components, can be accepted with tact and understood with reference to the unmet emotional needs or idealizing self states described in the diagram. Therapists, more easily than friends and lovers, can establish a role which is felt to be accepting and caring even while they refuse to reciprocate the patient's many and powerful invitations and provocations.

The process of integration proceeds through the establishment of a more continuous self-awareness, in which the therapist's knowledge of all the states and their summary in the diagram are main influences. It may also require, to a varying degree, the establishment of enough inner security and trust in the therapist for the original unmanageable experiences to be remembered or relived and placed in context. As these changes occur patients may symbolize them by redrawing their diagrams; for example Barbara, in Chapter 5, who used the image of islands for her states, first drew bridges between them and then overlapped them, and Paul, in Chapter 6, shrank down the depiction of his negative self state to the size of a parrot on the shoulder of the man-sized positive one.

The Dialogue of Therapy

The therapist is faced with a subtle human and conceptual task in which the two overarching requirements are to avoid collusive reciprocations of problem procedures and to provide understandings and experiences which foster integration and revision. The broad patterns detected in the reformulation process and recorded in the descriptions of problem procedures and the diagram represent the individual's organizing procedural knowledge which was laid down in the past and which constitutes the (largely unreflected-upon) system within which daily acts and experiences unfold. By learning to link the wide range of detailed acts and experiences to these broad patterns the patient can reflect upon them and gain control over what has been automatic; the first requirement on the therapist during the working phase of therapy is therefore to provide a shared experience of recognizing and not repeating the damaging procedural patterns. Only after this is established can less constrained explorations of possible alternative ways of being be embarked upon with the therapist or elsewhere.

In many ways the sequence of activities which occur in the course of the whole therapy (listening, acknowledging, exploring, reflecting and transforming through joint work) is repeated in each of the detailed segments of dialogue between patient and therapist. Before reformulation is completed the joint work is directed towards the completion of the account and description; after it, the work is more concerned with locating events in terms of this joint understanding.

Supervision of Therapists

Every therapist–patient pair is different, but CAT therapists are expected to follow the techniques and accept the underlying assumptions of the method. In order to teach these and know how far therapists are following the method these assumptions and techniques must be spelled out. Current research into therapist's interventions conducted by Dawn Bennett is addressing this issue; in what follows a simplified version of that work, used as a basis for classifying therapist interventions, has been combined with ideas from Leiman's Dialogic Sequence Analysis to suggest a way of analysing therapy transcripts which can make supervision more precise.

The Microanalysis of the Therapy Dialogue

The method of analysing patient–therapist dialogue which I propose here is currently being developed and will doubtless undergo changes with more experience. It is aimed at the work of supervision, where it promises greater precision than is normally possible; it could also offer trainees a means of detailed reflection on their work, when applied to audiotaped and transcribed excerpts from their own sessions. With more development it could contribute to process research, but this topic is not addressed here.

The method involves the detailed analysis of the exchanges between patient and therapist. The underlying assumption, based on CAT theory, is that every act or utterance can be understood as originating in one pole of a reciprocal role pattern and as being addressed, explicitly or implicitly, to the other pole (which may be represented by real or imagined others or by an aspect of the self). During the reformulation stage, as Leiman reports (personal communication), this type of analysis of quite short excerpts can detect, often in the first session, the patient's main underlying procedural patterns. In this it reflects and formalizes in CAT terms the practice of experienced dynamic therapists in arriving at their case formulations. Applied to later sessions, as proposed here, the analysis aims to locate the patient, at any given moment, in terms of the reformulation, by identifying the currently operating self state and by naming which role in which reciprocal role pattern or procedure is being played by the patient. The therapist's responding communications may also be classified in terms of the current understandings of what constitutes good and bad practice, as described below.

The material brought by patients and attended to by therapists may consist of *reported* past or current acts and experiences, *imagined* events or situations such as images or descriptions of dreams and fantasies and *enacted* behaviours and communications within the therapy relationship. Both reported and imagined events or stories may refer to (be metaphors for) the therapy relationship. The aim will be to locate each of these within the patient's system.

The therapist's responses to reported, imagined and enacted phenomena should (1) aim to explore their details and meaning, (2) should heighten the patient's understanding by helping them link such events to the history, reformulation letter and SSSD, (3) should avoid reinforcing (by reciprocation) problem procedures, and (4) should aid integration of dissociated self states. These activities, carried out in an accepting, acknowledging and carefully attending way, constitute the specifically professional therapist role in relation to the patient. Patients, to start with, will largely repeat their familiar problem procedures, but in time will begin to reciprocate with a working patient role, by questioning, learning, thinking, trying out alternatives and by using the jointly created tools of self-reflection.

The practical procedure for analysing an interchange between patient and therapist will require:

1. Listing and numbering the patient's self states (1, 2, 3, 4, and so on), the reciprocal role repertoire of each (A to B, C to D, E to F and so on) and the procedures generated by each core role (A1, A2, B1, C1 and so on). Once this is done, statements or events may be located by self state, role or procedure. In many cases the identification of the core reciprocal role concerned will be an adequate description.
2. Recording and transcribing sequences of the therapy dialogue and breaking up the dialogue into segments, each segment representing a single role enactment or story and the therapist's response.
3. Having available a classification of Therapist Interventions.

The following classification of therapist responses lists appropriate interventions and notes whether the opportunity for such interventions was taken or not. It also lists unhelpful or damaging interventions. Patients' participation in the work of therapy is also coded. As noted above, this coding is provisional and will doubtless be modified in many ways with more experience.

A CLASSIFICATION OF THERAPIST INTERVENTIONS

Code the whole excerpt or, if clear separate themes emerge, code each theme or enactment in turn.

Appropriate Interventions

Code by number and letter. Where opportunity not taken, add X.

1. *Acknowledgement*
   a. Facts/context explored
   b. Meanings/feelings explored
2. *Linking*
   a. Linked to other themes
   b. Linked to therapy relationship
   c. Located on diagram
   d. Diagram revised/extended
3. *Non-collusion*
   a. Notes invitation to collude
   b. Corrects initial/past collusion
   c. Links a or b to diagram
4. *Non-reinforcement*
   a. Patient's version of events or story (reflecting problem procedure) is challenged
5. *Countertransference*
   a. Identifying countertransference used empathically
   b. Reciprocating countertransference used to explore procedures
   c. 'Shaking transference tree'; exploring relationship issues
   d. Linking a, b, or c to diagram
6. *Pace control*
   a. Hot up, confront
   b. Slow down to avoid provoking resistance/state shift
7. *Homework*
   a. Negotiated agreement to perform work
   b. Task clearly located on aspect of diagram
8. *Exits*
   a. Work on alternatives to procedures threatening therapy or self-harm

   b.   Once procedures recognized, discussion/rehearsal/homework related
        to alternatives

                    Unhelpful or Damaging Therapist Interventions

  9. *Avoiding/diverting/ignoring*
      a.   Blocking, moving away from significant theme/enactment
      b.   Introducing irrelevant tasks
      c.   Introducing tasks at inappropriate moment
 10. *Reciprocations/collusions*
      a.   Implicit or explicit reciprocation of problem procedure
      b.   Reinforcing dissociation
 11. *General tendencies*
      a.   Avoiding silence, not allowing space to patient
      b.   Doing all the work, not involving patient in discussion/reflection

                                   ● ● ●

                       CODING PATIENTS' PARTICIPATION

Patients' explicit working at therapy, as opposed to enactments of problem procedures, may be classified as follows:

   Pa. Reflects, argues, revises what therapist proposes
   Pb. Works on, understands location of events on diagram
   Pc. Independent use of or elaboration of diagram

Microanalysis in Practice

This method of analysis will now be illustrated by applying it to the transcript of
the first phase of the eighth session of a patient. The interchange can be summarized as follows. The patient arrived having failed to do a homework assign-
ment and complaining of a headache which he attributed to a row with his
father. The therapist enquired further and suggested a link between his feelings
about his father and her, and located these feelings and his headache on the
diagram. The microanalysis of the sequence serves to demonstrate how the
work of the therapist was derived from her application of general therapeutic
and specific CAT skills and methods.

Case Example: Adam

Reformulation of Adam, aged 28, had produced an agreed Self States
Sequential Diagram describing two self states. **Self state 1** was described in

terms of Role **A** involving *contemptuous abuse* in relation to Role **B** *angry and needy*. **Self State 2** described role **C**, *protective care* in relation to role **D** *safe (suffocated)*. Role **B** generated three procedural loops: **B1** described a sequence of hope followed by disappointment, frequently leading to substance abuse (possibly representing a switch to either **A** or **C** in relation to self). **B2** was a procedural loop involving perfectionism (self-to-self) and striving to please (self-to-others) often leading to disappointment and a switch to **B3**, passive resistance. In the following account the coding is applied to short segments. (Therapist coding in parentheses.)

(1) The session opened with the patient explaining that he had had a bad headache for the past three days (*Reported*) and had not done the agreed homework. (*Enacted*) (*PT invites TH to play A by enacting B2*.) (2) The therapist asked him to say a bit more. (*1 ab*) (3) It appeared that he had offered to help his sister with a problem (*Reported? PT in role C or B2*) and that (4) this had led to an angry phone call from his father. (*Reported PT in B to father's A.*)

(5) The therapist asked how it had felt being in the crossfire. (*1b*) (6) The patient said he felt both angry for being criticized and guilty for not having spoken first to his father. But, if he had, 'he'd have gone over the top'. (*Reported. PT in B to father in A.*) (7) The therapist, after two attempts, got the patient to consider whether there was a link between the impact of that phone call from his father and his feelings about coming to the session without the homework, noting that he had been very tense on arrival *(2b)* PT: 'Yes I do feel tense and I don't feel well and I did think you might have a go at me.' (*Enacted. PT in B.*) (9) TH: 'So you thought I would treat you like a bad boy?' *(1a, 3a)* (10) PT: 'Well last week you did not seem to accept the reasons I gave for missing the session the week before ... I felt a bit bothered you'd think I was wasting your time'. (*Enacted. PT in B.*) (11) The therapist then asked 'So how do I seem to be reacting?' *(1b)*, to which the patient replied 'You seem OK ... I'm surprised,' after which there was some joint laughter. (*Enacted. PT1a.*) (12) The therapist then returned to asking the patient if he could see a link between the phone call from his father and his feelings about her *(2b)*. (13) PT: 'I expected you to be like he was, which is stupid and illogical ...' (*PT self to self A to B.*) (14) The therapist questioned whether logic or intelligence was the issue, implicitly not accepting his abuse of himself *(4a)* and then (15) traced the sequence on the diagram *(2c)* suggesting that, because of his father's reaction to his attempts to be helpful (*B2*), he had felt let down and criticized, reaffirming his sense of himself in the angry and needy procedure *B3 (2c)*. (17) The therapist then returned to the patient's feelings towards her, after he had missed the session and expected her to be stern, by asking him to acknowledge that he might have felt angry with her *(5c)*. The patient would not accept that, but agreed that he 'might have been a bit frustrated', to which the therapist replied that 'frustration is a sort of mild anger'. (18) She went on to suggest a link between his avoidance of

anger through the use of his placatory procedure and his headache (*2d*). (19) The patient confirmed this by describing how the headache had actually started while he was talking to his sister and then, indicating the procedural loop *B1* on the diagram (disappointment and anger leading to substance abuse), said that after the talk he had smoked a large joint which had made him feel worse) (*PT c*).

This segment is an example of good CAT practice, with all the appropriate interventions being made. It is important to note that the use of the diagram was in no way mechanical; it was preceded by (1) the exploration of the patient's experiences, (2) the suggestion of a link between a reported external event and an enactment in the therapy relationship, and (3) the therapist's exploration of the patient's transference and her accepting that the patient might have negative feelings for her. Once these stages had been completed the main sequence of the reported event and of the enactment were traced on the diagram. The patient then proceeded to describe an additional unreported detail (his smoking of a joint) and to locate this on the diagram.

A second brief extract from a different therapy but concerned with a similar situation will now be presented. A group discussion of the transcript of this short extract evoked, at first, a good deal of disagreement about the possible different ratings which could be applied to the therapist's interventions in the absence of contextual information or of knowledge of the non-verbal exchanges, but by the time all the segment had been discussed there was general agreement with the ratings given below. (In presenting such material for supervision, the therapist would, of course, be able to add information concerning his or her intentions and countertransference feelings; in group supervision it might also be the case that differing interpretations of the material might represent accurate responses to different or contradictory aspects of the communication.)

Case Example: Roland

Roland was a 30-year-old patient whose reformulation at this stage had yielded the following descriptions:

Self State 1
A *Critical contempt* in relation to B *patronized, humiliated, revengeful, envious*.
Procedures
B1 *Unrealistic striving* leading to failure and self-blame or a switch to blaming the other (**A**).
B2 *Unrealistic expectations* of self leading to feeling overwhelmed and incapable so giving up and feeling contempt for self (**A**).

Self State 2
C *Admiring* in relation to D *seeking admiration or admired*.

Procedures
D1 Grandiose fantasies, unrealistic schemes, leading to failure and a switch to blaming self or others (**A**).
D2 Seek perfect, admiring partner, feel mistrustful or patronized, leading to switch to reject (**A**) or provoke rejection (**B**).
D3 Seek perfect admiring partner, provoke dependence, feel trapped, leading to switch to criticize and reject (**A**).

The following excerpt is the opening exchange of session 5; Roland was late by 5 minutes, as he had been for the two previous sessions.

PT Yes, I know I'm late ...
TH Hm?
PT I had to see this guy on a business matter ...
TH You do find it hard to get here on time. (*So far, the therapist is in 1a offering acknowledgement*).
PT Well I always have good intentions (*the patient could be warding off the humiliated role **B** or could be feeling patronized—(**D2**)*.
TH You don't think perhaps you are making a bit of a point? (*1b*)
PT Oh no, it's not that, really it's not.
TH I suppose you've tried hard to get here. It's a shame, we could have used those 5 minutes. (*The patient declines to consider his lateness as motivated. The therapist does not link the suggestion that his lateness is motivated to the reformulation, although the suggestion would presumably imply that the patient was in **A**. Patient covertly **A**—critical contempt—to avoid humiliation—**B**.*
PT I really will try harder next week (*? seeking to be admired—**D2**—or to avoid role **B**.*)
TH I just wonder why you deprive yourself. I'm not asking you to work harder, but just to look at why. (*Therapist seeks to avoid being seen as critical—**A**—but? feeds PT sense of being patronized—**B** and fails to name clearly or link the covert negative action of the patient.*) (*2abc X*)
PT Well I just had to drive to Chelmsford to see this guy ...
TH I'm just concerned you don't miss out. (*2abc X*)
PT Tell you what then. Start the session half an hour later next week ... Oh I know you can't really. (*In this exchange the therapist's reiteration of concern and the lack of direct naming of the patient's enacted disdain could be heard as sarcastic (10a). This provokes an explicit contemptuous rejoinder—patient switches from **B** to **A**.*)

While this kind of microanalysis is time-consuming and could not be applied to all the material in ordinary clinical practice, the study of even short segments, such as the two above, offers a powerful way of ascertaining in supervision how well the reformulation fits the material, how well the therapist is using it, and how far the patient is learning to use it independently. In the case of Roland, a possible personal countertransference issue (the therapist's need to avoid confrontation) would clearly be taken up in supervision.

Reviewing Progress and Describing Alternative Procedures

In the usual practice of CAT a summary list of Target Problems and Target Procedures is rated each week, initially in terms of how well the latter are recognized and then on how far they are revised. The ratings are made by the patient in the session and are discussed with the therapist; their function is to help the patient to learn accurate self-evaluation and to ensure that both patient and therapist consistently link what is happening to the reformulation. Only when recognition is firmly achieved are revised, alternative procedures discussed in detail; at this point they may be written into the diagrams (as 'exits') or added to the Target Problem Procedure descriptions.

In working with borderline patients the continual reference to the diagram makes this weekly rating procedure redundant. In using the diagram it remains important, however, to review how far patients continue to follow *all* the negative procedural loops and enter *all* the negative self states.

There may, however, be phases in therapy when attention needs to be focused on a particular key procedure and in these instances the weekly rating of a verbal description or of a given procedural loop may be useful. This kind of focused attention is most likely to be needed where a procedure involves risk to the patient or threatens the continuation of the therapy; in such cases it will also be necessary to identify and rehearse alternatives with the patient without delay. As an example, the common, worrying danger of patients repeating self-harm may be considered. In such cases the procedural loop(s) leading to self-harm, describing the antecedents of the impulse or act, should be clearly described and should list, as exits, a range of rehearsed alternatives. These procedural descriptions, as well as aiding in the early recognition of destructive tendencies, serve to convey acceptance and understanding of the patient's impulses in a non-judgemental and non-disciplinarian way, an important consideration in people who have been abused and who often feel ashamed. In addition, involving the patient in working out possible alternative actions restores some of the sense of agency which may otherwise be sought by self-harm. Of possible alternative actions, seeking telephone contact with a friend or with the Samaritans or sitting down and writing to the therapist with the aim of bringing the writing to the next session are ways of restoring a sense of contact with others. Other actions are more individual: Connors (1996b) lists a number of methods used by patients in this way, including distraction, imagery, physical activity, drawing or writing, safe enactments of anger using objects and the use of self-soothing and comforting activities.

Other actions or symptoms which might endanger therapy may need a similar approach, but, in general, a comprehensive reformulation and the secure recognition of self states and problem procedures should be accomplished before alternatives are considered in any detail. Stable change is only likely to be achieved where all self states and negative procedures are identified accurately, reliably, in relation to each other and in the wider context of the patient's life.

Within the time limit of 24 sessions the process of revision will never be far advanced or securely established but, if integration has proceeded well, patients can maintain the therapeutic work and change will continue to occur without further help. Follow-up of patients completing therapy shows that psychometric scores frequently continue to fall after termination. The stability of personality disorders is maintained to a considerable extent by the constant elicitation from others of responses which appear to confirm dissociation and negative procedures, and a similar but benign process of confirmation can serve to maintain and extend the positive changes learned in therapy. During therapy itself a constant process of evaluation is important, both to sustain movement and identify blocks and to help the patient to learn accurate self-reflection.

Although the use of the SSSD in the session and in homework assignments involves the continuing evaluation of progress, it is still possible for patients and therapists to settle into what are essentially stagnant arrangements in which the appearance of therapeutic work conceals an inactive truce. Such states commonly follow an early phase of trust and active work and are the result of the fear of termination and of disillusion and disappointment (perhaps following early idealization), leading to the mobilization of hostile or distancing procedures. In other cases the anxiety aroused by contacting dissociated traumatic memories and feelings can lead to a return of dissociation and the mobilization of less exposed and more controlling self states. The rate at which the exploration of such memories can proceed will depend on the safety established in the therapy and the intensity of the trauma. Pacing should be explicitly under the patient's control in such cases. Where stalemate occurs it is probable that the therapist will have played a part in stabilizing the situation, either by covertly joining in the process of avoiding powerful and disturbing feelings, or by forcing the pace and arousing too much anxiety, or by indirect and unrecognized forms of counterhostility.

It should be recognized that it is virtually inevitable that some unhelpful countertransference feelings will be mobilized and likely that they may find expression since the therapy of borderline subjects, especially in a time-limited format, is emotionally very demanding. It requires genuinely knowing and feeling what the patient experiences, while ensuring that the reality of the professional role and the limits implied by this and by the time restriction are kept clearly in view. Supervision of therapists needs to attend to both aspects; they must know that their sharing of the patient's pain must not be mistaken for an offer to take it away, that their acknowledgement and acceptance of the patient's destructiveness must not be taken as approval and that their genuine care and concern must be understood to include the (ultimately freeing) built-in certainty of the termination. The therapist is on loan to the patient, and the aim must be to give what can be given in that time and to make the disappointment for what cannot be given manageable. As Mann (1973) observed, many patients have spent their lives either seeking for someone to make them better or else avoiding any emotional connection because the pain of not getting their needs met is unbearable. A successful time-limited therapy is the way out of this dilemma, and therapists should be able to value the therapeutic use of what they give and of what they refuse.

It is common for negative and distancing procedures to begin to influence the therapy relationship around session 10–12, and for that reason we have recently introduced a *mid-term review* of the therapy at this time. For this, therapists prepare a letter to the patient summarizing what has been achieved and indicating any problems which seem to be operating in the relationship. This provides an opportunity to gather together examples of the avoidance or blocking of the therapeutic work and to link them with the reformulation. If there have been breaks in therapy for any reason the reactions to this may be considered in anticipation of the problems of termination. In supervision the drafting of the letter is an opportunity for reviewing possible subtle countertransference collusions on the part of the therapist and for considering whether new approaches are called for.

Termination

As in any time-limited therapy, the fact of the time limit needs to be kept on the agenda from the beginning. This involves noting the number of each session and responding to any sign that the patient is assuming that the rules do not apply. The contract for borderline patients is normally for 24 sessions with follow-up at 1, 2, 3, and 6 months. Alternatively it can be helpful in some cases, especially where the patient's commitment is uncertain or where substance abuse continues, to build in a review around session 10 at which time the number of further sessions (up to the total of 24) can be agreed, or made dependent on how the work proceeds. This enables the therapist either to cut short or to galvanize blocked or sluggish therapies.

The issue of termination usually comes onto the patient's agenda shortly after the middle of the contracted number of sessions, at which time the 'mid-term blues', reflecting the emergence of negative procedures after the early intense activity and excitement, have usually surfaced. This often takes the form of the re-emergence of early untrusting, symptomatic or distancing procedures. This is a necessary stage, permitting the patient to risk destructive behaviour in a context where the feared or expected consequences do not follow, and hence to learn in action the possibility of revising long-established patterns. The mood of the second half of therapy is, in consequence, uneven. It is hardly surprising that these patients, who have experienced loss and deprivation so fully in the past, find the fact that the therapist is going to leave them hard to accept, however fully the contract was known from the beginning. It can also be hard for therapists to avoid hurt reactions to the denigration of their work or to resist a wish to cover up the patient's anger by reassurance or to respond to it by displaying their own vulnerable feelings or forms of counterhostility. But not all the patient's feelings about termination are bad; for some patients, there is an accompanying relief that a potentially suffocating dependency is avoided, and at some level in most patients there is pleasure and confidence in being trusted to manage, and an appreciation of what has been given.

The more clearly these mixed feelings emerge and are acknowledged and understood the more likely it is that patients will be able to hold onto what they have learned. If they are too painful to find expression (or if therapists do not help patients to articulate them) there is likely to be a powerful negative reaction to termination. Therapists need to keep their nerves steady through this stage. If they are seriously concerned with the risk of suicide, they should seek an independent assessment, but this is rarely needed. It is almost never advisable to respond to the anxiety provoked by the patient's desperation by offering to extend the therapy. For one thing, it is often possible to complete the work of termination at the follow-up meetings, without denying the patient the experience of being able to survive separation. For another, a review of the patient's progress and further needs is more reliably done after an interval, and is best carried out by someone other than the therapist. Even when it is clear that more therapy is indicated, the experience of termination is usually a helpful one; moreover, in most settings, further therapy will usually be with a different therapist.

The Goodbye Letter

The issues around termination are discussed in the therapist's *goodbye letter*, usually considered with the patient at session 23 or 24. This letter should briefly rehearse the original difficulties and offer an accurate, plain, unvarnished summary of what has been achieved and of what remains to be done. What the patient has expressed in the way of sadness or anger should be described and if unexpressed negative feelings are suspected their probable and understandable emergence should be predicted. At the same time the positive achievements and the mutual work achieved in the relationship should be recorded and the patient can be reminded that the ideas and conceptual tools developed during the therapy will be taken away by him or her.

The main aim of the letter is to guard against the patient's coping with the loss of the therapist either by idealization or by denying any value to the experience. The process of mourning the therapy should allow the internalization of a realistic image of the therapist, adding a new and more positive voice to the patient's internal dialogue.

The Assessment of Outcome in Individual Patients

A satisfactory outcome for the individual patient can be defined in a number of ways. In CAT, with its essentially ideographic approach, the main criterion will be change in the patient's specific difficulties as indicated by a reduction in the Target Problems and, of more importance in the long run, by the revision of the Target Problem Procedures which were identified during the reformulation. With borderline subjects, a reduction in the degree of dissociation between states, the lessened extremity of the main reciprocal role patterns and control over the previously most destructive state switches and procedures will be particularly important. The evaluation of these changes during therapy and the follow-up period will be carried out by the therapist and patient, as part of the therapeutic process, but termination may provoke short-term reactions which make accurate estimation of the final status difficult, and an overall asessment, at which further needs for treatment can be considered, is more objective if carried out later and by someone other than the therapist. This needs to involve detailed enquiries related to the target problems and to the diagram, carried out through a semi-structured interview. This can be combined with a systematic enquiry into the presence and intensity of diagnostic DSM features, and with the readministration of the questionnaires used before the therapy.

Evaluating Outcome as an Indication of the Effectiveness of a Treatment Method

The assessment of a series of individual outcomes is the basis of estimating the power of the therapeutic method. For this, the individualized measures described above remain crucial, but nomothetic tests also have a part to play. While at present there are no inventories which have been shown to be sensitive to the form of partial dissociation characteristic of borderline patients, the level of dissociative phenomena indicated by the Dissociation Questionnaire (DIS-Q) (Vanderlinden et al., 1993) should fall with successful treatment and scores on questionnaires such as the Symptom Checklist (SCL-90) (Derogatis et al., 1973) measuring general symptoms, and the Beck Depression Inventory (BDI) (Beck et al., 1961) measuring depression should also show reductions. Given the interdependence of disorders at Levels 1 and 2 (as described in Chapter 3) and the usual association of DSM Axis I diagnoses with BPD, reductions in these inventory scores provide a reasonable if indirect indication of improvement in borderline status. Long-term maintainance of improvement will be reflected in less use of health service resources, in better patterns of self-care and of relationships and in improvements in other indices of social adjustment as well as in symptom reduction. In assessing general social adjustment account must be taken of the external obstacles associated with unemployment, poor housing and poverty, to which so many citizens of the wealthy but abusive and depriving societies of the late twentieth century are condemned.

Comparative trials of therapeutic methods are difficult to set up because of the immense variability in borderline symptomatology and severity and the practical and ethical issues involved. Outcome will be heavily influenced by patient selection: for example the exclusion of substance-abusing patients, those with suicidal or violent histories and those with extreme degrees of dissociation will improve outcome figures, as will the inclusion only of those functioning at a level which enables them to pay for therapy. Uncontrolled trials of particular treatments, even those which provide adequate details of the patient population, the intervention and the measures used, must be interpreted with caution. They can, however, serve to identify patient factors associated with treatment response and, in a persistent condition such as BPD, the demonstration of change over relatively short periods of time in a substantial proportion of patients establishes a claim for serious attention and for the inclusion of the approach in the inevitably expensive randomized controlled trials which could offer more solid evidence (if it were not for the fact that research funding in the UK for such studies is virtually unobtainable). Uncontrolled outcome studies can also be combined with detailed studies of the process of therapy and with the refinement of models of the therapeutic process, and can establish methods of ascertaining therapists' compliance with the model.

Unsatisfactory Outcomes

The causes of early dropping out of therapy are often difficult to identify but they are likely to include errors in the referral and assessment stages or the therapist's failure to contain early hostility and mistrust. Once reformulation is completed, the successful weathering of the 'mid-term blues' is a key stage in the therapy. If this is accomplished, a successful termination can be anticipated. In some cases, however, the therapist's failure to deal with the emergence of negative feelings or the patient's inability to tolerate the real disappointment and finite nature of the therapy can lead to the patient dropping out before the end, or to an unsatisfactory termination. Such negative outcomes may indicate problems or limitations of the treatment method itself, failures to apply the therapy skilfully or the taking on of unsuitable patients.

At present not enough data have been accumulated to draw any firm conclusions about the selection of borderline patients for CAT. Up to now, outpatient referrals have been accepted as long as there was no current serious substance abuse (a condition not, in fact, consistently observed) or any recent psychotic features. It does seem, on experience to date and in line with the experience of others, that successful outcomes are less often achieved in patients who continue to abuse alcohol or cannabis. If such patients fail to monitor and control use they should probably be discharged (something tender-hearted therapists find hard to do) and referred for detoxification or to more intensive programmes such as those described in Chapter 10, if such are available. Another group of potentially poor outcome cases are those with very marked dissociation; these patients often have features of MPD, such as already named and firmly differentiated subpersonalities including some with markedly paranoid features, and they often hint at particularly gruesome, half-remembered and undisclosed memories. In these cases a longer or more flexible time contract may be advisable. However, more cases and a longer follow-up period are needed before firm conclusions can be drawn about selection.

Whether successful or not, it seems that CAT is a safe intervention even for more severely disturbed patients. Of a total of well over 2000 outpatients treated with CAT at St Thomas's and Guy's, of whom I would estimate that at least 10% met borderline criteria, only four died by suicide during or shortly after their therapy. Of these, three were borderline patients with associated bi-polar affective disorders, and all were inpatients at the time of death. Where CAT is not an effective or adequate treatment it can still serve to clarify what the therapeutic issues are and indicate the appropriate further course. That there is a need for further therapy for a proportion of borderline patients after a 24-session intervention is hardly surprising. Unsatisfactory outcomes do need to be reviewed, however, if the approach is to be refined. Some of the issues raised by such cases are illustrated by the following example.

Case Example: Gregory

Gregory was a 39-year-old man referred for depression two years after he had been successfully treated for heroin addiction. He had injected for the last ten years of his addiction but he had remained physically healthy and had worked regularly, although in unsatisfying jobs below his potential. He was on no prescribed medication but used both cannabis and heavy alcohol consumption to deal with intense feelings of loneliness. Gregory had had a large number of sexual encounters but his only sustained relationship was with a partner who visited irregularly; when together they spent most of the time smoking cannabis. In the past he had been transiently involved in cross-dressing and he had had some homosexual encounters.

Gregory was referred by his GP with a request for long-term psychotherapy, but as there were no possibilities of obtaining this in the NHS he accepted CAT at his assessment interview. In his early meetings with his (female) therapist he was cooperative and agreed to keep a diary recording his alcohol and cannabis use, with the aim of greatly reducing his intake. A self state sequential diagram was constructed with the following self states:

1. Based on his early experiences in the family: *Brutal neglect in relation to powerless, abused, abandoned.*
2. Enacted through substance abuse but also experienced as empty despair: *Blanked off in relation to absent.*

3. Based on his own involvement in looking after a handicapped nephew as well as on his wish to find care: *idealized caretaker to ideally cared for*.

The first self state generated relationship procedures dominated by the fear of humiliation and rejection; with men these involved him in being arrogantly dismissive, with women in being a conquering and abandoning Don Juan.

Gregory came to the fifth session having been depressed, he said, by the exclusively negative contents of the diary he had kept. He handed the diary to the therapist. The therapist asked about his feelings after the last session. He replied: 'I felt resentful ... There wasn't enough time ... the sessions seem to be getting shorter and shorter ... I felt cut off ...'. The therapist remarked that at the end of that session he had been talking very fast about what he suppressed with alcohol and had mentioned sexual feelings and confusion. The patient said he had thought about the question of what he suppressed and the answer was 'just pain'. The therapist then read from the part of the diary he had written just after the last session: 'Therapist dressed seductively, it stopped me talking' and suggested that there had been at least two feelings going on and not enough time to deal with them. The patient replied 'the last session felt like *minutes*'. The therapist then referred back to another comment from the last session, concerning Gregory's fear that, after talking about his deeper feelings, he was going to have to leave therapy in order to get away from the exposure. She referred this to the procedure emanating from self state 1, based on the fear of humiliation, and also suggested that he should not go faster than felt safe. This led to his expressing the feeling that he must rush if he was going to get anything from the therapy. A little later in the session the therapist read another entry in the diary concerning fantasies of rape and decapitation and asked if they were centred on her. He replied that, in some ways, that was the case; it was an expression of anger, but he reassured her that he was a non-violent man and could not possibly do anything of the sort in reality. The therapist asked in detail about any episodes of sexual violence in his life (there were none, to her relief) and suggested that, having established that, he might feel it safer to talk about and understand what was in his mind. The rest of the session involved Gregory, now in tears, in rehearsing, with relation to the diagram, and with empathic support from the therapist, all the ways in which he experienced and maintained his pain. The image of decapitation was seen to represent how he himself felt when the session was stopped and was linked to his childhood experiences (summarized in self state 1).

Gregory dropped out of therapy after 18 sessions, three of which he had failed to attend without notice. All the themes of the session reported above returned many times and phases of close involvement alternated with blank sessions, returns to heavy drinking or other forms of distancing. After he had written saying he was not coming any more he was sent a letter linking this decision to his fear of exposure and to his long pattern of discarding the women he was involved with; he did not reply to this letter, or to an invitation from his assessor to come and discuss possible alternative therapeutic help.

There were many early indications that this might be the disappointing outcome, including his original wish for long-term therapy and the very powerful feelings generated by the end of the fourth session which were discussed in the summary above. While his ability to come off heroin suggested personal strengths, and while his engagement in this therapy gave much evidence of both intelligence and sensitivity, his continuing or recurring use of cannabis and alcohol was a negative feature. Gregory showed an extreme intolerance of being alone, a feature of borderline patients highlighted by Gunderson (1996), and this may have made termination too hard to face.

As is evident from the extracts given above, the therapist managed the patient's powerful feelings with skill and sensitivity. The conclusion has to be either that he was an unsuitable patient for therapy or that the CAT model was inappropriate, in particular in its firm time limit. It would certainly have been easier to have worked with this patient in a longer or more flexible time frame, but when the time came to face termination it is likely that the same acute difficulty would have had to be faced. It would clearly have been better had abstinence been established before the therapy, but in a sense both Gregory's use of alcohol and his use of people were evidence of his association of his underlying need with a humiliating sense of weakness, which only some form of therapy could have addressed.

CHAPTER 10

Borderline Personality and Substance Abuse Problems

TIM LEIGHTON

A belief in the association of 'personality disorder' with substance misuse or addictive disorders extends back into the early decades of the twentieth century. An early position is expressed by R.P. Knight (1937): 'Alcohol addiction is a symptom rather than a disease ... There is always an underlying personality disorder evidenced by obvious maladjustment, neurotic character traits, emotional immaturity or infantilism.' Broadly speaking the orthodox view has moved from seeing addiction as a symptom of underlying psychopathology to believing it to be a 'primary illness'. The position most in current favour, at least in American psychiatry, is exemplified by Vaillant, who bases his opinion on his own research and on his review of a number of prospective studies. He says: 'We must stop trying to treat alcoholism as if it were merely a symptom of underlying distress' (Vaillant, 1995, p. 118), and he found that, on the average, childhood psychosocial factors which were most strongly associated with poor adult mental health were not particularly predictive of alcoholism and the strongest predictors of alcoholism (family history of alcoholism, ethnicity and adolescent behaviour problems) did not predict adult mental health.

Nevertheless the situation is made very complex by a number of factors. There is much more research over longer periods of time into alcohol use as opposed to other drugs, and despite a growing acceptance that there is a great deal of commonality between alcohol and other drug problems, it remains the case that alcohol is a socially sanctioned, widely used drug, whose use is integrated, more or less comfortably, into many societies, whereas illicit drug use is seen as deviant and unacceptable. It might be that conclusions drawn about alcohol dependence might not hold true of other drug dependence. Moreover there are several psychiatric diagnoses, including borderline and antisocial personality disorders, that are associated with high rates of substance use disorders, up to severe dependence, and in samples of alcohol or drug-dependent

128

people in treatment, high rates of BPD, Narcissistic Personality Disorder and Antisocial Personality have been found. Several American studies have found rates of BPD between 16% and 45%, and the vast majority of subjects had at least one personality disorder diagnosis (see Kaufman, 1994, p. 67). There are special diagnostic problems with this population, since there is controversy as to how the substance dependence distorts the personality and causes a person to behave in ways that look like personality disorder.

There is one particular circumstance which is known to be predictive of future alcohol or drug problems and whose great significance for understanding the personality difficulties of many people with these problems seems to me to be under-recognized. This is the presence of severe alcohol or drug problems in one or both parents. There may well be a genetic predisposition to such problems, but in addition to this there is often an impact on the family environment due to parental drinking which is of just the kind likely, according to a CAT model, to produce problematic interpersonal and self-management procedures, and indeed to produce a failure of integration due to inconsistent, traumatic or neglectful parenting as described in Chapter 3. I do not claim that all substance-misusing parents are incompetent, but many clearly are, and I am convinced that the experience of having an alcoholic or addicted parent is often devastating. It is not always the obvious problems such as violent behaviour which do the most damage; problems which can remain hidden in the family such as emotional withdrawal, emotional blackmail, or consistently broken promises all have their effect. There is also evidence that in homes with alcoholic parents there is an increased rate of sexual abuse or inappropriate sexualized attention to the children. There is good evidence from outcome studies that these kinds of experience complicate drug and alcohol problems, make them more difficult to treat, and very often make the business of recovery and achieving a stable fulfilling life more difficult.

Current Models of Treatment

Treatment for drug- or alcohol-dependent people is offered in various models in the UK, but if we exclude pharmacotherapy such as methadone maintenance, we see the field divided between proponents of intensive versus non-intensive approaches, and between advocates of a '12 Step' philosophy and those of a Cognitive-Behavioural bent.

The '12 Steps' are the programme of the self-help movement Alcoholics Anonymous, which stresses that the addicted person is suffering from a 'threefold illness': physical, emotional and spiritual. The AA path to recovery consists of acceptance followed by a moral and spiritual readjustment of relationships and values in the company of and with the guidance of other once addicted people. There is no doubt that this philosophy has helped a very large number of alcoholics and addicts. A model of short-stay (4 weeks to 3 months) residential treatment based on introducing people to the principles of the 12 Steps was developed in the USA during the 1970s and 80s, and is known as the Minnesota Model. Originally for alcoholics, this model sees addiction as 'Chemical Dependence' and has been used to treat other drug addictions and related behavioural problems such as compulsive gambling or overeating (Anderson, 1981).

The traditional treatment setting for opiate addicts has been a different kind of therapeutic community, known as the Concept House, with a much longer period of stay of between 12 and 24 months (Wells, 1990). This also originated in the United States and arrived in the UK in the early 70s. These programmes stressed the breaking down of the 'street addict' culture, based on dishonesty and evasion, and attempted to instil a sense of personal responsibility and cooperation with others through a tough regime involving work in small teams and the assumption of greater responsibility as the resident rose through the hierarchical structure. There is also a programme of 'encounter' groups aimed at helping people to experience and understand their emotions and to conform to the requirements of the community.

Over the last decade approaches to alcohol and drug problems have been much influenced by Cognitive-Behavioural Therapy. Marlatt and Gordon (1985) developed a model of relapse based on an individual's ability to cope with a range of 'High Risk Situations'. The lack of adequate coping led to a decrease in self-efficacy, and this, coupled with 'positive outcome expectancies' about alcohol or drug use, made return to use more likely. Marlatt and Gordon's Relapse Prevention programme consisted in the identification and monitoring of high-risk situations, the assessment of coping ability and the application of a range of Cognitive-Behavioural and Coping Skills techniques. Beck and his colleagues have also developed a similar model, deriving from his work with depression, anxiety and personality disorders (Beck et al., 1993). The Cognitive-Behavioural approaches have been influential on the other treatment modalities, despite their association with a controlled drinking goal (traditional treatment tends to aim for abstinence) and with a rejection of the Disease concept. Hazelden, one of the most famous of the Minnesota Model treatment centres in the US, has for a long time combined a 12 Step approach with Ellis's Rational Emotive Therapy, didactic and psychoeducational group therapy and family or couples work.

During this period there have also been a number of psychoanalytically inspired therapies, usually modified considerably from classical analytic technique, which have maintained the importance of attending to unconscious psychological structures and the role of transference and countertransference in the treatment of drug and alcohol addicts. An example of this is the self-psychology influenced Modified Dynamic Group Therapy of Edward Khantzian and colleagues (Khantzian et al., 1990). This concentrates on vulnerabilities and deficits in affect tolerance, self-governance, self-esteem and relationships.

The Cognitive-Behavioural, Psychodynamic, and 12 Step approaches have sometimes been seen as distinct and separate, but in practice there has often been an eclectic approach and in some cases an attempt to create an integrated model.

Clouds House

The treatment setting within which this author has worked for the past 11 years is a residential treatment centre in Wiltshire, England, known as Clouds House. This centre has about 35 beds for alcohol- and drug-dependent people who are treated together within the same programme. Clouds House is a Minnesota Model centre in that it helps its residents towards abstinence from all mood-altering chemicals and introduces them to the 12 Step programme of Alcoholics Anonymous/Narcotics Anonymous. We recommend that people should continue to attend meetings of AA or NA after they complete their treatment. However the treatment programme has been in constant development and has always offered a great deal more than an introduction to the 12 Steps. The treatment consists mainly in the opportunity to participate in a community with a culture of recovery, in which each resident could identify, experience and reflect upon his or her interpersonal difficulties as they arose in the treatment group and with the staff, and could make a start on modifying these. These patterns of difficulty were related to those which the individual had experienced in the outside world, and were linked to the person's drinking or drug use. Each day the residents attend a 90-minute group therapy session: the model used is very close to Yalom's Interpersonal Group Therapy. The individual treatment plan would typically include such target problems as suppressed or out-of-control anger, low self-esteem, difficulty trusting or feeling close to others. The average stay is six weeks, and during this time the resident would receive a great deal of feedback from the peer group, and have the opportunity to help others in turn. The counselling relationship helps the resident to keep focused on the target problems and allows for reflection and discussion of the group and community experience. The staff may recommend to the more vulnerable individual that he or she should go on to spend three to six months in a 'secondary unit', which is a less structured residential setting, similar to a 'half-way house' with a programme of therapy building on what was worked on at Clouds. About half our completers go on to such a house.

A Changing Population

It has been noticed by our staff that over the last 10 years the people who are referred to us for residential treatment show on the average a greater degree of disturbance. They are less likely to be in marriages or stable sexual relationships, or in employment. They have a more chaotic life style, frequently with a history of involvement in criminal activity, which might predate their involvement with drugs. This has affected our completion rates, in particular because the staff have had to ask more people to leave the centre for behaviour unacceptable to the community. There are social and political reasons accounting in part for this change, and there is evidence that some drug users are less well prepared for treatment and less actively involved in their referral than they used to be. That this change is probably taking place across the field is supported by the preliminary findings of the National Treatment Outcome Research Study (NTORS). This large government-sponsored study found higher than expected levels of psychological distress in drug addicts entering treatment in 1995, especially those referred to residential treatment.

As a result of this shift the staff at Clouds have had to become more interested in the difficult client, the type of person with whom we tended to do less well, who was more likely to drop out, and who perhaps was very difficult to help in any setting. At Clouds we had always tried to open our doors as widely as possible, and our residents ranged from overtly successful, functional, well-resourced individuals to completely chaotic, damaged and fragmented people who had very little coping ability. Because the majority of our patients were funded through the NHS or jointly with Social Services, but some were privately funded, and because we took alcoholics and drug addicts together, this heterogeneity was even more marked. We seemed to be able to help a great range of people, and something about the treatment centre seemed to be very therapeutic, but this success, it seemed, could not be explained by the traditional model, and individual outcome was very unpredictable. The differences between the personalities and histories of our residents seemed just as important as the admittedly important similarities. The treatment staff did not have adequate conceptual tools to cope with these differences, and often had great difficulty in creative treatment planning. We often took refuge in formulaic procedures which we all knew would be good enough for some but not for others. This was frustrating. There was also no adequate way of understanding the emotional and behavioural effect on staff members of our patients' personalities.

Through this experience we came to feel that although addiction was a phenomenon with a wide range of severity, in nearly every case that we saw it manifested as a very serious set of problems that reflected a deep disturbance in interpersonal and intrapersonal relationship. This disturbance was of various kinds, but it usually involved internal conflict, and frequently involved state shifts and swings of mood and motivation which could not adequately be dealt with by traditional cognitive-behavioural approaches alone. In the treatment centre setting, the staff were paying more attention to analysing their own feelings and responses to the addicts in treatment. An awareness of pressures to respond in ways which repeated previous relationships entered the daily discussion and training seminars. While we were not offering analytic treatment, psychodynamic concepts were useful in understanding what was going on, and in formulating a strategy for action, even if it was as simple as seeking help to avoid being invited into a punitive or controlling or submissive or whatever relationship and trying to offer a different experience. The ideas of transference and countertransference, and projective identification were used to describe the interpersonal processes, although we found that the concepts themselves seemed to want to stay in the staff's unconscious! The other idea which was helpful was that of splitting, particularly in explaining highly polarized reactions in the staff team towards individual patients, and also in understanding sudden shifts in relationship. These ideas began to be used by treatment staff as an explanatory language to interpret current treatment procedures and to suggest new avenues of approach, not necessarily as part of a well worked out theory of personality, or of addiction. In other words, countertransference feelings seemed like a clinical reality, and the concept could be used pragmatically without having a clear understanding of how those feelings arise, or how the personality might be structured, or what exactly is the relationship between current behaviour, aims, feelings and thoughts and childhood experiences and fantasies. This was the context into which the theory and practice of CAT has been introduced over the past four years.

Addiction, Borderline Personality Structure, and Contemporary Psychodynamic Theory

The connection between addiction and borderline and/or narcissistic personality structure has been pointed out by various psychoanalytic authors (e.g. Knight, 1937; Wurmser, 1974; Kernberg, 1967, 1975; Rinsley, 1988; Hartocollis and Hartocollis, 1980; McDougall, 1989; Berger, 1991). There has been a progressive move away from the classical analytic view, in which addiction was connected to the regressive gratification or repression of instinctual demands, towards seeing it as an attempt at self-healing or coping with unmanageable affect. Krystal and Raskin (1970) see compulsive drug use as resulting from a failure of the holding environment, whereby the child's vulnerable self was not helped to tolerate anxiety and other unpleasant feelings in a traumatic situation, integrating these into the self structure, but was left threatened by primitive, overwhelming, psychosomatic affect. The effects of drugs, in addition to other dissociative mechanisms, are able to act as a protection against such states. Kohut (1977a) feels that the drug in addiction provides a substitute for a deficit in self structure, and he relates this to the deficit in narcissistic personality disorder. He says that 'the narcissistically disturbed individual yearns for praise and approval because he cannot sufficiently supply himself with self-approval or with a sense of strength through his own inner resources'. For the addict, Kohut, believes, the drug becomes 'a substitute for a self-object that failed him traumatically at a time when he should have had the feeling of omnipotently controlling its responses in accordance with his needs as if it were a part of himself'. This failure leads to a catastrophic lack of self-esteem and confidence. Ingesting the drug provides a feeling of soothing acceptance and/or merger. Inevitably the relief is only temporary, leading to a pattern of insatiable repetition. Khantzian and Mack (1989) have stressed the function of 'self-governance', and point out how the programme of AA is designed to make up for and correct defects in this function.

From an 'object relations' point of view, Krystal (1977) also gives a vivid account of an addict patient's split transferences with members of a treatment team, and points out that he or she is probably 'not experiencing a simple splitting of the transference into one love and one hate relation. The picture will be quite complex, and quickly changing.' He goes on to describe what in CAT terms would be seen as the sequential enactment of a reciprocal role repertoire, with switches in relationship triggered by disappointment or other difficult interpersonal situations.

CAT Theory, Borderline Personality and Addiction

CAT theory is helpful in modelling and understanding addictive behaviour from a variety of perspectives. An obvious feature of addictions is that they consist of continuing repeated use of mood-altering chemicals or behaviours despite harmful consequences. This idea links addictive patterns to CAT's Problem Procedures, and it is not hard to see how alcohol or drug use could play its part in a variety of Dilemmas, Traps or Snags. It is also clear that if the ingestion of a drug is 'mood-altering', then a theory of drug use must include an account of these mood changes: for some problematic users it is apparent that in a very short time a complete change of state may be effected, so that they think, feel and behave differently, and others experience them differently, as though they have undergone a 'change in personality'.

On an individual basis it is possible to describe how drug use affects a person's behaviour, the kind of thoughts and feelings they have before using and afterwards, the kind of situations which seem to produce cravings, and the effects of the using on self-care and relationships. Indeed this is the territory in which Cognitive Therapy is making its contribution. The CAT model may be used to develop these descriptions into a set of clear procedural sequences, in which the function of the drug use may be recognized. A particular individual may have learned to use drugs in any of the following ways: (*intrapsychic*) to soothe, to reduce anxiety, to feel confident, to feel powerful, to quieten inhibiting or critical inner voices, to relieve psychotic symptoms, to relieve boredom, to feel pleasure; (*relationally*) to allow closeness or affection, to allow sexual contact, to distance oneself, to feel superior, to punish the other, to dissociate.

This list could be considerably extended. It is clear that as a class chemically dependent people suffer from marked procedural restriction. The drugs are so effective in producing the desired mood change, that other less damaging ways of managing painful or difficult situations are not easily persisted with. It is also common for addicted people to have grown up in a family in which feelings were routinely medicated with chemicals, so early role-modelling of other ways of coping was not apparent. This restriction in the coping repertoire means that the progressively negative consequences of drug use are responded to with further use, thus setting up an accelerating spiral into severe dependence.

This is particularly true of those chemically dependent people who have suffered abuse or neglect. Various estimates have been made of the prevalence of sexual molestation among those who receive drug addiction treatment. Bollerud (1990) estimates 75% of female patients to have been sexually abused, and there are probably high rates of physical and sexual abuse among the male population in addiction treatment also. Several American studies, including the large Los Angeles epidemiologic catchment area study (Stein *et al.*, 1988), have found significantly higher lifetime prevalence of drug abuse/dependence among those who were sexually abused in childhood (36.6% vs 16.5% for the non-abused) and also a much higher prevalence of alcohol abuse/dependence (26.2% vs 5.5%).

The Level 1 reciprocal role procedures commonly developed by such people are the same as those described in Chapter 3: neglecting, abandoning and abusing in relation to deprived, guilty and either rebellious or crushed. Kaufman (1994) notes that female addicts in particular are often in competition with their mothers who are seen as authoritarian and overcontrolling. The patterns of behaviour which are elaborated to mitigate these core reciprocal roles, for example perfectionism, passivity, placation or submission, are clichés of the alcoholism and addiction field. At Level 2, dissociation, which can be achieved with or without the use of drugs, may be manifest in various 'schizoid' procedures usually involving intellectualization and living in a 'world without feelings', grandiosity and the devaluation of others. Evidence that survivors of childhood sexual abuse use drugs or alcohol to 'chemically dissociate' is provided by, for example, Roesler and Dafler (1993).

It is also striking that many addicted people cannot use words to name their feelings and as a result have difficulty differentiating or even being aware of their emotional states. Whether this is developed as a dissociative coping strategy, or whether it is a result of not being helped in childhood to develop a language of feelings is not clear, but it has obvious implications at Level 3, that of self-consciousness. Although dependent people often know theoretically that their difficult feelings provoke a strong impulse to use drugs or drink, and they may be able to describe specific examples from the past, it seems extremely difficult for them to make this connection in the experiencing present. It is not at all uncommon for, say, an alcohol-dependent person to become agitated or upset in an interpersonal situation, including an individual or group therapy session, to be more or less unaware of this feeling even if it is pointed out by others, to experience later an impulse to drink leading to a 'bender', and then to be unable to recognize any connection at all between the feeling state and the drinking.

To summarize the connections between BPD and addiction, it is my belief that a treatment population of addicted people who show clear dependence plus a range of interpersonal and social difficulties are likely to show patterns of experiencing and behaviour similar to those described as Borderline or Narcissistic Personality Disorder. Some will have experienced the serious trauma which according to the CAT account leads to the development of problematic procedures at three levels. These people have the added difficulty that their use of chemicals to cope has escalated into addiction.

Others, who might be described as 'neurotic' alcoholics or addicts, have had a less severely damaging upbringing, but are very often trying vainly to satisfy a tyrannical inner parent. Alcohol and drugs offer an escape, and also a way in which their rage may be experienced, usually in a highly self-destructive manner. Guilt and rebellious rage are dealt with by perfectionism and a need to be in control, while a craving to conform and submit to society's expectations is contrasted with the chaos, aggression and degradation of the intoxicated state. These are less volatile and fragmented than the 'true' borderline addicts, but the erosion of self-esteem concomitant upon the destructive effects of the addiction leads to a personality organization which has the fragility of NPD, where a hint of criticism is experienced as a devastating attack which must be fended off or retaliated against.

There is also a proportion of addicted people who seem to have become so through a combination of genetic vulnerability and a drinking or using culture, despite a 'good-enough' family environment and the development of a reasonably solid sense of self. Such people are of course damaged by their addiction but as a rule they are helped to recover fairly easily, and their recoveries are relatively unproblematic.

CAT in theory and practice ought to be able to assist the addicted population considerably, in that it has been found helpful with a range of problems including Borderline Personality Disorder, as well as with behaviours that have a relationship with addictive behaviours, such as eating disorders and self-harm (Cowmeadow, 1994; Denman, 1995). And indeed, our experience so far, which is illustrated below in a few case examples, is that CAT is a highly promising approach. However, the therapy of addicted people is notoriously problematic, and indications are that while CAT has a unique and powerful contribution to make, there are some characteristics of chemical addictions which may make CAT in its weekly outpatient format less effective than it is with other related disorders. I will describe these in the next section and suggest principles which are likely to maximize its effectiveness. It is worth noting that of 17 cases described in this book, 9 had substance abuse histories (Emma, Ch. 1; John, Ch. 3; Tom, Ch. 5; Philip, Ch. 6; Ivy, Nick and Jim, Ch. 7; Elaine, Ch. 8; and

Gregory, Ch. 9). Of four cases regularly abusing alcohol and the one using cannabis continuously during the therapy, only two had favourable outcomes.

Treatment Implications

The psychotherapy of addicted people is generally agreed to be difficult, and indeed many models of therapy exclude such people as being unlikely to benefit. Ryle, asked about the limitations of CAT, has expressed the view that CAT is an appropriate and safe intervention for most psychological problems except frank psychosis or chaotic substance abuse. The experiences of the therapists encountering severe drug and alcohol problems in their CAT outpatient practice at Guy's and St Thomas's have not been different to those of other therapists the world over: addiction usually seriously disrupts the therapy, there is unreliable attendance, patients may arrive intoxicated, and even when good productive work seems to be done in the therapy session, progress is easily obliterated by drug-using episodes. It is often a dispiriting experience for both therapist and patient. It is usually better to try to get such patients referred to a more intensive specialist addiction treatment service. This does not mean that the therapy is not worth doing. We have had a number of patients referred to Clouds recently who have previously had CAT at Guy's, and although it was not sufficient to help them control the addiction, it was felt to have been a useful part of the journey, and the insights gained are very helpful during the residential treatment and in recovery thereafter.

It is important, I believe, to consider why addictive behaviour is so difficult to modify. Behavioural and cognitive theories of appetitive and motivational distortion have been used to try to help alcohol-dependent people to control their drinking, but controlled drinking for many has turned to be a much more difficult achievement than the theory would predict. There are probably very complex reasons for this, but one of the important ones may be to do with the 'intoxicating' effects of alcohol and other drugs, which have often been dismissed by some psychologists keen to see addiction simply as 'behaviour', subject to the same laws as other behaviour. However for the vast majority of the addicted people we see, I believe ingesting a drug results in a major Level 2 state shift. The person seems to lose touch very quickly with the 'motivated self' and attitudes, intentions and behaviour change radically. The actual ways in which they change depend on the individual person and to some extent on which drug or drugs have been used. The persistence of drug effects may make the attempt to use CAT tools such as the diagram next to impossible.

With addicted people, it is important not to be too optimistic about the ability of the 'motivated self' to prevail in stressful situations, or after an alcohol or drug using episode has begun. I also feel that it is vital to recognize the deep distress of the addicted person, and to offer if possible a structured support system that might include a residential stay at a treatment centre, or an intensive day care programme, preferably combined with involvement in a self-help group such as Narcotics Anonymous.

It will be gathered from the foregoing remarks that I believe strongly that addicted persons with a high level of disturbance will be able to make significant life changes for the better only if they become abstinent. In most cases this will entail complete abstinence from all mood-altering drugs. Some of our patients may require appropriate medication if suffering from severe depression. There is some evidence that antidepressants do not interfere with abstinent recovery and do help to facilitate progress and prevent relapse. It is difficult to predict whose depression will remit fairly quickly without pharmacological help, and whose will persist to threaten recovery.

It has been found by some clinicians that people on well-controlled methadone maintenance can be helped to make progress in therapy, but my experience is that such people are at very high risk for illicit drug use and heavy alcohol use. Despite the belief on the part of many drug workers in the UK that complete abstinence is 'an unrealistic goal' for the more entrenched and chaotic drug user or drinker, I have seen many hundreds of severely addicted people from every social class and with histories of trauma and disrupted early lives make excellent recoveries based on abstinence. The key has been the instillation of hope that such a recovery is possible, and this is usually brought about through contact and communication with ex-addicts in recovery. Belief in this possibility is vital for the professionals involved as well, together with a realization that the stages of recovery, including preparing for abstinence, detoxification, learning to stay drug free, and gradually adjusting one's inner world and relationships to achieve more satisfaction and choice in life, is a long process, often requiring several years. During this process various brief interventions play their part as staging posts on the journey. This is where CAT can play a most important role.

Advantages of CAT

The structure and therapeutic tools of CAT offer specific advantages for working with addicted people who have recently achieved abstinence and are either in an intensive addiction treatment programme, or have recently left, or who have managed to get clean without such interventions. My experience is based on a CAT project at Clouds in which we have offered formal 16- or 20-session CAT for selected individuals, while incorporating tools such as the Psychotherapy File, SDRs and Rating Sheets into our standard treatment programme. The formal CAT is usually offered to those who have completed the residential 6-week programme, and who attend weekly as outpatients. I have seen three cases in which we started CAT during the residential programme, and the first 8–10 sessions take place twice weekly, with reformulation at session 5 or 6. The therapy continues with the same therapist after the patient returns home or goes to a 'half-way' house for a further 8–10 weekly sessions.

This is a very promising format as it offers continuing support during the stressful and anxiety-provoking transition from the residential community to a less structured environment. The opportunities to employ such a format have been limited due to our rural location. Two case examples are described below to illustrate this work with borderline patients.

The model offers four major advantages. First, it provides a way for an addict to identify, recognize and interrupt/modify procedural sequences which had consistently led to a poor result. This type of cognitive work was already familiar to our treatment staff, for example in asking addicts to recognize high-risk situations, and 'run the whole reel' (i.e. anticipate the consequences beyond the initial rewarding behaviour). Testing incorrect beliefs (e.g. every time I have a craving, I have to use) and replacing irrational self-statements with more positive, enhancing ones is a standard part of Relapse Prevention. A second major advantage of CAT is that it connects the current procedures to the person's story, including experiences in childhood. Third, it provides for developing a language for feelings and states. A fourth advantage of the model, of particular relevance for our Borderline patients, is in its potential for gathering and organizing the dissociated self states. A map of states with their prevailing reciprocal roles can be created which should include the relationship with the drugs and drug associations.

CAT offers a useful way of understanding countertransference feelings and attitudes as invitations into reciprocal role procedures. Staff members are often invited to play an idealized parent role, or else might be experienced as condemning and rejecting, or seductive and intrusive. The early development of a jointly created Self States diagram aids the staff members in anticipating and recognizing the roles they may be invited into, and helps the patients to recognize in a new way what is happening for them: in particular it seems helpful to acknowledge the powerful destructive rage which can be turned on the therapeutic process. It may be possible to marshal resources to contain and resist this destructiveness and so prevent a sabotage of treatment such as premature self-discharge, antisocial behaviour leading to discharge by the staff, or relapse to drug use.

Case Studies

These examples have been conflated from various cases to illustrate some typical difficulties with more problematic clients, and the application of CAT tools to address treatment and recovery issues.

Case 1: CAT and the Containment of a Disruptive Patient

Richard is a 29-year-old man referred to treatment for his addiction to alcohol, opiates, and amphetamines. Richard has several times sought help, and it is clear to him that alcohol and drugs cause him great problems and he wishes to give them up. He says he wants to settle down and earn a living, perhaps to start a family. In view of his non-existent work record and the break up of his two relationships due mainly to his abusive behaviour while drinking, he often feels hopeless about these goals and repudiates them. He was referred to six weeks of residential treatment with funding available for a residential extended care of several months. It is clear that someone like Richard will do best with a long period of support from drug-free peers, a supportive living environment, and long-term help in building skills for living. Research indicates that the longer Richard can be retained in a treatment setting, the better his outcome is likely to be.

History.
Richard was brought up in a tough suburb of Manchester. He is the eldest of three brothers. When he was a child, his father was authoritarian and often violent when drinking, both towards his wife and his sons. Richard reports feeling scared and unsafe much of the time as a child, but as an adolescent he was able to develop a role as the leader of a gang of mates and thereby gain some status and a feeling of safety. He began to drink heavily and take a variety of drugs in his early teens and he and his friends were often in trouble with the authorities. He felt he had to be 'top dog', but maintaining this position led him into considerable conflict with others. He served several sentences in Youth Custody, and has served three adult jail sentences. The earlier convictions were for assault and burglary, the latter two were for drug offences involving petty dealing. He has had two fairly long-lasting relationships with girlfriends, and during these in particular, Richard has felt a powerful wish to 'sort himself out' and to 'get his life together'. He is experienced by those who get to know him as an intelligent, affectionate and likeable man, but one who is volatile and prone to sudden mood changes. He has mainly used alcohol, and he has a string of alcohol-related consequences including accidents and violence. He has also several times used heroin on a daily basis to the point of severe physical dependence, and he says he is psychologically dependent on amphetamines. He reports injecting the heroin and amphetamines as frequently as they are available, in various quantities up to a gramme of street heroin and two or more grammes of amphetamine sulphate per day. His 'habits' have been interrupted by prison sentences, and although he has used drugs in prison, his pattern has been to lose his physical dependence and to exercise to a good level of fitness. He uses a similar strategy in prison to achieve a feeling of safety as he used in childhood and adolescence: he gathers a small gang of friends and tries to maintain his 'top dog' position by intimidating others. If he does not feel in control in this way he feels extremely anxious and agitated. This leads to drug cravings. He often feels a powerful resentment towards authority figures of whom he is both afraid and extremely contemptuous. He often displays defiant behaviour which leads to more control from the authorities.

Behaviour in the centre.
In the treatment centre he began to behave in a way which was quite likely to get himself discharged. He was in a centre with a wide range of clients, both alcohol- and drug-dependent, and he was asked to mix as widely as possible with his group. He quickly gathered a little clique of drug users from a similar background to himself. This is quite usual and to be expected, but when challenged he found it hard to change this behaviour, and more worryingly, he began to be rude and intimidating to other members of the client group and to the night staff. There were, however, times, particularly during group therapy sessions, when Richard was more open about his behaviour and about his experience of himself. He said he felt like two different people, and when asked to enlarge on this, talked about his 'top dog' position, and another state in which he felt lonely and cut off from others.

Construction of the diagram.
In supervision the staff team talked about Richard's situation: some had reacted to his inconsistent presentation by feeling he was 'playing games' and had felt he should be discharged for making the community unsafe for others. However, when his procedure of intimidation was linked to his having had to cope and try to stay safe in many situations throughout his life—in his family, on the street and in prison—and when it was pointed out that this aim took precedence and prevented him from making any of his professed goals realistically attainable, the staff felt they had a better understanding. A diagram (Figure 10.1) was sketched out, based on two self states: one *aggressive control in relation to vulnerable* and the other *cut off, out of reach of feeling and others*. This seemed to help map both Richard's procedures and the staff's reactions (feeling vulnerable, wanting to reject and control). Richard's counsellor decided to present him with this diagram, explaining that it derived from what he had said about himself and inviting him to help modify the diagram if necessary.

Effect of the diagram.
The diagram was immediately meaningful to Richard, and produced a noticeable change of attitude. He was asked to reflect on certain new behaviours such as becoming more trusting and vulnerable with his peers, and it was found that the diagram enabled him to stay on this unfamiliar territory for longer and to resist flipping out of it when he felt insecure. He also learned that although the relationships offered at the centre were very different to those available in prison, the feeling of threat was similar, and his way of staying safe deprived him of the possibility of help. The aim of this intervention at this stage was primarily to lessen the likelihood of premature discharge. Later a 'snag' was identified in which Richard felt that if he 'made good' he would be rejected by his family and those of his background, and that he would be 'boring'.

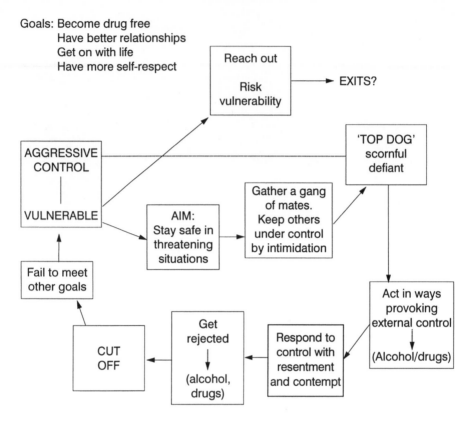

Figure 10.1   Richard A: draft SDR

I have met many Richards in treatment, and my colleagues agree that they cause difficult dilemmas for residential treatment staff. They are in great need of help and often want change very much, but they are very likely to discharge themselves or to provoke premature disciplinary discharge. Their ability to initiate and maintain change in the community is usually quite limited, at least partly due to instability of mood. The CAT approach, while not offering miraculous solutions, has shown itself useful in increasing retention and giving the client an experience of being understood. New insights should have immediate practical use, and the approach can be extended when the person undergoes necessary transitions such as the return to independent living in the community. I would strongly recommend Richard to seek mutual help in, for example, Narcotics Anonymous, and here again a CAT approach can help Richard to have realistic expectations of this and other resources and to make productive use of them.

Case 2: Multi-impulsive Behaviour

History.
Sarah is a 26-year-old woman, who was referred to residential treatment for her alcohol and drug dependency, but who has a long history of difficulties dating back to childhood. She was often in trouble at school and at home, and between the ages of 12 and 14 she occasionally ran away for a few days, usually staying with older youths in a squat, but once sleeping rough in a field overnight. She began to experiment with cannabis and alcohol at about this age. During adolescence she had problems with overeating, but during her adult life she has maintained a fairly skinny figure through using drugs and 'not bothering to eat'. She left school at 16 and from 18 she had a variety of jobs such as barmaid and club hostess, usually for short periods. When she was 21 she was raped, leading to a pregnancy. The child was given up for adoption at birth and Sarah kept this episode more or less to herself until telling a counsellor about it a year ago. She has had a number of boyfriends most of whom have been violent towards her, and she has had periods of prostitution which she says were to support her drug habit. Over the last few years Sarah has used increasing amounts of cocaine, alcohol and cannabis, with some opiate use. She has not been able to give up for more than a day or two. Sometimes she becomes suicidally depressed, although she has only once made a serious suicidal gesture, and on other occasions she makes superficial cuts on her arms with a knife or razor. She has a couple of recent convictions for shoplifting and a couple of earlier ones for soliciting.

Behaviour in the centre.
Sarah presented in a variety of ways, and provoked various emotional and behavioural reactions among the staff. She could appear somewhat submissive and compliant, saying that she definitely wanted help and wanted to stay at the centre. At these times she seemed vulnerable and counsellors felt protective towards her. More than one male counsellor identified that these feelings had a sexual undertone. Within the community she gravitated towards a couple of the male addict patients, both of whom had histories of violent behaviour. She said to her counsellor that she didn't want their attentions, which she felt were predatory, but she continued to 'hang out' with them. She said she felt sorry for them. At times, most markedly in group therapy, she seemed withdrawn, silent and cut off. At other times she seemed rebellious and rejecting of the staff's concerns. These concerns were stirred up considerably after it was discovered that Sarah was secretly inducing herself to vomit after meals, and after an incident when she was discovered by a nurse alone in her (shared) bedroom, holding a safety razor. She had made one superficial nick to her forearm.

Construction and use of the diagram.
The staff group's reaction to these behaviours was to become anxious and to discuss whether it was possible to keep her in the community. There was a guilty

and helpless feeling engendered, together with the idea that this could best be dealt with by 'getting rid' of her. It had to be recognized that if these behaviours were to continue she would end up by being discharged and would not get the help she needed. So it was decided to construct a diagram with Sarah's help. Her counsellor went to discuss with her the various self states we were observing and to ask her to elaborate on these. We came up with an *Ideal Care* state in which she either wished to take care of damaged others, or in which she was vulnerable and submissive, wishing to be understood and taken care of. In relationships, she would typically end up being *abused and overwhelmed*, and in relation to carers she would feel criticized or misunderstood, and withdraw in disappointment. She would either *angrily rebel*, pushing others away, or go into a *cut off, disconnected* state. She was able to agree these readily and ventured that she had often experienced herself as a 'split personality'.

The counsellor asked if she agreed that the self-cutting and vomiting behaviours could be seen as abusing herself, but Sarah felt they had more to do with being in a distracted, cut off state, devoid of real feeling. These behaviours together with drinking and using drugs 'took her pain away'. She thought the abuse state was mainly enacted with men.

At this point the self states had not been reliably linked to childhood experiences, as Sarah had not yet reported much about this period except to say that she was always in trouble. She said she didn't remember much about her early years. The staff decided not to probe into this but to base the reformulation on what was being enacted. A self states diagram was prepared (Figure 10.2). Sarah seemed to respond to the attempt to understand her in this way, and she agreed to a self-monitoring exercise, and to share her diagram with her group members, asking them to help her identify her states. At the same time a clear behavioural contract was drawn up under which she was to avoid self-cutting and self-induced vomiting, and she was to take responsibility to spend less time with her male peers and to try to develop communication and friendship with others in her group. It was made clear that unless she was seen to be doing her best to abide by this contract, her stay at the centre was in jeopardy. She was very scared by the contract as she was unsure of whether she would be able to keep to its terms, but she agreed to try. It so happened that she did induce vomiting on two further occasions, but she sought out staff immediately and reported this. She was expecting to be discharged, but it was pointed out that she was successfully addressing some of the other issues in the contract and that therefore she should carry on. We referred regularly to the diagram and encouraged her to use it to identify where she and others were on a daily basis.

The staff came to recognize that the wish to get rid of her was partly to do with cutting off from the anxious and conflicting feelings she induced in us. The diagrammatic reformulation allowed us to stand more of her for longer. Some of the team became aware that they felt abused by her angry, help-rejecting behaviour. We still had to send a clear message about what was and was not

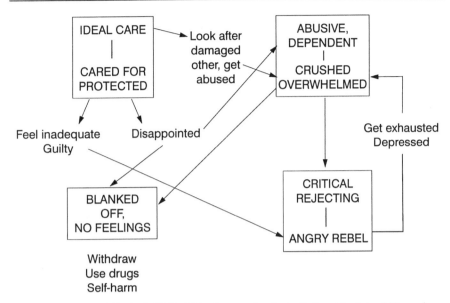

Figure 10.2   Sarah B: draft SDR. This diagram tracks both Sarah's state shifts and those experienced by the staff in relation to her

acceptable behaviour, and we had to arrange not to collude with her interpersonal procedures. We might well have had to discharge her, and she remained an uncertain prospect for secure recovery. We felt she would benefit from an extended stay in a structured environment, as not only would some of her procedures be likely to reinstate themselves, but also, like Richard, she had a snag based on beliefs that she could not and did not deserve to succeed in life. She is a high risk for drop out from any programme, residential or otherwise, and would almost certainly benefit from a moderately extended (24–40-session) individual CAT alongside involvement in Narcotics Anonymous and/or an aftercare group following her residential treatment.

CHAPTER 11

CAT of an Offender with Borderline Personality Disorder

PHILIP H. POLLOCK

There is a high incidence of Borderline Personality Disorder (BPD) within criminal populations (Meloy, 1988; Raine, 1993). Diagnostic criteria (DSM-IV, APA, 1994) include some impulsive and antisocial behaviours (e.g. reckless driving, physical fighting) and empirical studies with differing groups of offenders, including those who engage in drug misuse (McManus *et al.*, 1984), sexually deviant crimes (Kroll *et al.*, 1980) and murder (Gacono and Meloy, 1994), have shown notable associations between this diagnosis and criminal behaviours. The inclusion of certain antisocial behaviours within the criteria for the disorder (DSM-IV, APA, 1994) has prompted theorists and researchers to examine its common features with, and its differential diagnosis from, antisocial personality disorder. DSM-IV acknowledges the differing expression of violence by the individual with APD (aggression used for gain) and with BPD (aggression expressed in interactions with significant, caring others). For example, Benjamin (1993) pointed out that intense affect (e.g. rage, fear) occurs in the context of difficulties in relations with significant others, such as anticipated abandonment by a perceived caregiver. The resultant angry feelings may coerce care by controlling the caregiver or may provoke rejection and destroy this relationship (Pollock, 1996). Meloy (1988) proposed that, in close relationships, affective violence may be expressed impulsively by borderline subjects, often culminating in murder. Raine (1993) demonstrated that two specific features of BPD (unstable and intense interpersonal relationships and affective lability) were directly related to violence in those offenders diagnosed with the disorder. Raine also demonstrated that the greater the dimensional scores obtained on BPD measures the more violent was the index offence. A recent study by Pollock (1996) comparing male murderers with a sample of non-violent offenders revealed significantly higher mean scores on structured interview and self-report measures for borderline, passive-aggressive and self-defeating personality dimensions for the group of murderers. Comparisons on these dimensions considering offence types (e.g. sexual murder of a female compared to the killing of a male stranger) did not show significant differences. Although not unequivocal these findings support the theoretical proposal that borderline pathology is an important factor in understanding violent interpersonal behaviour. In summary, research findings support the view that aspects of BPD may be expressed through antisocial behaviours and may result in contact with forensic health services.

The Multiple Self States Model of BPD and Violence

Meloy (1988) and Fonagy *et al.* (1983) postulate that the violent and antisocial behaviour often exhibited by the offender with BPD is a reflection of attachment pathology, typically originating from 'hard' caregiving encounters with cruel, invalidating and abusing parents who are experienced as malevolent and painful (see also Meloy, 1992; Linehan, 1993). In CAT terms describing the internalized core of reciprocal role procedures (RRPs) is seen as central to analysing the connection between the violent act and his/her functioning. The relational repertoire of the violent BPD offender may be understood in CAT terms using the Multiple Self States Model (see Chapter 3).

An assumption of the Multiple Self States Model is that the BPD offender has a fragmented sense of self and others due to the alternating predominance of two or more discrete, conflicted and contradictory self states. The individual retains some awareness of the experiences of other self-states, unlike those with Dissociative Identity Disorder, and will often sharply oscillate between these disparate states of being, some of which are associated with crude and intense affects (Horowitz *et al.*, 1994) such as envy, rage and fear. Specific situations which evoke perceptions or memories of a previous trauma (for example a delayed return by, or implied criticism from, a partner) may be felt as repetition of the original event and result in an abrupt and unpredictable state switch (i.e. from idealized fusion to abandoned/deprived) and may mobilize feelings of panic from abandonment or rage at humiliation. Traumatic experiences with caregivers in the formative development of the child (e.g. sexual and physical abuse, emotional neglect) distort the acquisition of the individual's repertoire of reciprocal role procedures (Level 1), causing a number of specific personality deficits and incapacities. The individual is likely to internalize RRPs derived from malevolent and damaging parent–child interactions such as *aggressive predator* in relation to *victimized prey* (Meissner, 1988; De Zulueta, 1994), *controlling tyrant* in relation to *persecuted martyr*, or a *cruel/neglecting parent* in relation to *deprived/unfulfilled* child. These RRPs predominate and colour the future repertoire of transactions of the child, and later adult, affecting intimate relationships and self-management procedures and resulting in difficulties in several areas of his/her functioning. For example, the BPD offender may engage in parent-derived sadistic acts by creating sexual offence scenarios whereby reciprocal child-derived roles (e.g. impotent, abused) are induced in others, such patterns originating from internalized reciprocal roles derived from *attachment figure-to-attached person* relationships. Reckless misuse of illicit drugs may be observed in the individual's self-management procedures, representing a way of attaining a state of blissful fusion (with an imagined, idealized parent), a way of avoiding a state of emotional emptiness (child-derived) or a form of attack on the self.

Sudden changes in behaviour may represent oscillation between the two poles of an RRP (role reversal), a shift between alternative responses to the same other pole (response shift) or a switch to a different self-state in which an entirely different reciprocal role pattern operates. A self state switch may occur during an offence, for example when a previously idealized female victim is perceived as rejecting, frustrating and devalued prior to the act of rape (Meloy, 1988). Negative RRPs in BPD stem from a traumatic, preoccupied and unresolved attachment style resulting in restricted and pathological patterns of relating. Marlowe (1994) suggested that these partial, split-off RRPs remain unintegrated (i.e. in dissociated self states) throughout the individual's development and persist into adulthood.

BPD sufferers are seen to be incapable of conceiving their own mental state or that of others due to 'inhibition of mentation' (Morton and Frith, 1995); this is seen to be caused by their defensive avoidance of contemplating the abusing parent's state of mind (Fonagy, 1989). The CAT model suggests that an impaired capacity for self-reflection is further disrupted by state switches (Level 3; see Chapter 3). In this respect, the BPD offender's chaotic and confusing experience of relationships and the self, coupled with a lack of recognition and revision of self-perpetuating harmful RRP patterns and the accompanying raw affective states associated with some roles, renders containment and management very problematic. It is here that methodical formulation using CAT can be of value.

CAT with Offenders

A number of case studies have been reported which demonstrate the application of personal construct theory (Kelly, 1955) and CAT ideas to the reformulation of offender's personality functioning and offence behaviours. These include descriptions of the treatment of two violent females (Pollock and Kear-Colwell, 1994) and a subsequent investigation of the importance of the abusing-victimized RRP in seven violent female offenders. In these patients, experiences of dissociated states were found to be a prominent feature of their personality functioning (Pollock, 1996) and CAT was shown to be a valuable method of reformulating these cases and improving the offender's self-understanding and control of these dissociated self-states. A basic tenet of CAT reformulations in forensic cases is that the offence may be understood as the enactment between offender and victim of an identifiable reciprocal role, such as abusing-to-victimized representing an extreme example of forcing the victim to enact the complementary pole of the reciprocal role (see Ryle (1994a) for a reinterpretation of projective identification in CAT terms).

This pattern may at other times be enacted with the self (e.g. self-injury) or may be reversed, with others induced into the offending role. For example, the assault, binding, rape and murder of a stranger may represent the enactment of an *attacking/controlling* role in relation to the *impotent/abused* victim. Such patterns are frequently derived from aggrieved relationships, firstly with the offender's undermining and humiliating mother and, more recently, with a critical and controlling girlfriend. When the offender' behaviour can be understood as representing the enactment of a particular role, and equally when such a role is a feature of a dissociated self state, therapy must seek to counter dissociation and strengthen self-reflection and control. This may require the construction, with the offender, of a Self State Sequential Diagram (SSSD) and the use of this by the offender, as a tool for self-monitoring, and by clinical staff as a means of recognizing and avoiding collusion with the relevant procedures or for prediction of the offender's potential behaviour.

The following case study describes the use of CAT with a BPD offender. It includes selected excerpts of therapy dialogues to illustrate the use of this treatment with forensic populations.

Case Example: Lee

Lee is a 34-year-old man detained in a secure hospital for several years. He was convicted of a series of sexual offences against post-pubertal males for which he initially received prison sentences prior to being placed in secure psychiatric hospitals. He has received diagnoses of borderline personality disorder, factitious disorder (combined physical and psychological symptoms), sexual masochism and homosexual paedophilia. His problems remained unimproved despite a number of therapies (supportive, behavioural and cognitive-behavioural) with a variety of therapists, with all of whom Lee had terminated contact. His medication regime changed frequently depending on the presenting complaint (typically fabricated physical symptoms with no medical aetiologies). Lee displayed a chronic pattern of self-harm including genital and abdominal insertion of sharp objects, wrist-cutting and attempted overdosing. He was grossly obese and non-compliant to a diet-controlled regime for his diabetes. Lee had been dependent on psychiatric services for many years; he endured an open hospital for only two weeks out of 11 years before returning to secure accommodation following self-injury. Lee was born the eldest of four children into a poor family. His mother had an extensive psychiatric history including bipolar mood disorder and alcohol dependency. Lee's father worked overseas and was largely absent. His mother was reported to have been severely sexually and physically abusive to Lee (not his siblings) resulting, at times, in his hospitalization. He claims to have sexually assaulted both of his sisters and he experienced numerous episodes of sexual abuse by older boys after being detained in Borstal for theft, criminal damage and assaulting staff at school. Lee recalled one sadistic sexual assault by an older man which had caused physical injuries to his head and genital area. His lifestyle from the age of 17 to 26 years was itinerant, with no meaningful relationships, repeated incidents of self-injury and multiple admissions to hospital for nebulous physical complaints. He committed sexual assaults on young boys. These sexual offences showed a consistent feature in that Lee would offer help to the victim, then accost him violently, tie and sexually assault him, then force the victim to injure him during the assault.

Assessment

Lee completed a repertory grid (Kelly, 1955), read and discussed the Psychotherapy File and was requested to keep a self-monitoring diary of his moods, associated cognitions and reactions. His profiles on the Millon Clinical Multiaxial Inventory-2(MCMI-2; Millon, 1987) and the Personality Disorder Interview-IV (Widiger *et al.*, 1995) demonstrated borderline, histrionic, passive-aggressive and antisocial features with a score of 19 on the Hare Psychopathy Checklist-revised (PCL-R; Hare, 1991) suggesting a moderate level of psychopathic tendencies. On the Symptom Checklist-90-revised (Derogatis, 1983) Lee showed interpersonal sensitivity, anxiety, hostility and somatization. On the basis of Lee's presentation, an SSSD was constructed with him (Figure 11.1) and used as a pivotal tool in the subsequent therapy of 24 sessions for which he contracted. Two recurrent self states were identified and considered to reflect Lee's core relational configurations. Self state 2 is defined by a central RRP of a *rescuing/redeeming caregiver* in relation to a *perfectly cared for child*. Lee described this state as existing only in fantasy, and perceived it as unattainable and impelled by an intense fear of abandonment. Self state 1 consisted of a *sadistically attacking parent* in relation to a *terrorized, injured and hating child*. This can be seen to be akin to the 'stranger selfobject' described by Grotstein (1982) which, in CAT terms, represents the internalization of reciprocal role procedures characterized as *predator-to-prey* associated with sadism, violence and cruelty towards the self and others (Meloy, 1988).

Referring to Lee's SSSD, a number of procedural loops generated from the two main self states were defined as focal targets in therapy sessions. Lee's need to seek unattainable perfect care from a rescuing figure (derived from experiencing SS2) led to recurrent disappointment and unmet needs causing a state switch from SS2 to SS1, the central RRP of which originates from Lee's early

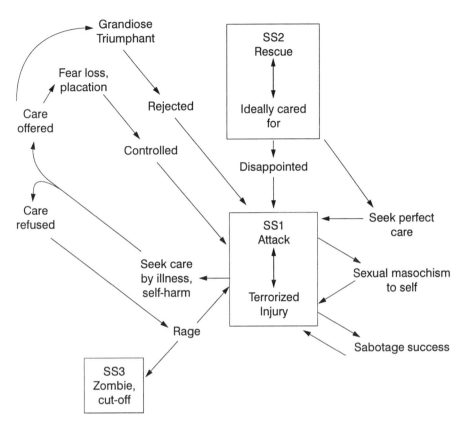

Figure 11.1   Lee: Self States Sequential Diagram

caretaking experiences. SS1 was often expressed in the enactment of an interpersonal offence, most typically in the form of a sexual attack on a young boy
and the enactment of both reciprocal roles of the RRP of SS1 at differing times
during the act. A frequent trap (Ryle, 1979) was also a product of SS1 in which
Lee would enact the underlying RRP with the self during sexual masochism,
representative of an identification with the attacking role of the RRP. A snag
from SS1 was also observed in which Lee would sabotage improvement due to
his self-hatred and belief that he was undeserving of positive steps towards
independence.

One specific procedural loop discusses Lee's attempts to gain needed care
from others by fabricating a variety of symptoms or cutting himself, forcing
nursing staff to attend to him. A procedural dilemma was subsequently
observed whereby if care was offered, he would triumphantly and arrogantly
destroy the relationship due to his expectation of rejection. When this outcome
did occur, Lee's feelings of rejection would lead to enactment of SS1.

Alternatively, he would fear loss of the relationship and placate the carer, resulting in feelings of being controlled similar to the state experienced with his mother.

A differing procedural loop occurred if care was refused. Lee typically experienced rage and fear culminating either in hate and emotional pain and a wish to attack others (e.g. in an offence) or a cut-off, 'shut down' and affectively blank zombie state (self-state 3, SS3) representing a response to his own intense rage or to a terrifying or terrorizing other. After a review of Lee's self-monitoring of his moods, reactions and behaviour and reference to the diagram the following dialogue at session 7 occurred between Lee and the therapist (*TH*):

TH I notice that you have recorded that you feel confused about how you should approach other people, particularly nursing staff, when you feel in need of attention or help or meaningful contact with them.

L Wouldn't you? they sit around all day, no interest in patients and then they ignore you unless you are agitated or something else.

TH What would that something else be? and what is the confusion about?

L Well, I begin to feel irritated, then paranoid, then worried and tense, then even more angry at them ... I then feel I have to give in to the urge to do 'something' ... I don't know.

TH Can I refer to the diagram we put together and the part of it which shows how you seek care from others, or not ... we agreed this was an area we should focus on ... it appears that you believe you can only do one of two things to obtain care ... you think you either have to harm yourself or claim to have physical symptoms to get others involved with you or you avoid others, withdraw and feel deprived ... is that the way it happens? neither of these ways of behaving work or lead to what you would wish for.

L Yeah, I have to do that because they're not interested and don't give a damn ... they won't pay any attention unless I do, and even then it's rubbish care, isn't it?

TH You feel they withhold the care you need at times?

L I deserve (*angry*), you can't depend on them or they palm you off with medication, big deal! ... that takes a lot of effort!

TH Have you ever sought to test out the possibility that others may willingly provide what you need? perhaps not all of them, it would be unrealistic to expect everyone to care ... but what about some members of staff who you get on well with, one you trust and have faith in?

L I don't know, they wouldn't do as much with me as they do when I do this (*refers to cuts on arm*), this ensures they do something ... same with physical things.

TH Where do you think that need to obtain care, even in some ways forcing others to provide it, comes from? when did you first experience that?

L When my parents didn't come to see me on my birthday ... I was in bed with a broken leg in the Borstal, as usual I waited and they didn't turn up

... I felt pure hate for them that day, especially her (*begins to become visibly angry and tearful*) and I thought why do my brothers and sisters get to stay at home and all that love ... she then 'phoned up drunk and said I was her favourite ... I cut myself and then hit one of the staff ... later I would cut myself and go to the hospital casualty ... if they admitted me I'd fight with the doctors and nurses and tell them where to stick their help.

TH And if they didn't?

L   I'd feel totally ... devastated, betrayed, disillusioned ... my temper would flare and I'd start to feel like committing an offence (*tearful*).

TH Against who?

L   A boy ... I'd think about it for a while and then it would become too much ... I'd either cut myself and not remember, or overdose or assault a young boy ... the perfect offence was abusing the boy and getting him to hurt me at the same time.

TH Like the last offence?

L   Yeah ... I abused him and he punished me at the same time ... it bonded me to him ... it felt secure in some way.

TH Why that young boy at that time in that way?

L   He reminded me of when I was abused ... he was unspoiled, then he was like my prey ... I was in control of it, he couldn't do anything ... that's when I tied him up.

TH So you could play out the 'brutal predator' you named here? (*refers to self state 1*) and you get punished at the same time? how did you feel afterwards?

L   Gutted ... full of anger and hate for myself ... even more confused.

TH How could you maybe do things differently? an exit from this pattern of manipulating care or getting no care, then ending up either harming yourself, thinking of harming others or ruining relationships (*referring to SSSD*) and feeling panicky about possible abandonment like you did when your parents let you down ... could you actively select a member of nursing staff you trust, approach him or her and openly ask for help with your feelings at the time ... you anticipate you'll not get the right care or it will be withheld ... let's see.

Lee's description demonstrated a shift between alternate poles of the RRP of SS1 (*attacking* to *hating/injured*). Within the course of the offence he assumes each role at differing times. This corresponds to Rappoport's proposal (cited by Meloy, 1992) that the offender attempts to 'resonate' with his/her victim. Following from this session, Lee reported approaching a member of nursing staff when feeling depressed and requesting help on three occasions over the next week. He recalled feeling disappointed that he did not feel satisfaction from these interactions but acknowledged the nurse's genuine attempts to help. He was able to further self-observe the switch between SS1 and SS2 in his SSSD and, although he felt anxious at 'the unknown' feelings of not enacting either pole of this RRP, he persisted. The predicted transference pattern emerged when Lee accused the therapist of being unavailable and witholding care when he was distressed and not being 'on tap' when required. Reference was made to the SSSD and the wish for an idealized rescuing therapist in relation to Lee's need to seek perfect care. The unrealistic expectation within this pattern was pointed out and he was encouraged to tolerate the care he received and learn to soothe and calm himself using cognitive and behavioural techniques.

An important trap for Lee (derived from SS1) was that of the 'punished martyr' whereby his self-hatred and guilt (in relation to a sadistic and controlling parent) led to sexual masochism which then served to confirm his belief regarding his unlovability. The following therapy conversation occurred to address this self-perpetuating pattern:

TH When you say that you have fantasies of abusing young boys, what typically happens?

L I don't get sexually aroused or anything ... I feel depressed, low ... then guilty and want to hurt myself ... no one could talk me out of that idea if I'm in it, it's like a compulsion ... I hate myself, then I'll harm myself, there's no pain.

TH So that self-harm is for a different reason?

L Yes and no ... it does both, I get care but I feel better for harming myself. My mother wouldn't hit me for a while, I'd be confused ... I'd do something to get into trouble and then she would hit me and I'd feel better, less confused, it would make sense, she'd say 'you're evil, you need to be beaten'.

TH But what about now? your mother has little or no contact with you, why do you still maintain that pattern of behaving? you act towards yourself in the same way your mother did to you ... you almost act sadistically towards yourself on her behalf.

Lee showed significant progress within the 24 sessions except for the trap involving sexual masochism which he found difficult to manage on occasions and described as 'almost a compulsion'. This required repeated reference to the diagram and tolerance for periodic relapses of this problem which, however, occurred less frequently and intensely during one year follow-up. Positive changes were observed from post-therapy testing on symptom measures and Lee began to undertake work training, attending a hostel and preparing for independent living.

Specific Clinical Issues

In the CAT of the BPD offender who has a violent history, a number of specific transference and countertransference patterns derived from the underlying RRPs of the offender's core repertoire are observable and particularly relevant.

The emergence of hostility and destructiveness is very common and often emanates from restricted and polarized RRPs such as *abusing/victimized, sadistic control/helpless, persecuted* which are reversible during abrupt state switches within the therapeutic relationship. This was observed in Lee's switch from relating to and perceiving the therapist as *idealized/rescuing* to *attacking/controlling*. On these occasions, there is a real potential for destructive acting out towards the therapist, to others or to the patient him/herself. Efforts must be made to use the CAT reformulation to contain the patient and also to aid the therapist in managing this situation and to avoid reciprocation of the role which the patient may be inducing (e.g. *aggressor, abandoning*). For Lee, the nature of the RRPs constituting both self states led to incidents within the therapy. When in SS1 the therapist was perceived as a persecutor who was threatening and abusing (the patient feeling vulnerable, controlled and despairing). This could be followed by an abrupt switch into SS2 in which the therapist felt urged to rescue the suffering patient from his despondency by considering initiation of medication and providing more time for Lee. The use of the SSSD and the therapist's non-collusion serve to guide the patient towards internalizing, over time, more adaptive and flexible RRPs such as *accept/sustaining* in relation to *nurtured*, a pattern modelled by the therapist. This represents a revision at stage 5 of the procedural sequence (Ryle, 1990) allowing a more adaptive choice of roles.

A further transference pattern may emerge in which the patient's perception of a persecuting therapist and his fear of sadistic control (e.g. self state 1) results in the emergence of paranoid feelings in the patient. Lee reported that the construction of the letter and SSSD at the beginning of therapy had made him feel anxious and he described 'seeing red eyes on the wall' of his bedroom and the therapist's consulting room; he stated that these interventions made him 'feel cornered and vulnerable'. Lee was encouraged to understand this reaction in terms of his RRP repertoire and his fear of attack at the hands of a sadistic and controlling parent. Lee also reported feeling anxious about the letter saying that it represented a loss or absorption of his identity by the therapist, although he responded positively to its contents and acknowledged its usefulness. Identification of such reactions is important given the relationship between paranoid states and violent behaviours (Hodgson, 1993).

Evaluation of CAT in Forensic Cases

The value of CAT reformulations in the treatment of offenders lies in its ability to locate where, in the complex self-perpetuating and harmful procedural patterns, individuals may engage in extremely destructive and damaging behaviour. The identification of the RRPs which are enacted between offender and victim represents a particular strength of such reformulations, providing a powerful aid to explaining to the offender the nature and causes of his actions and facilitating an exploration of the origins of these procedures. Many treatment approaches for offending behaviour fail to emphasize the need to define this interpersonal dimension between offender and victim, or fail to do so in a manner which provides relatively simple, concise and accessible descriptions.

The joint construction and use of the SSSD informs the therapeutic responses of the therapist by anticipating transference and countertransference patterns, and assisting the avoidance or early recognition of unintended collusion. Caring staff may also use the SSSD to devise individually designed care plans for offenders which provide consistent, helpful management.

The identification of abrupt switches between self states, which (as in the present case) may be experienced as unpredictable, difficult to comprehend and control, helps the offender to self-observe and manage his reactions, including those which may lead to the criminal act. The therapist's task in these cases very often includes making predictions of the offender's potential behaviour, predictions which influence discussions concerning release, rehabilitation and risk estimations. The SSSD helps the therapist to base such predictions on a detailed knowledge of the relevant aspects of the offender's functioning.

CHAPTER 12

CAT in Context

The aims of this final chapter are (1) to summarize the actual and potential clinical applications of CAT, alone or in combination with other approaches, to the treatment of BPD, (2) to consider how far CAT may be considered to be 'evidence-based', (3) to propose that CAT theory raises questions about other theoretical systems which deserve discussion, and (4) to place the treatment of BPD in a wider social context.

The Clinical Scope of CAT for Borderline Patients

As already indicated, time-limited CAT seems to be an adequate therapy for a considerable proportion of patients. In the remainder, however, longer or repeated interventions may be called for, and other treatments may be needed. This is not surprising since, given the long duration and complex psychopathology of BPD, no single intervention is likely to be adequate for all cases, and a comprehensive service should provide a range of treatments. Had such a service dedicated to the treatment of severe personality disorders been available when the patients described in this book were treated it would have been possible to consider in more detail the scope of CAT and its relation to other interventions. In reality, the underfunding and successive reorganizations affecting mental health services in Britain over the past decade and the low priority granted to psychological treatments meant that the available alternatives were very limited.

In this situation, the actual options for further treatment for patients not responding adequately to the CAT intervention were (1) a return to the psychiatric outpatient service or mental health centre which had referred them, (2) an attempt to find a trained cognitive-behavioural psychologist or nurse who might build on the CAT understandings with behavioural and problem-oriented work, (3) group therapy, for some patients, especially those who were socially isolated, where vacancies in suitable groups could be found, or (4) a further CAT treatment.

Between a quarter and a third of patients were referred on for one or other of these options, the remainder being satisfied with the changes achieved. This use of CAT to treat unselected borderline outpatients has, I believe, established that it can make an effective and economical contribution to the treatment of BPD. These results, and the process studies being carried out by Bennett (see Bennett and Parry, in press), have established that CAT is now ready for inclusion in comparative trials, as soon as funding and practitioners of a contrasting method who are willing to participate can be found.

Integrating Different Treatments

Of equal importance, the simultaneous or sequential combination of CAT with other psychological treatment approaches needs to be evaluated systematically. The combining of different treatments needs to be guided by an overall model of the treatment process; without this the programme can easily take the form of a confusing salad, in which each ingredient retains its purity, with no shared concepts or language. Because CAT originated in the integration of different theories and practices and continues to be permeable to ideas from other sources, and because many techniques can be incorporated within its practice, I believe that it could well provide a satisfactory framework within which to integrate different specific treatment methods.

I also believe that, for patients, an initial CAT reformulation represents the most powerful acknowledgement and description of the full extent of their experience and behaviour, and as a result is uniquely capable of recruiting their cooperation and of initiating an integrative process. Borderline pathology, even more strikingly than other forms of psychological distress, needs to be understood in terms of the high-level processes governing and the beliefs shaping the functions of 'the self'. Humane clinicians working in any theoretical system may, of course, provide integrating acknowledgements for their patients, but this depends on personal qualities and is not supported by theories which fragment the self into subsidiary structures and processes. The concept of the procedure describes something which someone experiences and does and should defy reification. The language of CAT is designed to avoid reductions of the patient's human experience and human responsibilities; whether in talking about them or in talking with them we aim to avoid reducing them to assemblages of maladaptive behaviours, dysfunctional schemas or conflicted internal objects. The jointly agreed descriptions of a patient's procedures should be rooted in the patient's words and self-reflections, and in using them we seek to maintain the symmetry between the human patient and the human clinician. For these reasons I believe that the collaboration involved in the process of reformulation and the understandings expressed in the letter and diagram provide the best basis for choosing and timing additional treatments.

Which additional treatments are called for will depend on the nature of the unresolved problems.

1. *Where integration has not been achieved*, the difficulty may lie in the therapist's failure to extricate him or herself from a collusive countertransference, in which case either further individual therapy, or a CAT, or group analytic group may be called for. In other cases the persistence of dissociation may reflect its extent and intensity and the presence of active and unaccessed traumatic memories. In such cases individual CAT should be enriched by the specific techniques developed for managing trauma-induced dissociation (see e.g. Kennerley, 1996).

2. *Where problem procedures have been recognized but not revised* the subsequent use of cognitive behavioural treatments, or the inclusion within CAT of some of the specific techniques developed in that field, may prove effective. In other cases group therapy (itself an effective first treatment for some borderline patients, see Pines, 1978) may provide the best way to extend the achievements of individual CAT (Maple and Simpson, 1995; Duignan and Mitzman, 1994). Other group interventions include social skills training and the various methods used in day hospital programmes to develop capacities and confidence.

3. *Where access to feeling remains incomplete*, some patients can use Art Therapy to create and externalize powerful images of experiences beyond the reach of words which complement the written and diagrammatic tools of CAT. For others, psychodrama may allow new understandings to be felt and new procedures enacted.

4. *Where patients are too disorganized to use outpatient psychotherapy* day hospital (Bateman, 1995) or inpatient regimes (Rosser *et al.*, 1987) may be clinically and cost-effective. Working in such settings with borderline patients is always difficult, because of their propensity to set up a network of dissociated relationships with fellow patients and staff, which serves to maintain dissociation. To combat and make use of this requires high levels of training and supervision; this can be aided by the use of CAT ideas. Individual reformulations shared with the group (perhaps, I fantasize, with diagrams printed on T-shirts, or carried by patients like passports) can help avoid this negative development, by highlighting the interpersonal expression of, and need to avoid the reinforcement of, problem procedures. Dunn and Parry (in a paper given at the ACAT Conference, 1997, to be published) describe the use of CAT methods in formulating care plans in a unit for severely disturbed borderline patients, where the creation of a common language for patients, staff and supervisors had a markedly favourable impact. Leighton (Chapter 10) and Pollock (Chapter 11) describe similar practices. Given that most borderline patients have successfully and harmfully extracted collusive reactions from clinical staff, this development seems particularly sig-

nificant and deserving of wider use and evaluation. This work stems from psychoanalytic writers such as Main (1957) and is an example of how CAT has modified such understandings and made them more accessible to clinicians and of direct value to patients.

Supportive Treatment

Having discussed a range of possible treatments, it should be acknowledged that in reality most borderline patients receive forms of 'supportive therapy'. At its best this can represent the offer of a defined, minimum degree of support and witnessing, combined with the very clear message that nothing else is on offer. Where this clear establishment of the limits is linked with reliably sustained availability, as can be the case in general practice, for example (see the case of Emma in Chapter 1), this may be truly helpful, but where occasional visits to a succession of junior psychiatric trainees are implied it is not. Unskilled sustained support can be very undermining by fixing the patient in the dependent role, a role which can easily be shaped into a collusive, idealized or subtly resistant one which undermines autonomy and risks ending in massive disillusion. For those undertaking supportive work with borderlines the kind of understanding offered by the multiple self states model and by diagrammatic reformulation would be a protection against such collusive involvements, and could open the way to a gradual handing over of responsibility to the patient.

All these treatment approaches (apart from unwise forms of supportive therapy) have in common an attempt to limit the chances of the patient becoming regressively dependent. I believe that this aim is correct and it is fundamental to CAT. But, to end this account, what the Jungians might call CAT's shadow side should be mentioned. As described in Ryle (1982, p. 136), I have known two seriously disturbed and deprived patients who were healed by prolonged and total physical dependency, resulting from injuries sustained in road accidents and the subsequent surgery. I wonder how far the prolonged regressive and ambivalent dependencies characteristic of many long-term dynamic therapies and psychoanalyses are of value; maybe those few patients who cannot recover with the combinations of the various active methods described above need real, intensive care.

Evidence-based Practice and Theory

One source of CAT was the research evaluation of dynamic psychotherapy and it can therefore claim some priority in the now fashionable call for evidence-based practice. CAT-associated research is summarized in Ryle (1995b); the scale and design of most of it leaves much to be desired, the work having been largely done in the course of clinical practice with minimal funding, but the accumulating evidence, including some from controlled trials, supports the claim for the general efficacy of time-limited CAT. The ongoing research into the treatment of borderlines from which most of the case material of this book is drawn will be reported elsewhere, but is reasonably encouraging.

While the jewel in the crown of any particular therapy is the demonstration of its capacity to achieve results as good as, or better than, existing methods, most advances in therapy have antedated their proof by controlled trial. The value of such trials, where they have been carried out, has often been reduced by the failure to use measures appropriate to the aims, in particular by a reliance on measures of the more accessible symptoms and behaviours rather than of the underlying structures and processes which may have more long-term implications. This being so, the pressure for evidence-based practice, while desirable, carries some risks in an era when cost-effectiveness as judged by managers can so easily be calculated on dubious premises. But this does not alter the fact that short, effective, evaluated therapies are needed by individual patients and by those currently excluded from therapy. In this respect CAT, having anticipated the need for brief and evidence-based approaches, may be a little smug, but it badly needs a more sustained research base.

The value of research goes beyond the production of evidence; it lies in the clarifying and challenging of the underlying assumptions and values informing therapies. This was well said 125 years ago by Claude Bernard (1967): 'we usually give the name of discovery to recognition of a new fact; but I think that the idea connected with the discovered fact is what really constitutes the discovery'. Researchers have often been accused of choosing measures which favour their particular therapy, and my own use of repertory grid techniques (for example, in Brockman et al., 1987) could be seen as an example of this, but in my view the reciprocal influence of using grid measurements in research and developing CAT methods in practice has been a fruitful one, generating many ideas connected with discovered facts.

In the real world, unfortunately, neither new discovered facts nor new ideas have had a major impact on practice, despite increasingly sophisticated research. This is partly because research in this field is so difficult to do and to judge, and partly because most therapists are trained by, and loyal to, institutions or movements dominated by organizational and intellectual orthodoxies within whose orbits what is accepted as evidence, what evidence influences practice and even what journals are read are narrowly circumscribed. Belief in this sphere is determined by non-rational influences even more powerfully than is the case in the less fragmented scientific communities described by Kuhn (1962).

Theoretical Debates

In this atmosphere, those aspects of CAT theory which have differentiated it from its sources and which represent criticisms of, or alternatives to, other systems have, so far, evoked little discussion. This differentiation has been accompanied by the revision of models of early development in the light of observational studies of infants and by the transformation of object relations notions inspired by Leiman's introduction of Vygotskian and Bakhtinian ideas. These ideas also question the cognitive therapy focus on individual schematic development and rational learning by pointing to the transmission of the parent's personal and culturally formed procedural patterns as the main early influence. The model of borderline personality proposed in this book, which replaces models of intrapsychic conflict with an emphasis on dissociation induced by childhood trauma, represents another critique of most current psychoanalytic thought and offers a model of structure largely absent from cognitive therapy. CAT is also differentiated from attachment theory, although there are convergences also, through its central interest in sign mediation and the power of culture in the formation of human personality. The constancies and variabilities of our biological endowment are seen in CAT theory as the stage on which the complex dramas of our cultural evolution are enacted. It seems to me that these are all issues which deserve debate.

The Social Context

While there are no simple correlates between social injustice and individual psychopathology, our borderline patients have usually suffered abuses, deprivations and denigrations both from their immediate families and from the wider society. Some of these are self-inflicted, in the sense that their borderline procedures frequently lead them into provoking repetitions of rejection and abuse, and it could be tempting to say that, as therapists, our job is confined to trying to influence those behaviours. I think to do so would be an evasion. Offering an acknowledgement of the reality of the patient's past experiences is at the heart of the CAT reformulation; we cannot, or anyway should not, minimize the extent to which the wider society of school, the employment exchange, the hospital or prison and our own waiting lists may continue to deprive and abuse. As therapists, we focus on early experience because it often explains where damaging procedures were learned and allows us to clarify what the individual was and was not responsible for, but we should not forget that patients live in the present. Hagan and Smail (in press) are critical of psychotherapists for failing to acknowledge the realities of social power and they propose a helpful, detailed process of 'power mapping' to depict how much power over their lives, bodies and circumstances patients have exercised in the past and continue to exercise in the present. These authors acknowledge that CAT does offer patients 'a plausible hypothesis ... formulated as a sympathetic and respectful statement of how they learned to cope with the conditions into which they were born—' but go on to say that 'there is a danger in such approaches of psychologising the materiality of social power'. In my view this (somewhat obscure) statement carries a danger of falsely dichotomizing the psychological and the material. Powerless adults are constrained both by the material realities of society and by the assumptions and values transmitted by that society. We must, of course, recognize that patients may need help in respect of their material realities, but we should not forget that the assumptions transmitted to children by parents and others and the social controls which maintain the basic inequalities of our society are largely instilled and enforced by psychological, not material means. The cultural formation of mind is central to the developmental theory of CAT, and clarity in describing how this has determined beliefs and behaviours is central to its practice.

Psychotherapists committed to work in the public sector could learn from power mapping. The material realities imposed by recent political changes in the UK must be of concern to psychotherapists and to their borderline patients who, long neglected, are particularly vulnerable. Over the past 50 years the National Health Service has been reasonably successful in making treatment available to all, irrespective of social power or wealth, and the advantages offered to patients by private care became increasingly invisible. These changes have been partially reversed in recent years by chronic underfunding, by the introduction of systems of management operating on assumptions derived from industry or supermarkets and involving the marginalizing of clinicians, and by an ideological shift. Despite our unprecedented productivity, the leaders of the developed world have declared universal health care, along with welfare and education, to be economically beyond our means and even, they would like to assert, morally dubious.

The egalitarian aims of the NHS are being subverted and the UK is moving towards a situation like that in the USA, where a substantial minority of citizens enjoy health standards and health care at third world levels. In such a situation, psychotherapy, which in the case of psychoanalytic approaches has always kept one foot in the private sector, could easily become a commodity, purchasable by the well-off or provided as a perk like the company car, but unavailable to the more deprived and distressed whose needs are greater. Borderline personality disorder, being persistent and severe, is likely to be particularly unpopular with private companies or health insurers, so treatment of it will be left to the depleted public services. Having developed and taught CAT with the precise aim of making therapy available to those in need, I find these developments obscene, and I am deeply perturbed by the passivity of the majority of psychotherapists in the face of them.

In this book I have expressed what I believe to be justified optimism about the possibility of helping borderline patients. Unless we defend our professions and the interests of those in need of our help, it will have been a fruitless enterprise.

The Psychotherapy File

An Aid to Understanding Ourselves Better

We have all had just one life and what has happened to us, and the sense we made of this, colours the way we see ourselves and others. How we see things is for us how things are, and how we go about our lives seems 'obvious and right'. Sometimes, however, our familiar ways of understanding and acting can be the source of our problems. In order to solve our difficulties we may need to learn to recognize how what we do makes things worse. We can then work out new ways of thinking and acting.

These pages are intented to suggest ways of thinking about what you do; recognizing your particular patterns is the first step in learning to gain more control and happiness in your life.

Keeping a Diary of Your Moods and Behaviour

Symptoms, bad moods, unwanted thoughts or behaviours that come and go can be better understood and controlled if you learn to notice when they happen and what starts them off.

If you have a particular symptom or problem of this sort, start keeping a diary. The diary should be focused on a particular mood, symptom or behaviour, and should be kept every day if possible. Try to record this sequence:

1. How you were feeling about yourself and others and the world before the problem came on.
2. Any external event, or any thought or image in your mind that was going on when the trouble started, or what seemed to start it off.
3. Once the trouble started, what were the thoughts, images or feelings you experienced.

By noticing and writing down in this way what you do and think at these times, you will learn to recognize and eventually have more control over how you act and think at the time. It is often the case that bad feelings like resentment, depression or physical symptoms are the result of ways of thinking and acting that are unhelpful. Keeping a diary in this way gives you the chance to learn better ways of dealing with things.

It is helpful to keep a daily record for 1–2 weeks, then to discuss what you have recorded with your therapist or counsellor.

Patterns That Do Not Work, but are Hard to Break

There are certain ways of thinking and acting that do not achieve what we want, but which are hard to change. Read through the lists on the following pages and mark how far you think they apply to you.

Applies strongly + +   Applies +   Does not apply 0

Traps

Traps are things we cannot escape from. Certain kinds of thinking and acting result in a 'vicious circle' when, however hard we try, things seem to get worse instead of better. Trying to deal with feeling bad about ourselves, we think and act in ways that tend to confirm our badness.

Examples of Traps

	+ +	+	0
1. *Fear of hurting others* Feeling fearful of hurting others* we keep our feelings inside, or put our own needs aside. This tends to allow other people to ignore or abuse us in various ways, which then leads to our feeling, or being, childishly angry. When we see ourselves behaving like this, it confirms our belief that we shouldn't be aggressive and reinforces our avoidance of standing up for our rights. * People often get trapped in this way because they mix up aggression and assertion. Mostly, being assertive—asking for our rights—is perfectly acceptable. People who do not respect our rights as human beings must either be stood up to or avoided.			
2. *Depressed thinking* Feeling depressed, we are sure we will manage a task or social situation badly. Being depressed, we are probably not as effective as			

we can be, and the depression leads us to exaggerate how badly we handled things. This makes us feel more depressed about ourselves.

3. *Trying to please*
   Feeling uncertain about ourselves and anxious not to upset others, we try to please people by doing what they seem to want. As a result: (1) we end up being taken advantage of by others which makes us angry, depressed or guilty, from which our uncertainty about ourselves is confirmed; or (2) sometimes we feel out of control because of the need to please, and start hiding away, putting things off, letting people down, which makes other people angry with us and increases our uncertainty.

4. *Avoidance*
   We feel ineffective and anxious about certain situations, such as crowded streets, open spaces, social gatherings. We try to go back into these situations, but feel even more anxiety. Avoiding them makes us feel better, so we stop trying. However, by constantly avoiding situations our lives are limited and we come to feel increasingly ineffective and anxious.

5. *Social isolation*
   Feeling underconfident about ourselves and anxious not to upset others, we worry that others will find us boring or stupid, so we don't look at people or respond to friendliness. People then see us as unfriendly, so we become more isolated, from which we are convinced we are boring and stupid—and become more underconfident.

6. *Low self-esteem*
   Feeling worthless we feel that we cannot get what we want because (1) we will be punished, (2) others will reject or abandon us, or (3) anything good we get is bound to go away or

turn sour. (4) Sometimes it feels as if we must punish ourselves for being weak. From this we feel that everything is hopeless so we give up trying to do anything which confirms and increases our sense of worthlessness.

Dilemmas (false choices and narrow options)

We often act as we do, even when we are not completely happy with it, because the only other ways we can imagine seem as bad or even worse. Sometimes we assume connections that are not necessarily the case—as in 'If I do *x* then *y* will follow'. These false choices can be described as either/or or if/then dilemmas. We often don't realize that we see things like this, but we act as if these were the only possible choices.

Do you act as if any of the following false choice rule your life? Recognizing them is the first step to changing them.

Choices About Myself

I act as if:

	++	+	0
1. Either I keep feelings bottled up or I risk being rejected, hurting others, or making a mess.			
2. Either I feel I spoil myself and am greedy or I deny myself things and punish myself and feel miserable.			
3. If I try to be perfect, I feel depressed and angry; If I don't try to be perfect, I feel guilty, angry and dissatisfied.			
4. If I must then I won't; it is as if when faced with a task I must either (1) gloomily submit, or (2) passively resist. Other people's wishes, or even my own feel too demanding, so I put things off, avoid them.			
5. If I must not then I will; it is as if the only proof of my existence is my resistance. Other people's rules, or even my own feel too restricting, so I break rules and do things which are harmful to me.			
6. If other people aren't expecting me to do things for them or look after them, then I feel anxious, lonely and out of control.			

7. If I get what I want I feel childish and guilty; if I don't get what I want, I feel frustrated, angry and depressed.

8. Either I keep things (feelings, plans) in perfect order, or I fear a terrible mess.

Choices About How We Relate to Others

I behave with others as if:

	++	+	0
1. Either I'm involved with someone and likely to get hurt or I don't get involved and stay in charge, but remain lonely.			
2. Either I stick up for myself and nobody likes me, or I give in and get put on by others and feel cross and hurt.			
3. Either I'm a brute or a martyr (secretly blaming the other).			
4 a. With others either I'm safely wrapped up in bliss or in combat;			
b. if in combat then I'm either a bully or a victim.			
5. Either I look down on other people, or I feel they look down on me.			
6 a. Either I'm sustained by the admiration of others whom I admire or I feel exposed;			
b. if exposed then I feel either contemptuous of others or I feel contemptible.			
7. Either I'm involved with others and feel engulfed, taken over or smothered, or I stay safe and uninvolved but feel lonely and isolated.			
8. When I'm involved with someone whom I care about then either I have to give in or they have to give in.			
9. When I'm involved with someone whom I depend on then either I have to give in or they have to give in.			
10 a. As a woman either I have to do what others want or I stand up for my rights and get rejected;			
b. as a man either I can't have any feelings or I am an emotional mess.			

Snags

Snags are what is happening when we say 'I want to have a better life, or I want to change my behaviour but ...'. Sometimes this comes from how we or our families thought about us when we were young; such as 'she was always the good child', or 'in our family we never ...'. Sometimes the snags come from the important people in our lives not wanting us to change, or not able to cope with what our changing means to them. Often the resistance is more indirect, as when a parent, husband or wife becomes ill or depressed when we begin to get better.

In other cases, we seem to 'arrange' to avoid pleasure or success, or if they come, we have to pay in some way, by depression, or by spoiling things. Often this is because, as children, we came to feel guilty if things went well for us, or felt that we were envied for good luck or success. Sometimes we have come to feel responsible, unreasonably, for things that went wrong in the family, although we may not be aware that this is so. It is helpful to learn to recognize how this sort of pattern is stopping you getting on with your life, for only then can you learn to accept your right to a better life and begin to claim it.

You may get quite depressed when you begin to realize how often you stop your life being happier and more fulfilled. It is important to remember that it's not being stupid or bad, but rather that:

(a) we do these things because this is the way we learned to manage best when we were younger;
(b) we don't have to keep on doing them now we are learning to recognize them;
(c) by changing our behaviour, we can learn to control not only our own behaviour, but we also change the way other people behave to us;
(d) although it may seem that others resist the changes we want for ourselves (for example, our parents, or our partners), we often underestimate them; if we are firm about our right to change, those who care for us will usually accept the change.

Do you recognize that you feel limited in your life:

	++	+	0
1. For fear of the response of others: for example I must sabotage success (a) as if it deprives others, (b) as if others may envy me, or (c) as if there are not enough good things to go around.			
2. By something inside yourself: for example I must sabotage good things as if I don't deserve them.			

Difficult and Unstable States of Mind

Some people find it difficult to keep control over their behaviour and experience because things feel very difficult and different at times. Indicate which, if any, of the following apply to you:

	++	+	0
1. How I feel about myself and others can be unstable; I can switch from one state of mind to a completely different one.			
2. Some states may be accompanied by intense, extreme and uncontrollable emotions.			
3. Others by emotional blankness, feeling unreal, or feeling muddled.			
4. Some states are accompanied by feeling intensely guilty or angry with myself, wanting to hurt myself.			
5. Or by feeling that others can't be trusted, are going to let me down, or hurt me.			
6. Or by being unreasonably angry or hurtful to others.			
7. Sometimes the only way to cope with some confusing feelings is to blank them off and feel emotionally distant from others.			

Continue overleaf if you want to:

Different States

Everybody experiences changes in how they feel about themselves and the world. But for some people these changes are extreme, sometimes sudden and confusing. In such cases there are often a number of states which recur, and learning to recognize them and shifts between them can be very helpful. Below are a number of descriptions of such states. Identify those which you experience by ringing the number. *You can delete or add words to the descriptions* and there is space to add any not listed.

1. Zombie. Cut off from feelings, cut off from others, disconnected.
2. Feeling bad but soldiering on, coping.
3. Out-of-control rage.
4. Extra special. Looking down on others.
5. In control of self, of life, of other people.
6. Cheated by life, by others. Untrusting.
7. Provoking, teasing, seducing, winding-up others.

8. Clinging, fearing abandonment.
9. Frenetically active. Too busy to think or feel.
10. Agitated, confused, anxious.
11. Feeling perfectly cared for, blissfully close to another.
12. Misunderstood, rejected, abandoned.
13. Contemptuously dismissive of myself.
14. Vulnerable, needy, passively helpless, waiting for rescue.
15. Envious, wanting to harm others, put them down, pull them down.
16. Protective, respecting of myself, of others.
17. Hurting myself, hurting others.
18. Resentfully submitting to demands.
19. Hurt, humiliated by others.
20. Secure in myself, able to be close to others.
21. Intensely critical of self, of others.
22. Frightened of others.
23.

The Psychotherapy File was developed by Dr Anthony Ryle, Consultant Psychotherapist, Department of Psychiatry and Senior Fellow, United Medical & Dental Schools (UMDS) of Guy's and St Thomas's Hospital, London.

For further information about Cognitive Analytic Therapy—CAT—please contact the CAT Coordinator, Munro Clinic, Guy's Hospital, London SE1 9RT

APPENDIX 2

Repertory Grid Technique

Repertory grid technique is derived from the work of George Kelly and linked with his Personal Construct Theory (Kelly, 1955). The use of grids to study psychotherapy was one of the factors leading to the development of CAT; applications of grid technique to psychotherapy research are described in Ryle (1975).

In essence, grid technique is simple, although the mathematical aspects can scare off the innumerate (of whom I am one). The aim is to study an individual's thought processes by focusing on how he/she sees the similarities and differences in a class of *elements* (things, phenomena, people, etc.). The procedure depends upon selecting the field of interest and listing the relevant elements; these could be brands of chocolate or current hits or computers (but would be confined to only one of the categories). In psychology these elements are usually people, but they can be relationships between people (see the dyad grid used with Claudia in Chapter 8) or, as in several examples in this book, they can be states.

Having selected the elements, the person's own way of comparing/contrasting them is elicited. To do this in Kelly's mode, the person is asked to select any three elements at random and to note ways in which two are similar to each other and different from the third. This procedure is repeated with different elements until no new terms are generated. The terms define the individual's *personal constructs*. In some cases other sources of constructs may be used, such as interviews or therapy sessions, and it is also possible for the observer to supply constructs in order to cover issues of particular interest, as in the states grid used here. This practice is frowned on by pure Kellyans on the grounds that *personal* constructs should be those elicited from the person, using his or her terms. If constructs are supplied it is important to make sure that the subject can use them and he/she should be invited to add others.

Having assembled a list of elements and constructs, the grid is completed by the subject systematically rating every element according to how well it is described by every construct. Constructs are bipolar (e.g. black vs white) and orthodox Kellyans present them in that way, but my preference is to use descriptions of one pole for rating (e.g. black), as an individual's other pole, on analysis, may turn out to be something other than the obvious opposite (e.g. not white, but coloured or not black, but Caucasian). In CAT terms, constructs highly correlated can represent *if-then* dilemmas, those with high negative correlations *either-or* dilemmas. The resulting rows and columns of figures (the grid) are analysed mathematically, with a principal component analysis. The cases in the present book were analysed using 'Flexigrid' (Tschudi, 1990; University of Oslo). The output from this analysis provides the following kinds of measure (presented here in largely non-technical language):

1. How far any two constructs are used similarly is indicated as a *correlation*.
2. How similarly any two elements are described is recorded as an *'element distance'*, a measure calculated with reference to the average distance between all the elements.
3. A principal component analysis extracts from the grid mathematical *components*; after the first component is abstracted the remaining variation is similarly analysed to give the second principal component and so on. Each construct and each element will be located by a loading on these components; the psychological meaning of a component is indicated by these loadings.

Displaying the Results Graphically

The two-component maps (graphs) presented in this book give a simplified summary of construct–construct, element–element and construct–element relationships. Elements appearing close on the map are conceptually similar, those at opposite ends of the first (horizontal) or second (vertical) component are opposite in terms of the constructs defining that component. To avoid clutter, constructs are written around the edge, located according to their loadings on the two components by extending a line out from the intersection of the components (which are drawn at right angles to each other after a mathematical rotation) through their exact location; elements are located at the point indicated by their loadings.

Interpretation of Maps

The whole procedure is, in essence, a way of demonstrating (in terms of distance and in terms of meaning) similarities and differences in the way an individual makes sense of the elements selected for study. These ways are idiosyncratic and are therefore useful information about the person; how the world is construed will to a large extent determine how the person proceeds in it. This 'how' can depend on the implications of certain terms; a person doing a grid where the elements are people, who construes strength and dangerousness as highly correlated, will act differently from one who construes strength and supportiveness as going together. The relations between elements can also be of interest, for example the similarity of the self to key others or to ideal or feared versions of the self may be of particular interest.

The States Grid

This grid is one in which the elements are the individual's states, identified through the procedures described in Chapter 3. The constructs which are provided are chosen on theoretical grounds, seeking to assess the mood, sense of self and others, access to emotion and control of emotion characteristic of each state. The degree to which these apply to each state will be rated on a 1–5 scale. The following is the list:

I feel: overwhelmed by feelings; weak; happy; angry; sad; guilty; out of control; unreal; cut off from feelings.
I: trust others; depend on others; control others; want to hurt others.
Others: seem critical; envy me; attack me; admire me; care for me.

References

American Psychiatric Association (1994). *Diagnostic and Statistical Manual of Mental Disorders* (DSM IV). Fourth Edition. Washington, DC: American Psychiatric Association.

Anderson, D. (1981). *Perspectives on Treatment: the Minnesota Experiment*. Center City, MN: Hazelden.

Bateman, A. (1995). The treatment of borderline patients in a day hospital setting. *Psychoanalytic Psychotherapy*, **9**, 3–16.

Beck, A.T., Freeman, A. and associates (1990). *Cognitive Therapy of Personality Disorders*. New York: Guilford Press.

Beck, A.T., Ward, C.H., Mendelson, M., Mock, J.E. and Ezbargh, J.K. (1961). An inventory for measuring depression. *Archives of General Psychiatry*, **4**, 561–571.

Beck, A.T., Wright, F.T., Newman, C.F. and Liese, B.S. (1993). *Cognitive Theory of Substance Misuse*. New York: Guilford Press.

Benjamin, L. (1993). *Interpersonal Diagnosis and Treatment of Personality Disorders*. New York: Guilford Press.

Bennett, D. and Parry, G. (in press). The accuracy of reformulation in cognitive analytic therapy: a validation study. *Psychotherapy Research*.

Berelowitz, M. and Tarnopolsky, A. (1993). The validity of borderline personality disorder: an updated review of recent research. In P. Tyrer and G. Stein (Eds), *Personality Disorder Reviewed*. London: Gaskell.

Berger, L.S. (1991). *Substance Abuse as Symptom*. New York: Analytic Press.

Bernard, C. (1967). *An Introduction to the Study of Experimental Medicine*. New York: Dover.

Bollerud, K. (1990). A model for the treatment of trauma-related syndromes among chemically dependent inpatient women. *Journal of Substance Abuse Treatment*, **7**, 83–87.

Brewin, C.R. (1996). Scientific status of recovered memories. *British Journal of Psychiatry*, **169**, 131–134.

Brockman, B., Poynton, A., Ryle, A. and Watson, J.P. (1987). Effectiveness of time-limited therapy carried out by trainees: a comparison of two methods. *British Journal of Psychiatry*, **151**, 602–609.

Brockman, R. (1990). Medication and transference in psychoanalytically oriented psychotherapy of the borderline patient. *Psychiatric Clinics of North America*, **13** (2), 287–306.

Bruner, J. (1986). *Actual Minds, Possible Worlds*. Cambridge, MA: Harvard University Press.

Burkitt, I. (1996). Social and Personal constructs: a division left unresolved. *Theory and Psychology*, **6** (1), 71–77.

Chadwick, P., Birchwood, M. and Trower, P. (1996). *Cognitive Therapy for Delusions, Voices and Paranoia*. Chichester: Wiley.

Connors, R. (1996a). Self-injury in trauma survivors. 1. Functions and meanings. *American Journal of Orthopsychiatry*, **66** (2), 197–206.

Connors, R. (1996b). Self-injury in trauma survivors. 2. Levels of clinical response. *American Journal of Orthopsychiatry*, **66** (2), 207–216.

Cowmeadow, P. (1994). Deliberate self-harm and cognitive analytic therapy. *International Journal of Short-Term Psychotherapy*, **9**, 135–150.

Crittenden, P.M. (1990). Internal representational models of attachment relationships. *Infant Mental Health Journal*, **11** (3), 259–277.

Denman, F. (1995). Treating eating disorders using CAT: two case examples. In A. Ryle (Ed.), *Cognitive Analytic Therapy: Developments Theory and Practice*. Chichester: Wiley.

Derogatis, L.R. (1983). *SCL-R 90: Administration, Scoring and Procedures Manual II*. Toronto: Clinical Psychometric Research.

Derogatis, L.R., Lipman, L.S. and Covi, M.D. (1973). SCL-90: an outpatient rating scale: preliminary report. *Psychopharmacotherapy Bulletin*, **9**, 13–29.

De Zulueta, F. (1994). *Traumatic Roots of Destructiveness: From Pain to Violence*. London: Whurr.

Dolan, B., Evans, C. and Norton, K. (1995). Multiple Axis II diagnoses of personality disorder. *British Journal of Psychiatry*, **166**, 107–112.

Donald, M. (1991). *Origins of the Modern Mind*. Cambridge, MA: Harvard University Press.

Duignan, I. and Mitzman, S. (1994). Measuring individual change in patients receiving time-limited cognitive analytic group therapy. *International Journal of Short-Term Psychotherapy*, **9** (2/3), 151–160.

Dunn, J. (1995). Intersubjectivity in psychoanalysis: a critical review. *International Journal of Psychonalysis*, **76**, 723–738.

Dunn, M. (1994). Variations in Cognitive Analytic Therapy technique in the treatment of a severely disturbed patient. *International Journal of Short-Term Psychotherapy*, **9** (2/3), 119–134.

Feldman-Summers S. and Pope, K.S. (1994). The experiences of 'forgetting' childhood abuse: a national survey of psychologists. *Journal of Consulting and Clinical Psychology*, **62**, 636–639.

Fonagy, P. (1989). On tolerating mental states: theory of mind in borderline patients. *Bulletin of Anna Freud Centre*, **12**, 91–115.

Fonagy, P. (1991). Thinking about thinking: some clinical and theoretical considerations in the treatment of a borderline patient. *International Journal of Psychoanalysis*, **72**, 639–656.

Fonagy, P., Moran, G.S. and Target, M. (1983). Aggression and the psychological self. *International Journal of Psychoanalysis*, **74**, 471–485.

Freud, S. (1933). *New Introductory Lectures on Psychoanalysis*. Standard Edition, Vol. 22. London: Hogarth Press.

Fyer, M.R., Frances, A.J., Sullivan, T. *et al.* (1988). Co-morbidity of borderline personality disorder. *Archives of General Psychiatry*, **45**, 348–352.

Gacano, C. and Meloy, J.R. (1994). *The Rorschach assessment of Aggressive and Psychopathic Personalities*. Hillsdale, N.J: Erlbaum.

Grotstein, J. (1982). Newer perspectives in object relations theory. *Contemporary Psychoanalysis*, **18**, 43–91.

Gunderson, J.G. (1996). The borderline patient's intolerance of aloneness: insecure attachments and therapist availability. *American Journal of Psychiatry*, **153**, 752–758.

Gunderson, J.G. and Austin, V. (1981). The diagnostic interview for borderline patients. *American Journal of Psychiatry*, **138**, 896–903.

Gunderson, J.G. and Phillips, K.A. (1991). A current view of the interface between borderline personality disorder and depression. *American Journal of Psychiatry*, **148**, 967–975.

Gunderson J.G. and Sabo, A.N. (1993). The phenomenological and conceptual interface between borderline personality disorder and PTSD. *American Journal of Psychiatry*, **150**(1), 19–27.

Hagan, T. and Smail, D. (in press). Power mapping. 1. Background and basic methodology. 2. Practical application. The example of child sexual abuse. *Journal of Community and Applied Social Psychology*.

Hare, R.D. (1991). *The Psychopathy Checklist-Revised*. Toronto: Multi-health Systems.

Hartocollis, P. and Hartocollis, P.C. (1980). Alcoholism, borderline and narcissistic disorders. In W. Fann, l. Kanakan, A. Pokorny and F.R. Williams (Eds), *Phenomenology and Treatment of Alcoholism*. New York: Spectrum.

Higgitt, A. and Fonagy, P. (1992). Psychotherapy of narcissistic and borderline personality disorder. *British Journal of Psychiatry*, **167**, 23–43.

Hodgson, S. (1993). *Mental Disorder and Crime*. London: Sage.

Horowitz, L., Rosenberg, S., Baer, B., Ureno, G. and Villasenor, V.S. (1988). Inventory of Interpersonal Problems: Psychometric properties and clinical applications. *Journal of Consulting and Clinical Psychology*, **56**, 885–892.

Horowitz, M.J. (1979). *States of Mind*. New York: Plenum Press.

Horowitz, M.J., Milbrath, C., Ewart, M., Sonnebon, D. and Stinson, R. (1994). Cyclical patterns in states of mind in psychotherapy. *American Journal of Psychiatry*, **151**, 1767–1770.

Huizinga, J. (1924; many editions since 1955). *The Waning of the Middle Ages*. Harmondsworth: Penguin Books.

Janet, P. (1965). *The Major Symptoms of Hysteria*. New York: Hafner Publishing.

Kaufman, E. (1994) *Psychotherapy of Addicted Persons*. New York: Guilford, Press.

Kelly, G.A. (1955). *The Psychology of Personal Constructs*. New York: Norton.

Kennerley, H. (1996). Cognitive Therapy of dissociative symptoms associated with trauma. *British Journal of Clinical Psychology*, **35**, 325–340.

Kernberg, O. (1967). Borderline personality organisation. *Journal of the American Psychoanalytic Association*, **15** (3), 641–685.

Kernberg, O. (1975). *Borderline Conditions and Pathological Narcissism*. New York: Jason Aronson.

Kernberg, O. (1984). *Severe Personality Disorders: Psychotherapeutic Strategies*. New Haven, CT: Yale University Press.

Kernberg, O.F., Selzer, M.A., Koenigsberg, H.W., Carr, A.C. and Appelbaum, A.H. (1989). *Psychodynamic Psychotherapy of Borderline Patients*. New York: Basic Books.

Khantzian, E.J., Halliday, K.S. and McAuliffe, W.E. (1990). *Addiction and the Vulnerable Self: Modified Dynamic Group Therapy for Substance Abusers*. New York: Guilford Press.

Khantzian, E.J. and Mack, J.E. (1989). Alcoholics Anonymous and contemporary psychodynamic theory. In M. Galanter (Ed.), *Recent Advances in Alcoholism*. New York: Plenum.

Knight, R.P. (1937). The dynamics and treatment of chronic alcohol addiction. *Bulletin of the Menninger Clinic*, September, 1937.

Kohut, H. (1971). *The Analysis of the Self*. New York: International Universities Press.

Kohut, H. (1977a). Self-deficits and addiction. In Research Monograph 12, *National Institute on Drug Abuse*.

Kohut, H. (1977b). *The Restoration of the Self*. New York: International Universities Press.

Kohut, H. (1979). The two analyses of Mr Z. *International Journal of Psychoanalysis*, **60** (3), 3–27.

Kolb, J. and Gunderson, J. (1980). Diagnosing borderline patients with a semi-structured interview. *Archives of General Psychiatry*, **37**, 37–41.

Kroll, J., Pyle, R. and Zander, J. (1981). Borderline personality disorders inter-rater reliability of the diagnostic interview for borderlines. *Schizophrenia Bulletin*, **7**, 269–272.

Krystal, H. (1977). Self and object representation in alcohol and other drug dependence: In Research Monograph 12, *National Institute on Drug Abuse*.

Krystal, H. (1977). Self and object representation in alcoholism and other drug dependence: implications for therapy. In Research Monograph 12, *National Institute on Drug Abuse*.

Krystal, H. and Raskin, H.A. (1970). *Drug Dependence: Aspects of Ego Function.* Detroit: Wayne State University Press.

Kuhn, T.S. (1962). *The Structure of Scientific Revolutions.* Chicago: University of Chicago Press.

Leiman, M. (1992). The concept of sign in the work of Vygotsky, Winnicott and Bakhtin: further integration of object relations theory and activity theory. *British Journal of Medical Psychology,* **65**, 209–221.

Leiman, M. (1994a). Projective identification as early joint action sequences: a Vygotskian addendum to the procedural sequence object relations model. *British Journal of Medical Psychology,* **67**, 97–106.

Leiman, M. (1994b). The development of Cognitive Analytic Therapy. *International Journal of Short-Term Psychotherapy,* **9** (2–3), 67–82.

Leiman, M. (1995). Early development. In A. Ryle (Ed.), *Cognitive Analytic Therapy: Developments in Theory and Practice.* Chichester: Wiley.

Leiman, M. (1997). Procedures as dialogic sequences: a revised version of the fundamental concept in Cognitive Analytic Therapy. *British Journal of Medical Psychology,* **70**(2), 193–207.

Linehan, M.M. (1993). *Cognitive Behavioural Therapy of Borderline Personality Disorder.* New York: Guilford Press.

Luborsky, L. and Crits-Christoph, P. (1990). *Understanding Transference: The CCRT Method.* New York: Basic Books.

Lucas, F.L. (1956). *Greek Poetry for Everyone.* Boston: Beacon Press.

Main, T.H. (1957). The ailment. *British Journal of Medical Psychology,* **30**, 129–145.

Malan, D.H. (1976). *The Frontiers of Brief Psychotherapy.* London: Hutchinson.

Malan, D.H., Heath, E.S., Bacal, H.A. and Balfour, F.H.G. (1975). Psychodynamic changes in untreated neurotic patients. *Archives of General Psychiatry,* **32**, 110–126.

Mancuso, J.C. (1996). Constructionism, personal construct psychology and narrative psychology. *Theory and Psychology,* **6** (1), 47–50.

Mann, J. (1973). *Time-Limited Psychotherapy.* Cambridge, MA: Harvard University Press.

Maple, N. and Simpson, I. (1995). CAT in groups in A. Ryle (Ed.), *Cognitive Analytic Therapy: Developments in Theory and Practice.* Chichester: Wiley.

Marlatt, G.A. and Gordon, J.R. (Eds) (1985). *Relapse Prevention: Maintenance Strategies in the Treatment of Addictive Behaviours* New York: Guilford Press.

Marlowe, M.J. (1994). Cognitive Analytic Therapy and borderline personality disorder: restricted reciprocal role repertoires and subpersonality organisation. *International Journal of Short-Term Psychotherapy,* **9**, 161–169.

McDougall, J. (1989). *Theatres of the Body: a Psychoanalytic Approach to Psychosomatic Illness.* London: Free Association Books.

McManus, M., Alessi, N.E., Grapentine, W.I. and Brickman, A. (1984). Psychiatric disturbance in serious delinquents. *Journal of American Academy of Child Psychiatry,* **23**, 602–615.

Meissner, W.W. (1988). *Treatment of Patients in the Borderline Spectrum*. Northvale: Jason Aronson.

Meloy, J.R. (1988). *Violent Attachments*. Northvale: Jason Aronson.

Meloy, J.R. (1992). *The Psychopathic Mind: Origins, Dynamics and Treatment*. Northvale: Jason Aronson.

Mersky, H.T. (1992). The manufacture of personalities: the production of Multiple Personality Disorder. *British Journal of Psychiatry*, **160**, 327–340.

Millon, T. (1987). *The Millon Clinical Multiaxial Inventory—2* Minneapolis: National Computer Systems.

Morton, J. and Frith, U. (1995). Causal modelling: a structural approach to developmental psychopathology. In D. Cicchetti and D.J. Cohen (Eds), *Manual of Developmental Psychopathology* (pp. 357–390). New York: Wiley.

Millon, T. (1993). The borderline personality: a psychosocial epidemic. In J. Paris (Ed.), *Borderline Personality Disorder: Etiology and Treatment*, Washington, DC: American Psychiatric Press.

Mollon, P. (1993). *The Fragile Self: The Structure of Narcissistic Disturbance*. London: Whurr.

Mollon, P. (1997). The memory debate: a consideration of clinical complexities and some suggested guidelines for psychoanalytic therapists. *British Journal of Psychotherapy*, **13** (2), 193–203.

Musil, R. (1995) (Trs. S. Williams and B. Pike). *The Man without Qualities*. New York: Knopf.

Nurnberg, H.G., Raskin, M., Levine, P.E., Pollack, S. Siegel, O. and Prince, R. (1991). Hierarchy of DSM III-R criteria efficiency for the diagnosis of borderline personality disorder. *Journal of Personality Disorders*, **5** (3), 211–224.

Ogden, T.H. (1983). The concept of internal object relations. *International Journal of Psychoanalysis*, **64**, 227–241.

Paris, J. (Ed.) (1993). *Borderline Personality Disorder: Etiology and Treatment*. Washington, DC: American Psychiatric Press.

Patrick, J. (1993). The integration of the self-psychological and cognitive-behavioural models in the treatment of borderline personality disorder. *Canadian Journal of Psychiatry*, **38**, Suppl. 1, S 39–S 43.

Perris, C. (1994). Cognitive therapy in the treatment of patients with borderline personality disorders. *Acta Psychiatrica Scandinavica*, **89**, Suppl. 379, 69–72.

Perry, J.C. and Herman, J.L. (1993). Trauma and defense in the etiology of borderline personality disorder. In J. Paris (Ed.), *Borderline Personality Disorder: Etiology and Treatment*. Washington, DC: American Psychiatric Press.

Pines, M. (1975). Group analytic psychotherapy of the borderline patient. *Group Analysis*, **11**, 115–126.

Pollock, P.H. (1995). Cognitive analytic therapy with offenders: a case of spree serial murder. Paper presented at the ACAT conference, Guy's Hospital, November.

Pollock, P.H. (1996). Clinical issues in the cognitive analytic therapy of sexually abused women who commit violent offences against their partners. *British Journal of Medical Psychology*, **69**(2), 117–127.

Pollock, P.H. (1996). *The MCMI-2 Profiles of murderers* (unpublished).

Pollock, P.H. and Kear-Colwell, J.J. (1994). Women who stab: a personal construct analysis of sexual victimisation and offending behaviour. *British Journal of Medical Psychology*, **67**, 13–22.

Putnam, F.W. (1989). *Diagnosis and Treatment of Multiple Personality Disorder*. New York: Guilford Press.

Putnam, F.W. (1994). The switch process in Multiple Personality Disorder and other state-change disorders. In: R.M. Klein and B.K. Doane (Eds), *Psychological Concepts and Dissociative Disorders*. Hillsdale, NJ: Erlbaum.

Raine, A. (1993). Features of borderline personality and violence. *Journal of Clinical Psychology*, **49**, 277–280.

Rapaport, D. (1992). Psychiatric report on John Wayne Gacy. Cited in Meloy, J.R., *The Psychopathic Mind: Origins, Dynamics and Treatment* (pp.147–148). Northvale: Jason Aronson.

Reich, J.H. and Green, A.I. (1991). Effect of personality disorder on outcome of treatment. *Journal of Nervous and Mental Diseases*, **179**, 74–82.

Rinsley, D.B. (1988). The Diopsas revisited: comments on addiction and personality. *Journal of Substance Abuse Treatment*, **5**, 1–8.

Robbins, M. (1989). Primitive personality organisation as an interpersonally adaptive modification of cognition and affect. *International Journal of Psychoanalysis*, **70**, 443–459.

Roesler, T.A. and Dafler, C.E. (1993). Chemical dissociation in adults sexually abused as children: alcohol and drug use in adult survivors. *Journal of Substance Abuse Treatment*, **10**, 537–543.

Ross, C.A. (1994). *The Osiris Complex. Case studies in Multiple Personality Disorder*. Toronto: University of Toronto Press.

Rosser, R.M., Birch, S., Bond, H. *et al.* (1987). Five year follow-up of patients treated with inpatient psychotherapy at the Cassel Hospital for Nervous Diseases. *Journal of the Royal Society of Medicine*, **80**, 549–555.

Rutter, M. (1987). Temperament, personality and personality disorder. *British Journal of Psychiatry*, **150**, 443–458.

Ryle, A. (1975). *Frames and Cages*. London: Sussex University Press.

Ryle, A. (1979). The focus in brief interpretive psychotherapy; dilemmas, traps and snags as target problems. *British Journal of Psychiatry*, **135**, 46–64.

Ryle, A. (1982). Psychotherapy: a Cognitive Integration of Theory and Practice. London: Academic Press.

Ryle, A. (1985). Cognitive Theory, object relations and the self. *British Journal of Medical Psychology*, **58**, 1–7.

Ryle, A. (1990). *Cognitive Analytic Therapy: Active Participation in Change*. Chichester: Wiley.

Ryle, A. (1991). Object relations theory and activity theory: a proposed link by way of the procedural sequence model. *British Journal of Medical Psychology*, **64**, 307–316.

Ryle, A. (1992). Critique of a Kleinian case presentation. *British Journal of Medical Psychology*, **65**, 309–317.

Ryle, A. (1993). Addiction to the death instinct? A critical review of Joseph's paper 'Addiction to near death'. *British Journal of Psychotherapy*, **10**(1), 88–92.

Ryle, A. (1994a). Projective identification: a particular form of reciprocal role procedure. *British Journal of Medical Psychology*, **67**, 107–114.

Ryle, A. (1994b). Persuasion or education? The role of reformulation in cognitive analytic therapy. *International Journal of Short-Term Psychotherapy*, **9**(2/3), 111–118.

Ryle, A. (1995a). Transference and countertransference variations in the course of the cognitive analytic therapy of two borderline patients: the relation to the diagrammatic reformulation of self states. *British Journal of Medical Psychology*, **68**, 109–124.

Ryle, A. (Ed.) (1995b). *Cognitive Analytic Therapy: developments in theory and practice.* Chichester: Wiley.

Ryle, A. (1995c). Defensive organisations or collusive interpretations? A further critique of Kleinian theory and practice. *British Journal of Psychotherapy*, **12** (1), 60–68.

Ryle, A. (1996). Ogden's autistic-contiguous position and the role of interpretation in psychoanalytic theory building. *British Journal of Medical Psychology*, **69** (2), 129–138.

Ryle, A. and Beard, H. (1993). The integrative effect of reformulation: cognitive analytic therapy with a patient with borderline personality disorder. *British Journal of Medical Psychology*, **66**, 249–258.

Ryle, A. and Marlowe, M.J. (1995). Cognitive Analytic Therapy of borderline personality disorder: theory, practice and the clinical and research uses of the self-states sequential diagram. *International Journal of Short-Term Psychotherapy*, **10**, 21–34.

Safran, J.D., Crocker, P., McMain, S. and Murray, P. (1990). The therapeutic alliance rupture as a therapy event for empirical investigation. *Psychotherapy*, **27** (2), 154–165.

Safran, J.D. and McMain, S. (1992). A cognitive-interpersonal approach to the treatment of personality disorders. *Journal of Cognitive Psychotherapy: an International Quarterly*, **6** (1), 59–68.

Sandler, J. (1976). Countertransference and role-responsiveness. *International Review of Psychoanalysis*, **3**, 43–47.

Sandler, J., Dare, C. and Holder, A. (1973). *The Patient and the Analyst.* London: Allen & Unwin.

Schacht, T.E. and Henry, W.P. (1994). Modelling recurrent relationship patterns with Structural Analysis of Social Behaviour: the SASBY-CMP. *Psychotherapy Research*, **4** (3 & 4), 208–221.

Siren, O. (1963). *The Chinese on the Art of Painting: Translations and Comments.* New York: Schocken Books.

Soloff, P.H. (1993). Pharmacological therapies in borderline personality disorder. In J. Paris (Ed.), *Borderline Personality Disorder: Etiology and Treatment.* Washington, DC: American Psychiatric Press.

Soloff, P.H., Lis, J.A., Kelly, T., Cornelius, J. and Ulrich, R. (1994). Risk factors for suicidal behaviour in borderline personality disorder. *American Journal of Psychiatry*, **151** (9), 1316–1323.

Soloff, P.H. and Millward, J.W. (1983). Developmental histories of borderline patients. *Comprehensive Psychiatry*, **24**, 574–588.

Spitzer, R.L., (1983). Psychiatric diagnosis: are clinicians still necessary? *Comprehensive Psychiatry*, **24** (5), 399–411.

Stein, G. (1992). Drug treatment of the personality disorders. *British Journal of Psychiatry*, **161**, 167–184.

Stein, J.A., Golding, J.W., Siegel, J.M., Burnam, M.A. and Sorenson, S.B. (1988). Long-term psychological sequelae of child sexual abuse: the Los Angeles epidemiological catchment Area study. *Lasting Effects of Child Sexual Abuse* (pp. 135–154). Newbury Park, CA: Sage.

Steiner, J. (1979). The border between the paranoid-schizoid and the depressive positions in the borderline patient. *British Journal of Medical Psychology*, **52**, 385–391.

Steiner, J. (1990). Pathological organizations as obstacles to mourning: the role of unbearable guilt. *International Journal of Psychoanalysis*, **71**, 87–94.

Stern, D. (1985). *The Interpersonal World of the Infant.* New York: Basis Books.

Stone, M.H. (1993). Long-term outcome in personality disorders. In P. Tyrer and G. Stein (Eds), *Personality Disorder Reviewed.* London: Gaskell.

Szostak, C., Lister, R., Eckardt, M. and Weingartner, H. (1994). Dissociative effects of mood on memory. In R.M. Klein and B.K. Doane (Eds), *Psychological Concepts and Dissociative Disorders.* Hove, UK, and Hillsdale, NJ: L. Erlbaum.

Toomela, A. (1996a). How culture transforms minds: a process of internalisation. *Culture and Psychology*, **2** 285–305.

Toomela, A. (1996b). What characterises language that can be internalised: a reply to Tomasello. *Culture and Psychology*, **2**, 319–322.

Treasure, J. and Ward, A. (1997). Cognitive analytical therapy in the treatment of anorexia nervosa. *Clinical Psychology and Psychotherapy*, **4**(1), 62–71.

Trower, P. and Chadwick, P. (1995). Pathways to defense of the self: a theory of two types of paranoia. *Clinical Psychology: Science and Practice*, **2**, 263–278.

Tulving, E. (1985). How many memory systems are there? *American Psychologist*, April, 385–398.

Tyrer, P. (1996). Comorbidity or consanguinity? *British Journal of Psychiatry*, **168**, 669–671.

Tyrer, P., Alexander, J. and Ferguson, B. (1987). Personality Assessment Schedule. In P. Tyrer (Ed.), *Personality Disorders: Diagnosis, Management and Course*. London: Wright.

Tyrer, P. and Stein, G. (1993). *Personality Disorder Reviewed*. London: Gaskell.

Vaillant, G. (1995). *The Natural History of Alcoholism Revisited*. Cambridge, MA: Harvard University Press.

van der Hart, O. and Horst, R. (1989). The dissociation theory of Pierre Janet. *Journal of Traumatic Stress*, **2** (4), 397–412.

van der Kolk, B.A., Pelcovitz, D., Roth, S., Mandel, F.S., McFarlane, A. and Herman, J.L. (1996). Dissociation, somatization, and affect dysregulation: the complexity of adaptation to trauma. *American Journal of Psychiatry*, **153** (7), 83–93.

van Reekum, R., Links, P.S. and Boiago, I. (1993). Constitutional factors in borderline personality disorder: genetics, brain dysfunction and biological markers. In J. Paris (Ed.), *Borderline Personality Disorder: Etiology and Treatment*. Washington, DC: American Psychiatric Press.

Vanderlinden, J., Van Dyck, R., Vandereycken, W., Vertommen, H. and Verkes, R.J. (1993). The Dissociation Questionnaire (DIS-Q); development and characteristics of a new self-report questionnaire. *Clinical Psychology and Psychotherapy*, **1** (1), 21–27.

Wells, B. (1990). Psychosocial Interventions. In Ghodse and Maxwell (Eds), *Substance Abuse and Dependence* (pp. 164–165). Basingstoke: Macmillan.

Westen, D. (1990). Towards a revised theory of borderline object relations: implications of observational research. *International Journal of Psychoanalysis*, **71**, 661–693.

Widiger, T.A., Frances, A., Spitzer, R.L. and Williams, J.B.W. (1988). The DSM III-R personality disorders: an overview. *American Journal of Psychiatry*, **145**, 786–795.

Widiger, T.A., Mangine, S., Corbitt, E.M., Ellkis, C.G. and Sorenson, S.B. (1995). *Personality Disorder Interview-IV; A Semi-Structured Interview for the Assessment of Personality Disorders*. Odessa, FL: Psychological Assessment Resources.

Wortham, S. (1996). Are constructs personal? *Theory and Psychology*, **6** (1), 79–84.

Wurmser, L. (1974). Mr Pecksniff's Horse: psychodynamics in compulsive drug use. *Psychodynamics of Drug Dependence* National Institute on Drug Abuse, Research Monograph 12.

Yeomans, F., Selzer, M. and Clarkin, J. (1993). Studying the treatment contract in intensive psychotherapy with borderline patients. *Psychiatry*, **56**, 254–263.

Young, J.E. and Lindemann, M.D. (1992). An integrative schema-focused model of personality disorders. *Journal of Cognitive Psychotherapy: an International Quarterly*, **6** (1), 11–23.

Index

Related titles of interest from Wiley...

Cognitive Analytic Therapy
Developments in Theory and Practice
Anthony Ryle

Explores the current state-of-the-art theory and practice through case histories and accounts of the application of CAT to particular patient groups.

0-471-95602-3   210pp   1995   Hardback
0-471-94355-X   210pp   1995   Paperback

Cognitive-Analytic Therapy
Active Participation in Change
Anthony Ryle

A new integration in Brief Psychotherapy.

0-471-93069-5   282pp   1991   Paperback

Cognitive Therapy of Anxiety Disorders
A Practice Manual and Conceptual Guide
Adrian Wells

Up-to-date account of the practical application of cognitive therapy for anxiety disorders emphasising the design and implementation of pure cognitive therapy skills.

0-471-96476-X   328pp   1997   Paperback

Cognitive Psychology and Emotional Disorders
2nd Edition
J. Mark G. Williams, Fraser Watts, Colin MacLeod and Andrew Mathews

Explains how emotion affects: conscious and nonconscious processing; memory bias and memory deficits; attentional bias; schematic processing; judgements; and thought and images.

0-471-94430-0   416pp   1997   Paperback

Visit the Wiley Home Page at http://www.wiley.co.uk